JOURNEY TO THE EDGE OF THE WORLD

headline

BILLY CONNOLLY

JOURNEY TO THE EDGE OF THE WORLD

First published in 2009
by HEADLINE PUBLISHING GROUP

1

Cataloguing in Publication Data is available from the British Library

ISBN 978 0 7553 1885 8

Designed by Nicky Barneby @ Barneby Ltd
Set in Minion and FF Legato
Printed and bound in Great Britain by Butler Tanner and Dennis Ltd

Headline's policy is to use papers that are natural, renewable and recyclable products
and made from wood grown in sustainable forests. The logging and manufacturing processes
are expected to conform to the environmental regulations of the country of origin.

HEADLINE PUBLISHING GROUP
An Hachette UK Company
338 Euston Road
London NW1 3BH

www.headline.co.uk
www.hachette.co.uk

The text of this book is taken directly from interviews with Billy Connolly, from his video diaries and from his commentaries in the course of filming the ITV1 series 'Billy Connolly's Journey to the Edge of the World', with some additional research material included as background.

CONTENTS

Part Three

Part Four

ACKNOWLEDGEMENTS

Grateful thanks to: Cameraman Tim Pollard and Sound Recordist Mark Atkinson; Scenery Cameraman Nick Martin; Production Manager Helen Breslin; Series Producer Mark Jones.

Also to: Producer/Directors Chris Malone, John Moulson and Barnaby Coughlin; Assistant Producers Christian Collerton, Tom Barrow, Kevin Forde and Ben Smith and Series Researcher Dominic Aston. Taking care of all the logistics back at base were Production Executive Karen Stockton, Production Co-ordinator Kay Beaumont and Travel Consultant Richard Fish. Editors Daniel Ward, Kim Horton, Tris Harris and Andy Drayton. Stephen Edwards colour graded the pictures. The music for the series was composed by Nainita Desai and Malcolm Laws; the audio for the shows was mixed by Dion Stuart. The opening titles and maps for the series were designed by Liquid TV. I'm grateful for the part they made in giving the series its high production values.

I'd like to thank Executive Producers Bill Jones and Fiona Keenaghan and Commissioning Editor at ITV Network Jeff Anderson for their support and encouragement.

Photographs for this book were taken by Christian Collerton (including the front jacket photo), Tom Barrow, Kevin Forde, Ben Smith, Mark Atkinson (including the back jacket photo), Mark Jones, Russell Daigle and Eric Walsh. I'd also like to thank Kevin Morgan, Content Director at ITV, and Lyndsey Weatherall and Peter Gray in the ITV Press Office.

And for the book, my thanks to Val Hudson, designer Nicky Barneby, Graham Green, Lorraine Jerram, Sarah Douglas and all at Headline Publishing Group.

And most particularly to writer Wendy Holden for making the book so good.

Lots of people we encountered were so helpful with their time and facilities and I'd especially like to thank Rod Raycroft from Yukon Tourism, Newfoundland and Labrador Tourism, Parks Canada, Eco Tours British Columbia, the crew of the *Akademik Ioffe* and Quark Expeditions. Their local knowledge was invaluable. I met many, many people on my trip who touched me with their generosity and kindness, the like of which I have never encountered before. It goes without saying but without the local people we filmed with there would be no series. And no book! Thank you all.

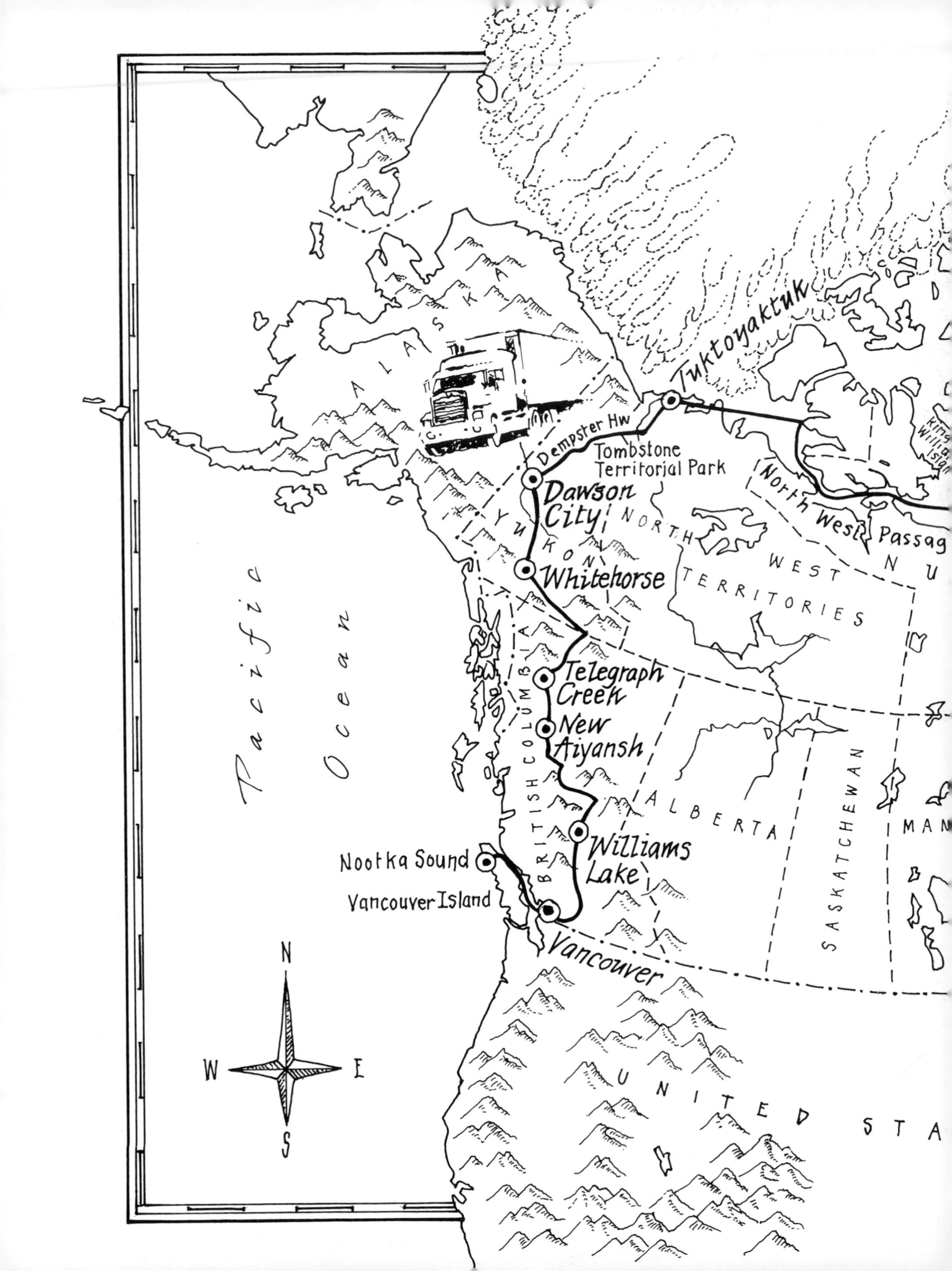

ALASKA
Tuktoyaktuk
Dempster Hw
Tombstone Territorial Park
Dawson City
YUKON
NORTH WEST TERRITORIES
North West Passag
Whitehorse
Pacific Ocean
BRITISH COLUMBIA
Telegraph Creek
New Aiyansh
ALBERTA
SASKATCHEWAN
MAN
Williams Lake
Nootka Sound
Vancouver Island
Vancouver
N
W
E
S
UNITED STA

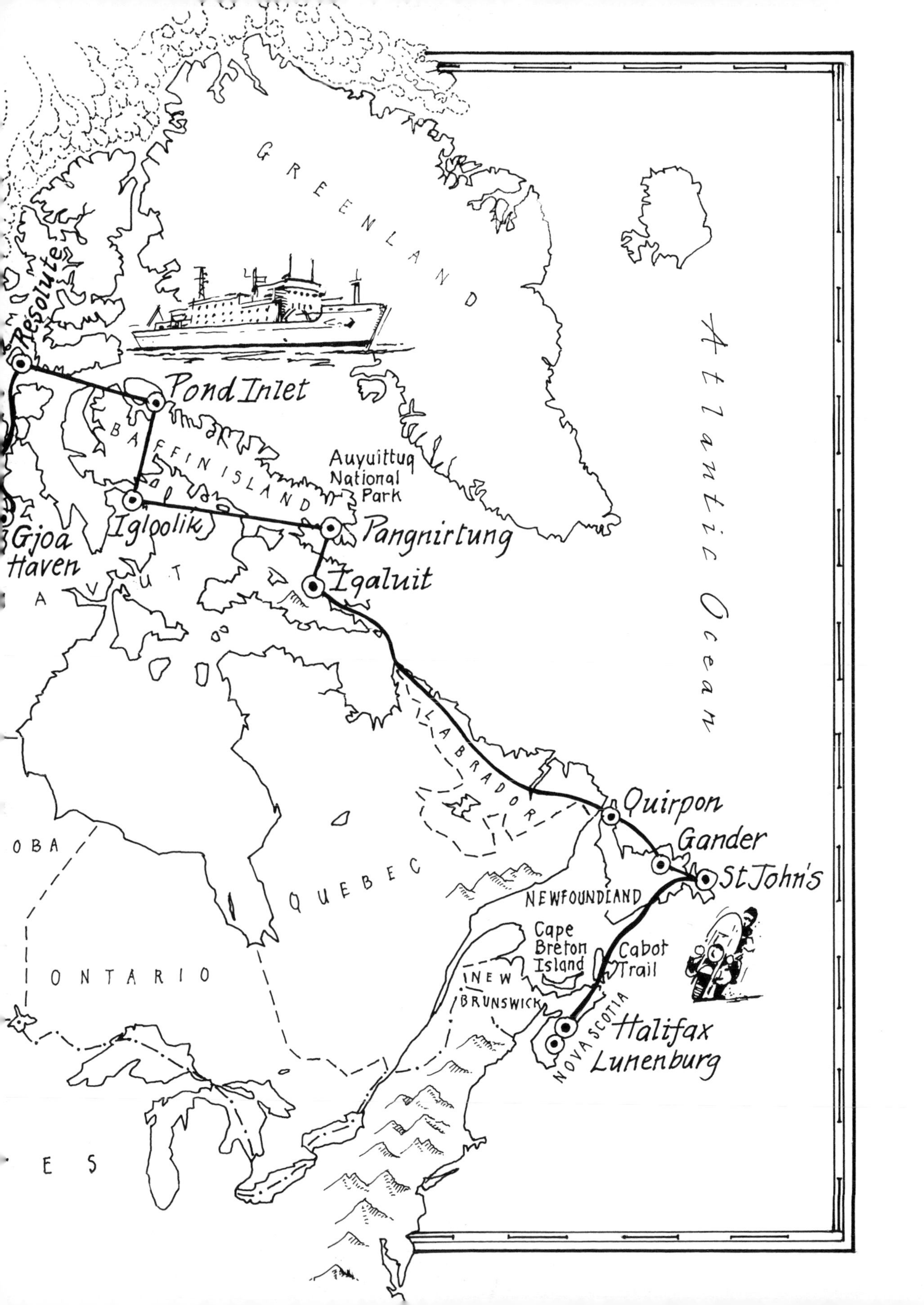

GREENLAND
Resolute
Pond Inlet
BAFFIN ISLAND
Auyuittuq National Park
Igloolik
Pangnirtung
Gjoa Haven
Iqaluit
Atlantic Ocean
LABRADOR
Quirpon
Gander
St John's
NEWFOUNDLAND
QUEBEC
Cape Breton Island
Cabot Trail
NEW BRUNSWICK
NOVA SCOTIA
Halifax
Lunenburg
ONTARIO

INTRODUCTION

I'VE ENJOYED TRAVELLING ever since I was a boy and went on my first proper journey, from Glasgow to Blackpool. Once I'd reached the Golden Mile, I thought I'd ended up on the dark side of the moon.

I grew to like the look of the world even more when I was in the Territorial Army and then as a young hitchhiker. Although I sound very Scottish and behave in a Scottish way, I am a world citizen and enormously proud of that. I especially like how beautiful the world is and how much space there really is. People think we're all living shoulder to shoulder and there's no room left. It's lovely to be able to go somewhere like the Arctic and show that it just simply isn't the truth. When you see the breadth and height there is to that barren wilderness, it is completely overwhelming to find yourself confronted with this enormous space and a silence that you think you can hear.

In travelling to the top of the world via the fabled Northwest Passage, I was not only making a unique journey but also living out some boyhood dreams – before I get too old. For centuries the Northwest Passage has been icebound, but these days, for just a few weeks in the summer, the ice melts. That means loafers like me are given a wee window of opportunity to follow some of the most extraordinary men in history on what was once their quest for the holy grail of world exploration – not to mention all the romantics and nutters; people with broken hearts or hoping to fall in love; the mavericks and adventurers, fantasists and those fleeing poverty and injustice.

The timing of my journey was perfect, as the Arctic is losing its great silence and isolation. An invasion of modern-day speculators is flooding in to make new fortunes and squabble over ancient territories. I hate the way humans are given the blame for everything, though. I'm bored rigid with those who refer to our world as an 'environment'. I can't take another evening of watching programmes or reading articles telling me that if only we would do this or that there would be more spotted bears and it's all our fault. My message to them is simple: Shut Up.

The human race isn't given enough credit. Sure, we have made some horrible mistakes but we have also done some immensely big and good things. That's what keeps the ball going around and around. Best of all, there are still delightful folk who get on with their lives harmoniously; with nature and with each other. Those people who cook your meals or deliver things, who cut your hair or chop your logs, who catch your fish or make your shoes, who herd your cattle or push their children on the swings. They don't have a spokesman and I would like to be their guy.

Many of the people I would meet on the course of my great adventure had an innate appreciation that things don't need to be extraordinary to be beautiful. They understand that there is deep beauty within ordinariness and plainness and a lack of desire for richness and sparkliness; the kind of beauty that can be found in people's eyes and in their hearts and souls. The sort of goodness you can tell by the shake of a hand, especially if it is a big, happy, handsome handshake at the end of a chance encounter.

So, come with me on this journey to the edge of what we know. Meet some of the people who live up there, far from the rest of the world. Read the stories of those who have lived and breathed and died in this incredible country of epic journeys and brave hearts, and who are still doing so … in their own quiet way.

PART ONE

What would the world be, once bereft of wet and wildness? Let them be left. O let them be left, wildness and wet; Long live the weeds and the wilderness yet.

Gerard Manley Hopkins (1844–1889)

BLUENOSE II
LUNENBURG N.S.

NOVA SCOTIA

To launch my journey across the New World on the schooner *Bluenose II*, the symbol of Nova Scotia, is to begin with a sense of this land's remarkable history.

This iconic piece of wood and steel and cloth, rope, linen and cotton is a replica of the most famous ship in Canada, built in 1921, and known to just about every Canadian because it is on their smallest coin – the dime. In between brutal seasons of fishing for cod and scallop on the notorious Grand Banks, the original *Bluenose* raced the fishing schooners of neighbouring American states such as Massachusetts. The undisputed Queen of the North Atlantic, she thrashed the Americans every year for seventeen years, and there is nothing Canadians love more than thrashing Americans.

Casting an expert eye

Bluenose II was built in 1963 to the original plans. Many of those who helped build her had worked on her predecessor too. As a former shipyard worker, I was impressed by this lovely beast the moment I set eyes on her; even more so when I had to hoist her sails or take the wheel. I like the noises ships make, especially when the engine goes off and you're lying in bed at night and can listen to the creaking. It reminds me of camping under canvas.

I'm not such a great sailor as my wife, Pamela. It's not my cup of tea or my glass of rum or whatever the expression is. I've got a wee dinghy and Pamela has a gin palace, with berths for eight guests, which is an entirely different fish. I can't even read charts or anything. If it was up to me we'd have headed for Ireland instead

Opposite: The most famous vessel in Canada

THE *HALIFAX HERALD* newspaper launched the International Fisherman's Trophy in 1920 and a fierce rivalry was begun. In the first competition, the Nova Scotian schooner *Delawana* was beaten by the *Esperanto*, a fishing vessel out of Gloucester, Massachusetts.

The following year, after *Bluenose* had been built at the Smith and Rhuland dockyard in Lunenburg, she beat *Elsie* from Gloucester, wresting back the trophy. She hung on to it for the next seventeen years. The symbol on Canadian stamps for many years in the 1920s and 30s and again sixty years later, she also won competitions for the largest catches of scallops and other fish on the Grand Banks. After the Second World War, she was sold as a freighter to work in the West Indies, eventually foundering on a reef off Haiti in 1946.

Nine years later, in 1955, *Bluenose* was inducted into the Canadian Sports Hall of Fame, the first non-human inductee at the time. Her symbol still appears on the Nova Scotia licence plate and has appeared on the Canadian dime since 2002. Her daughter, *Bluenose II,* was completed in 1963 and sold to the Canadian government in the early 1990s. She serves as a symbol of the province and a tourist vessel but, in deference to her predecessor's unbeaten record, she does not race.

of Nova Scotia, in completely the wrong direction, but on a ship like *Bluenose II* I was as happy as a clam, and clams are apparently very happy things.

Pier 21, Halifax, Nova Scotia

WALKING AROUND PIER 21 IN Halifax, Nova Scotia, is an emotionally charged experience. This is a special place in Canadian hearts – their Ellis Island, the port where millions of immigrants landed to settle in the New World.

Unless they were of native descent, all the Canadians currently inhabiting the country arrived there from somewhere else. One in five can trace a link back to Pier 21. During the Second World War, more than 500,000 Canadian servicemen left to help the Allies from this historic pier. Their convoys reached Britain in 1939 but they didn't go to battle straight away, which meant they spent a lot of time stationed at British bases with nothing else to do but get to know the local women. Among the immigrants who arrived in Canada after the war were 48,000 war brides and 22,000 children, all under the age of six, many of whom had never met their fathers. There is something I love about a guy going to war and coming back with two or three other people.

The post-war convoys also carried thousands of Jews and other refugees from war-torn Europe. It must have been a wonderful thing, coming from the uncertain into the next unknown, but knowing that this unknown – even though they had no idea what to expect – had to be better. Sighting land after a week-long passage through the mist and the fog must have come as such a relief. It would have been a release from the past and the terrible grip of the North Atlantic. There must have been a collective sigh of relief as friends and families met up on the pier. One Italian-Canadian who visited recently apparently broke down when he recalled arriving in North America after the war and almost being shipwrecked during the voyage. When he reached Canadian soil, he fell to his knees and kissed it.

I was intensely moved by the whole experience of Pier 21. I felt haunted by the courage of the immigrants in leaving their homes and families in Germany, Holland, Italy or Russia, arriving in an unknown country in the middle of the night. These displaced people never expected to see their loved ones or their home again.

Opposite: 'Aye aye, Captain!'

FOUNDED IN 1749, Halifax has a long and proud history of welcoming refugees, workers and newcomers seeking greater opportunities. Pier 21 is still known as the historic Gateway to Canada.

In the first part of the twentieth century Canada actively encouraged immigration under the assisted passage scheme. Men would arrive first, find themselves a job and send money later for their families to follow. From 1869 until the early 1930s, Pier 21 also processed 100,000 children (now referred to as British Home Children) under the British child emigration scheme, a (we must presume) well intentioned but nevertheless poorly executed plan to relocate the poor and orphaned to work on Canadian farms and in domestic service.

By keeping its borders open during and after the Second World War, Canada offered a lifeline of personnel and supplies to and from Britain. Fifty thousand Canadian servicemen who sailed to war in Europe from Pier 21 never returned. Canada has continued to provide sanctuary for thousands of evacuees – men, women and children – fleeing religious or ethnic persecution across Europe: more than one and a half million between 1928 and 1971. Through its ports have passed a diversity of cultures and languages that ultimately enriched the country and made it what it is today. Those grateful immigrants have gone on to bear the children and grandchildren that make up the current Canadian population.

Immigrants arriving at Pier 21's red-brick dockyard building were carefully processed before being allowed to board trains for destinations across the country where they would start their new life. Everyone was questioned and examined, their papers checked and their backgrounds investigated. Some stayed for just a few hours. Others were put into temporary camps until they received landed immigrant status, once homes and jobs could be found.

Pier 21 was finally closed on 28 March 1971, forty-three years after it opened, when air travel became preferable to a North Atlantic crossing. With so many Canadians making pilgrimages back to Pier 21 over the following decades to reflect on their arrival, it was decided to restore the immigration shed and transform it into a heritage site and immigration museum. It was officially opened on Canada Day (1 July), 1999, and has been immortalised in song and folklore ever since.

They were putting themselves through a kind of bereavement in the hope of a second chance.

Desperate to be accepted, they stood waiting in the immigration hall, not understanding the language and uncertain what to expect from the country or the climate or the people. They didn't even know if the food was going to be the same. They must have looked at the uniformed strangers who were going to judge them and wondered, 'What if they turn me away?'

Many of the war brides had no idea how huge Canada was and fully expected their husbands to be meeting them which, of course, they weren't. Instead these women were herded into makeshift barracks where they had to wait for travel documents, papers and authorization. It must have been so difficult. I have never been an immigrant in that way and I would hope never to be one. I don't think I'm equipped with that kind of strength and character.

Now that Pier 21 is a tourist attraction and a symbol of Canada's immigrant heritage, it is a much happier sort of place. It isn't nearly as sad, weary, lovelorn and tearjerking as it once was. This is a good place where people still wave to ships, the magical way they wave to trains and don't to cars and motorbikes, for some reason. It's so great to see people waving white hankies as loved ones arrive or sail away.

When the nine-storey American cruise ship *Carnival Victory* pulled into its berth next to Pier 21 in the early morning fog, I was

Welcoming a cruiser to Halifax

Town crier Peter Cox greets visitors

keen to see who disembarked. I had this romantic notion I might meet someone making a pilgrimage to relive the momentous day they'd first arrived. Maybe a war bride or perhaps one of the thousands of kids born of that unity between the men who went off to fight and the women they met on the other side of the world? Instead, one of the first people down the gangplank looked like a latter day Rob Roy, whose Scottish garb put my checked trousers into the shade. So much for romanticism.

What *was* romantic and mystical and ghostly was the piping in of the ship by men and women dressed as nineteenth-century Scottish highlanders. God's music is what I call it. The tune on the bagpipes was jolly and welcoming, which was nice because there was often such sad music associated with these long sea voyages. In Ireland especially, families used to hold a sort of funeral for people emigrating because they knew they were never going to see them again. They called it an 'American wake', enjoyed while you were still alive, because going to Canada or America was like dying.

Peter Cox, Halifax's stentorian town crier, called out a welcome to the disembarking passengers, something he does for the three ships that arrive every day. The town crier for the past twenty-eight years, Peter wore a magnificent black and red cape with old navy buttons. He sported a big white beard and looked the part completely. Best of all, he had a special musicality to his voice. With his great noise and the wailing of the pipes, the passengers of the *Carnival Victory* could at least hear that they were arriving in Nova Scotia, even if the fog obscured everything from view.

In the research department of Pier 21's former immigration hall, the names and details of everyone who passed through have been painstakingly catalogued. Those seemingly endless lists gave a sort of funerary feel to the place, but in truth few of those who arrived in Canada were sad to leave their old countries; most were happy for the chance to start a new life. They could hardly believe what it meant to be in a free country – to choose where they lived and what work they did, to move freely and without subjection to religious bigotry. Their energy, enthusiasm and hope seeped from the walls of Pier 21 just as much as the sadness did. It was a strange mix.

I was curious to know how many Billy Connollys had passed through from Ireland or Scotland, because my family traces its roots back to both countries. To my surprise, research coordinator Steve Schwinghamer came up with thirty-five straight away, right back in the time of the Irish potato famine. Thirty-five Billy Connollys? God knows what the Canadians did to deserve that.

He found one William Connolly who'd hailed from Glasgow and arrived in Canada via Liverpool in 1949. He ended up in Saint John, New Brunswick, the day before my birthday, which felt like a weird coincidence. I didn't even know the guy, yet I started feeling all kind of tingly and quivery. Having had this smiling idea to look for Billy Connollys I didn't know, I suddenly began to wonder if I was joined at the hip to this one. I had this overwhelming desire to track him down because there was a Billy Connolly in our family, my father's uncle, who we always thought had emigrated to New York. It might have been the same guy. That's what the whole immigration thing does for you. It's a bit like going to a funeral of someone you didn't know – you get emotionally involved after a very short period of time. Such places are extraordinary.

Steve explained that most visitors to Pier 21 have a similarly individual and direct connection to the past. The names on those lists aren't just anonymous entries; they are the direct ancestors of those who come asking about them. The entries themselves are fascinating, full of the sort of detail that really brings names to life. For example, all those arriving had to list how much money they carried and state whether or not they were physically or mentally able. Steve told me that many people who'd proudly claimed over the years that they'd come to Canada 'with nothing' were often

PIER 21 HAD A RIGOROUS SYSTEM of processing and questioning. Having been quizzed about their health and morality, new arrivals would be searched for hidden food packages. Some people went to ingenious lengths to smuggle in food they didn't think they'd be able to get in Canada – southern European staples such as pepperoni, salami and giant wheels of cheeses, for example, and one German woman dressed a sausage as a baby, complete with bonnet.

Hungry immigrants were given cornflakes to eat as soon as they landed but many were insulted, as for many Europeans (especially the Dutch) corn was animal food not considered fit for human consumption. In protest, they'd tip the contents of the little cereal boxes onto the floor until there was a carpet of cornflakes. One young woman so loved the new food she was offered that, not understanding it was to be had with milk, would eat it from the box like a snack.

shown to have arrived at Pier 21 with considerable sums. I could just imagine some of the immigrants reinventing themselves once they'd arrived in the New World.

Others had embellished their previous lives, such as claiming they'd been heroic rebels fighting the Brits in Ireland only for their families to discover, later, that they'd really been policemen or in some other respectable job back home. Maybe they didn't exactly lie, maybe they just put a little gloss on who they were and what they'd been to get a better start. I researched my genealogy once, desperately hoping that I came from a long line of sheep stealers, but there was nothing. We were just people who got married and had babies and died.

I especially liked the story Steve told me about one elderly gentleman who came with several younger members of his family looking for his own entry in the record books. Poor old fella, it had completely slipped his mind that he'd arrived on the doorstep of Canada in the company of a young woman who was not his wife. He had some serious explaining to do to his children and grandchildren. Maybe he didn't think her name would be listed alongside his. He was busted eighty years on for travelling with a bit on the side.

* * *

I WAS PUT THROUGH MY PACES in the immigration hall by customs officer Sheila Humes, who pretended to interview me as if I were a new arrival. I have no idea if, in a real situation, I would have been allowed into the country, but my interview went something like this:

'Good morning.'

'My name is Connolly. I'm fresh off the boat.'

'From what country?'

'I'm from Scotland.'

'And what do you plan to do here in Canada?'

'I plan to make the best of myself.'

'Have you got something lined up as a job?'

'I have absolutely nothing but my excitement.'

'Your excitement? Well, it's got to be channelled somewhere.'

'I couldn't agree more. I was hoping you'd come up with something.'

'What are your skills? What did you do in Scotland?'

'I did pretty much nothing but follow fire engines.'

'Well, maybe you could be a fireman?'

'I do have a Nova Scotia tartan baseball cap. Does that get me anything?'

'Not really. Are you going to stay in Nova Scotia?'

'I don't know. I think it looks like a charming place, but I might have a look at the rest and see. It depends on the employment opportunities.'

'Oh, I thought you chose Nova Scotia because it means "New Scotland". You'd be welcome here.'

Customs officer Sheila Humes interviews another Scot

'I chose Nova Scotia because the ship stopped here and threw me off!'

'Oh well. I'm going to say you have no money. You have your enthusiasm. I think we can introduce you to someone from the volunteer section and channel that enthusiasm.'

'That's a good idea. I'm quite healthy.'

'You haven't got tuberculosis or anything?'

'I don't.'

'You don't have a criminal record or anything like that?'

'No. Nothing— Do you have a lie detector machine?'

'No, I'm sorry, we don't. But usually I can tell by your eyes – and a smile helps.'

'Ha ha. People have fallen for that before.'

'Oh, I can tell. We have security in case the twinkle is too much.'

'Absolutely. The twinkle when you drinkle. But I would advise you to get a lie detector machine, 'cause I'm sure guys like me come sidling up every other day.'

'We do have them, but most often they're caught.'

'I have my heart set on becoming a lumberjack.'

'We've got opportunities in every province in Canada. This is a country to come to. If you've got the enthusiasm, you can be anything you want to be.'

'And I have nothing against maple syrup whatsoever. I won't hear a word against it.'

'Oh, it's great on pancakes.'

'It's great on most things, I find. It's very good on your body. It makes your underwear stay in place – all that tackiness stops it sliding around.'

'You are bad! Maybe I shouldn't let you in…'

'Maybe I'll be a bad influence on the other lumberjacks?'

'Well, they might be a bad influence on you because they're quite the characters.'

'I'm looking forward to spending some nice time in your country. I'll treat it gently. Before you know it, I'll have a pet moose and a beaver to chop trees down.'

'Welcome. Enjoy your visit. More Scots in Canada… Great.' ”

St Paul's Church and the Halifax Explosion

HALIFAX HAS ANOTHER claim to fame that it would probably prefer not to have – that of the Halifax Explosion of 6 December 1917. The *Mont-Blanc*, a French munitions ship carrying more than 2,000 tons of explosives and all sorts of other nasty things destined for the war in Europe, was coming into dock in Halifax harbour when it collided with a Norwegian ship, the *Imo*, sailing out; the *Imo* was bound for New York to pick up relief supplies for Belgium.

A huge fire broke out and raged for half an hour, attracting crowds. Then there was an almighty explosion. It was not just a bang; this was the biggest manmade explosion ever until the atomic bomb was dropped in the Second World War. The *Mont-Blanc* was blown clean out of the water. The shockwaves created a tsunami in the harbour that flooded the town.

I'd never even heard of this disaster and yet 2,000 people were killed and another 9,000 injured. Twenty-five thousand people, almost half the population, were made homeless. Astonishing. Bits of that boat were blasted for miles. Windows went in everywhere. Part of the ship's anchor landed more than two miles away. Some pieces travelled four miles through the air and flew into the chancel of St Paul's church, Halifax, where there's still a bit stuck in the wall. St Paul's is a beautiful, white wooden church – its original design was based on that of a church in London drawn by one of Sir Christopher Wren's pupils. King George II gave permission for it to be built in 1749 and, the oldest place of Protestant worship in Canada, St Paul's was used as a makeshift morgue after the disaster and the vestry as an emergency hospital.

Once the initial crisis was over, someone noticed that the piece of debris which had passed through a window at St Paul's had left an eerie impression of a man's head. Someone else claimed to recognize it as a profile of Reverend Jean-Baptiste Moreau, an assistant at the church in the 1750s, to whom – he said – the impression bore an uncanny likeness. When the rest of the congregation asked him how he knew, he claimed he'd once seen a picture of Moreau. So, they laminated the glass, keeping the broken bit between two panes, and there it still is – the Explosion Window – for all to see.

Halifax's famous 'Explosion Window'

Isn't that brilliant? I love that kind of thing. Identifying Moreau in that jagged hole in the window was an attempt at spirituality which probably flabbergasted people back then, whereas today it just feels like some sort of happy accident. Personally, I thought the man in the window looked more like the Scottish actor Alan Cumming…

Titanic Graves, Halifax, Nova Scotia

FAIRVIEW LAWN CEMETERY is notorious for having the largest burial site of *Titanic* dead anywhere in the world bar the ocean. As the closest mainland port with railroad connections to the sinking, Halifax was chosen as the final resting place of those whom the rescuers were able to fish from the icy waters.

Of the 1,517 souls who died when the White Star liner sank off the Grand Banks on 14 April 1912, just 328 bodies were picked up. Of those, more than 200 were brought to Halifax, fifty of which were shipped back to the US or Europe. The remainder were buried in Fairview Lawn.

Paying my respects at the *Titanic* graves

There is still something magical about the *Titanic* and about the final resting place of her passengers and crew. Of all the hundreds of ships that have been lost, none has more mystery. Even as a boy, I read about the disaster in *Reader's Digest* and it moved me. I remember reading how those in the lifeboats waved to those still onboard as the ship took on water. The fathers left behind, standing on the deck waving back to their families, puffed on their cigars until they glowed red in the dark. That image stayed with me all my life.

The White Star Line initially decreed that all the black granite graves would be of equal size regardless of rank, status or a passenger's accommodation. This was so that the class system which had been so abused as the ship went down would finally be disregarded in death. Wealthier families, however, insisted on paying extra for larger, more elaborate headstones with longer inscriptions, so the disparity remains. Few relatives ever travelled as far as Nova Scotia to visit the graves they'd paid for.

* * *

"I LIKE GRAVEYARDS *and I particularly like to shine a spotlight on the great unsung, for whom I have a special place in my heart. That's why I love reading obituaries. When you open the paper it's the only good news out there. Obituaries should be moved to the front page in my opinion. You'll see some picture of a wee fat lady with curly hair, the kind you'd see every day in the supermarket, only it turns out that she rescued kids from Nazi clutches. Or there'll be one of those little balding men who look like ordinary Joes, but the obituary says they invented great things or found cures for diseases.*

Graveyards can have the same effect because you discover wonderful things about ordinary people. A visit to a cemetery is life-enriching and always enlightening. I never feel sad in cemeteries; I find peace and a kind of joy in them. There are so few gravestones with nasty things written on them. Instead relatives pen little poems or sweet sentiments of the kind you'd normally mock and scorn, but in graveyards they take on another persona. It's seeing people at their best.

I looked at Buddhism for a while when I first met Pamela – she put me on to it – and I took a lot of nice things away from the doctrines. One of them was that whenever you see a little corpse in the street, like road kill, you say to yourself: 'This is the way of all things, and it will be the same for me, too.' That's a great life lesson. Doing that regularly made me lose my fear of death. It gave me a benign attitude to dying and makes it feel natural for me to wander around a graveyard and note all the ordinary people remembered: 'This is the way of things.' There's great solace in that. ”

I love the irony that most of the people who visit Fairview Lawn Cemetery have arrived in Halifax by cruise ship. Just after breakfast, they disembark from a vessel not dissimilar to the *Titanic*, get on a coach and the first thing they go to see in the whole of Nova Scotia is a site commemorating the sinking – of a ship! Doesn't that make you smile? Immediately after breakfast, too. Just when they thought it was safe to get back in the water...

Each name in the *Titanic* section of the cemetery faces Newfoundland, the land nearest to where she sank. The layout of the graves is said to accidentally mimic the bow of a ship, with several long rows at the front and a shorter, curving one added at the rear as more bodies were washed up in the months following the disaster. There is even a gap in the rows said to indicate where the iceberg struck. Strangely, the 'bow' of the boat-shaped row of

The graves curve like a ship's bow

graves faces north-east, which is exactly the direction *Titanic* was pointing when she was discovered on the seabed in 1985.

Sporting a Panama hat, Blair Beed, local historian and grandson of the undertaker's assistant who helped man one of the rescue boats, showed me around the graves. He told me that locals had always regarded the graveyard as a 'bit of a curiosity' until the movie *Titanic* was released in 1997. Suddenly, everyone wanted to visit the graves; they realized they had a celebrity in their midst.

The officers of the Halifax coroner listed everything that was found on each of the bodies rescued from the *Titanic*, from the clothing they were wearing and the documents they were carrying to what jewellery and tattoos they may have had. The authorities used this archive information to try to identify each body, even in recent times, but sometimes the technique backfired.

'The trouble is,' Blair explained, 'a man who might have been in love with Mabel, had since moved on to Grace. If they mentioned in the paper that a body was found with the name Mabel tattooed on it, then Grace didn't necessarily know who he was. That's the problem with tattoos. You can't erase the past.'

Many of the forty unidentified bodies buried at the cemetery were later identified from their belongings, however, including a Jenny Henriksson who had the letters 'JH' sewn into her undergarments. She was the only female JH on the ship's manifest.

One of the first graves Blair showed me was that of Londoner Everett Edward Elliott, a twenty-four-year-old coal trimmer who worked in the engine room and went down with his ship. His family paid extra for a headstone denouncing the malicious rumour circulating at the time that crew members had saved themselves at the expense of passengers, including women and children. I could almost hear the trumpet sound as I read the text describing him as one of the 'heroic crew' who 'died on duty'. A poetry inscription insisted: '*Each man stood at his post, while all the weaker ones went by, and showed once more to all the world how Englishmen should die.*'

There was the grave of a Scottish violin player, a man named John 'Jock' Marhume, interred in his bandsman's uniform. And a twenty-eight-year-old electrical engineer named Robert Norman from Glasgow, who'd helped a fellow second class passenger into a lifeboat and then remained onboard to play the piano during the final hymn as the ship went down. The archives list that he was fair haired with a high forehead, that he carried a gold watch and

chain, a pocket knife and diary, and had five pounds four shillings and sixpence on him when he was found.

It touched me enormously that the relatives of the dead wanted everyone to know of their loved ones, even though they believed the only visitors would be Nova Scotians. The parents of one lost child paid extra for a poem which read: '*Think of my soul in the heaven of rest I'll sail the wild seas … no more the tempest may sweet pour the wine … and tears I am safe evermore.*'

Perhaps the most moving of all the graves was that of the Unknown Child, one of fifty-four children under the age of ten who lost their lives. His was the second body to be plucked from the icy waters by sailors using searchlights. The discovery of this little two-year-old blond-haired, blue-eyed boy without a lifebelt moved rescuers to tears. They vowed that if no one claimed or identified the child, they would pay for his coffin and headstone themselves, which is what they did. His epitaph reads: '*Erected to the Memory of an Unknown Child Whose Remains Were Recovered After the Disaster to the "Titanic", April 15th 1912.*' In recent years, visitors have started to leave little teddy bears and trinkets and toys on the boy's grave, even tickets to the movie about the disaster.

Ten feet away was the grave of Alma Paulson, aged twenty-nine, a third class passenger from Sweden, who was lost with her four children on her way to meet her husband Nils in Chicago. Nils was a former miner who'd found a job as a tram conductor. He'd saved for two years to pay for his family's passage. Only Alma's body was recovered but her children were all listed on her tomb – aged two, four, six and eight. Romantic legend had it that the Unknown Child was really her youngest son Gösta, buried opposite her completely by coincidence. DNA testing finally disproved that. When the scientists opened Alma's grave to take a DNA sample, they found that she'd been buried along with her mouth organ. Reports from survivors stated that she'd played it to her children to keep them calm as she promised a ship was coming to save them. Visitors often leave teddy bears on Alma's grave too because they assume her children are buried with her, but sadly they aren't.

* * *

Opposite: Alma Paulson, buried without her children

ONE UNREMARKABLE GRAVE with a simple inscription receives more attention than most. It is that of J. Dawson, a young man in his early twenties who shovelled coal in

PAULSON
ALMA PAULSON
AGED 29 YEARS
WIFE OF NILS PAULSON
LOST WITH FOUR CHILDREN
APRIL 15, 1912.
IN THE "TITANIC"
TORBURG DANRIA AGED 8
PAUL FOLKE AGED 6
STINA VIOLA AGED 4
GOSTA LEONARD AGED 2
206

Titanic*'s boiler room. He was identified from his union card. His real name was Joseph Dawson from Dublin and his grave reads* 'J Dawson. Died April 15, 1912' *and then gives the number 227, which meant he was the 227th body to be pulled from the water.*

In the movie Titanic, *Hollywood actor Leonardo DiCaprio played a third class passenger called Jack Dawson who drowned after falling in love with Kate Winslet's character. Since then, Joseph Dawson's grave has become an international shrine. The grass around it is worn away by the feet of weeping women, young and old, caught up in the fictional story. There are plastic flowers on his grave permanently, to help tour operators find it when they pull up with coachloads of tourists, eager to see this grave above all others.*

Blair told me he had seen a photograph of Joseph Dawson in the archives and he wasn't even a particularly handsome-looking fellow. He had light-coloured hair and a moustache and he died in his work dungarees. Yet hundreds of women identify him with Leonardo DiCaprio, which I find truly wonderful. A coach full of giggling Japanese tourists fresh off a cruise ship arrived while I was there, to take photographs. They seemed quite happy to forget poor Joseph the stoker from Dublin, focusing their affections instead on Jack Dawson, romantic hero.

Blair Beed's grandfather helped retrieve the bodies

Young Joseph has become like a dead rock star, and it isn't even him! I can't think of a single incidence where something similar has happened – that a dead man has become a sex symbol posthumously. I love that! There's something so showbusiness about that which really pleases me. It shows that it is never too late. Good on him, I say! ”

Lunenburg, Nova Scotia

LUNENBURG WAS A NICE PLACE. It had a foghorn that went all night. As I lay in my bed listening to it, I was reminded of Scotland when I was a boy. Each New Year's Eve my father would open the window so we could hear the ships' horns going off down in the Clyde. The changing fortunes of the River Clyde and the decline in shipbuilding have strong parallels with the fate of Lunenburg and of a fish that changed the world.

Since records began in 1925, more than 600 fishermen have been lost from Lunenburg after setting out to catch cod; seven schooners foundered in 1927 alone. That's a huge contribution from this tiny community. A memorial in the town lists the dead, many of whom share the same surname. Whole families were

LUNENBURG OLD TOWN was formally established in 1753 as the first British colonial settlement in Nova Scotia outside of Halifax and named after King George II of Hanover, also known as the Duke of Braunschweig-Lunenburg.

Additional settlers, 'foreign Protestants' from Switzerland, Germany and France who were encouraged by the British to colonize, swelled the existing population and helped build a model town. They protected it against attack from the native Indians and the French. Fishing and shipbuilding sustained it over the years. Many of the town's buildings still date from the late 1700s and attract thousands of tourists every year. Lunenburg, which is on the South Shore of Mahone Bay, is now a UNESCO World Heritage site.

In the 1950s Lunenburg sent the first fishing fleet to the famous Grand Banks of Newfoundland, where shallow plateaus and warmer Gulf Stream waters encourage fish to feed. The Fisheries Museum of the Atlantic, on the picturesque Lunenburg waterfront, commemorates the proud fishing heritage of this part of the Canadian coast. Visitors can even chat to some of the 'old salts' who once fished the North Atlantic, but whose role now is largely symbolic.

Ralph Church and Bobby Beringer, cod fishermen

wiped out – fathers and sons, brothers and uncles – often on the same boat, in the course of carrying on a fishing tradition passed down from generation to generation. It really stops your heart in its tracks to think that this pretty, touristy town with its restaurants and souvenir shops once had such a harsh past.

Half-brothers Ralph Church and Bobby Beringer, who took me out fishing on their boat *Crystal Ann*, are a dying breed. They come from a rare species of man who used to make a living (and a very hard living it was) fishing for cod in the treacherous waters off Newfoundland and Nova Scotia on Canada's eastern seaboard. I can remember at school reading about the infamous Newfoundland Banks in childish wonder. My teachers told us it was impossible the world could ever run out of fish; there were so many millions in the sea. Who would have thought that the cod would become almost extinct? To suddenly be in a boat on the Grand Banks felt like the strangest thing to this boy from Glasgow.

When Ralph and Bobby were growing up, the Lunenburg wharf

was full of scallop, cod and haddock draggers, part of an industry that was the lifeblood of this region.

'There used to be sixteen dories going down to the Grand Banks every day and they'd come home full of fish,' Ralph reminisced, as we headed to sea. 'Then they started net fishing with big trawls behind the boats and after a while it seemed like they cleaned all the fish up. Now we're back to the handlines, catching much smaller fish.'

As there are just three boats fishing out of Lunenburg these days, for limited catches of cod, hake and pollock, these two men have had to become part of the growing tourist industry, taking oafs like me out 'jigging' for cod. The new rules state that they're allowed to catch up to sixty fish but Ralph and Bobby said there was 'no way in hell' they ever would.

'One or two would be good these days, and anything under three feet has to be thrown back, which is most of them,' Ralph told me. 'Even when we do catch something, the price is way down on what we used to get.'

Ralph and Bobby told me the cod once swam so thick that they'd freeze solid in the ice of the bay. These days visitors to Lunenburg can only buy what they call 'second-hand fish' from Russia or elsewhere. The place that was once the fishing capital of Canada, a boom town where oysters and lobsters were poor man's food, has lost its heart. Most people moved away, looking for a new living. Lunenburg became a place for old men, tourists and T-shirt sellers, as well as speculators who buy up the old houses and sell them on at prices beyond the reach of the locals. It's the same story the world over.

Lunenburg's historic quay

INTRODUCED AFTER THE Second World War, industrial-scale trawling using huge factory ships, many of them foreign, stole the livelihood of local fishermen. People have described the scale of industry off the Newfoundland shores as like 'cities at sea'.

The Canadian government initially imposed a 200-mile exclusion zone around its coast, but then allowed locals to fish it just as heavily, hoping to cash in on the world's growing hunger for cod. In 1992, it was finally realized that one of the world's most abundant populations of fish had suddenly collapsed. Stocks were at less than one per cent of what they had been in the 1960s. Canada's 1993 cod moratorium, which limited catches and put an end to cod fishing for several years to allow stocks to replenish, finally did for Lunenburg and many fishing towns like it. More than 500 years of fishing came to an end, forcing 40,000 people out of work.

Even after fifteen years of the ban, the fish have not come back in significant numbers. Global warming, a thriving seal population and overfishing have all been blamed but the future of cod fishing in Newfoundland is in serious doubt.

'You know, young people got to leave and find somewhere to make an awful pile of money or they can't afford to buy any place here,' Bobby said with a sigh. 'Maybe I'm wrong, but I don't see where it's better.'

These big men with strong hands and hearts knew exactly where and how it went wrong for the fishing industry of Nova Scotia and they were very honest about it. 'We were a lot to blame,' they admitted. 'We took the little fish out as well as the big fish.'

This sort of land breeds strong people. They have the same eyes as people who live in the desert or in wilderness areas where they can see to the horizon. They call it the 'eight-mile stare'. They look at you with their eyes kind of screwed up against the sun, or the glare of the snow. They give you that eight-mile stare even when they don't need to. And when you learn about their lives you understand why.

Bobby told me he was involved in a tragic fishing accident many years ago in which five of his friends were killed onboard the *Cape Aspey*, a scallop trawler that went down in forty-mile-an-hour winds. Everything that hit the boat froze. The fishermen tried to smash the ice off with picks, but when the vessel slowed to allow more men up on deck, she took on too much water and sank. Investigators reckoned there was seventy tonnes of ice accumulated on her that night, the weight of which eventually rolled her over.

'That was a bad night,' Bobby said. 'Last of January 1993, half past eleven at night. Wind chill was about thirty-five below zero. We were a hundred and fifty miles offshore. I'd sooner forget about that night.'

He and some of the crew managed to get into the life raft in survival suits but five didn't make it. Two didn't even get off the boat. The rest of them spent the night in the life raft, taking on water and ice, before they were found at dawn by search and rescue planes and plucked from the ocean.

'That was a nice sound – the search planes,' he said. 'They started dropping great big orange flares and lit the whole water up all around us. That was a good feeling because before then I didn't think we'd ever be found.'

I would never have known Bobby's story unless I'd squeezed it out of him. He wasn't a braggart; just an ordinary guy getting on with his life. I love people who have done extraordinary things but who don't boast of it. Salt of the earth, they are.

Fishing in this part of the world must be the hardest way to make a living. I can't imagine anything more dangerous or life-threatening than going hundreds of miles offshore in the middle of winter to try to catch fish. Or being out on a boat at thirty-five below and a hundred and fifty miles offshore with ice clinging to you and wondering if you're going to get home.

Our fishing trip was far less demanding, mercifully. Jigging is the old romantic method which involves using some mackerel bait on a circular hook and trailing a single line through your fingers to catch a fish, just as they did a hundred years ago. Bobby told me to spit on my bait in Lunenburg tradition but I said a wee prayer instead. After a long time out at sea, I eventually caught some mackerel, some pollock and even a small cod.

I love catching fish. Something very primal happens when it's just you and the sea, waiting for something to happen and then there's that nudge at the end of your line. It's like being in touch with some alien force; a little knock from another place, another time. You get all excited, as if it was the last thing on earth you expected even though you have all this equipment and that is exactly what you set out to do. Then up they come – six or seven at a time – and it's a joy. There's something very real and right about it.

Bobby and Ralph were such warm, nice human beings. They weren't at all as you'd imagine Nova Scotian fishermen to be – you know, made of leather and wearing yellow oilskins all day. They were big softies. They take off their woolly pullovers and go home

Small fry compared to the cod

An old salt and his fish

and are just granddads to their families. We got along great and talked about everything from cooking mackerel to taking Viagra. They told me how fish was preserved, first in salt and later, when the catches got so big, in ice. They gave me some salt cod to try, a traditional dish in these parts, but I much preferred the icing-laden doughnuts they had brought along to dunk in our coffee. I was surprised to hear that they would rather eat fish than steak any day. You'd think that a guy who'd been fishing all day would want a nice juicy steak when he got home but, no, they'd rather have some fried cod and potatoes.

It was strange, though, being out at sea with those men. dI was happy to be with them and laugh with them and I was sad to see them go. But even though they had a great devil-may-care philosophy, it was like we were at the end of some game that had been played for a century or two which was almost over. It'd be a great shame if that's the end for that whole way of life in Nova Scotia, but you never know.

Highland Games, New Brunswick

I AM CONSTANTLY SURPRISED BY the enduring nature of culture. Everyone thought that when Europe became one, its culture would flop into one big jelly mould and that we'd evolve a European culture, instead of one that was uniquely Scottish or Dutch or Belgian. Surprisingly, though, individual cultures have flourished and flowered, with people becoming deeply interested in each other's cultures as well.

Take New Brunswick: it started off inhabited by the Mikmaq Indians, was then settled by the French and English with a large influx of Scots and Irish, and has now absorbed a broad spectrum of residents who range from Chinese to Spanish. Of all the cultures adopted by this maritime province, Scottish has to be the noisiest.

People often start to research their own heritage when they reach middle age or when they move away from their home ground. I think that's what probably sparks events such as highland games in countries far from the Highlands. The Scots are the only people I know who use the word 'exile' for its emigrants; you never hear of someone being an English exile in Canada. In one way it's endearing and in another way it's kind of pathetic – the Scot abroad missing the homeland; a longing they reinforce with festivals. I bet half the people in Scotland have never been to a highland games in their life, and yet something draws them to those kinds of events the farther they get from their homeland. It's like a second wave of Scots reaffirming themselves with Gaelic and music, adding a modern twist.

Kilts a'flying

The twenty-seventh annual New Brunswick Highland Games reflect the potent Scottish heritage in this part of the world resulting from the disastrous Highland Clearances. Forcibly evicted from their homes and sent to a foreign country, that extraordinary band of strong and wonderful people hugged their culture to them like a security blanket. They did this partly, I think, in response to the great wilderness, the enormous unknown they faced when they arrived. Confronted with such vastness they clung to what they knew – anything to bring them solace.

Their descendants have kept that culture so intact that Scottish historians sometimes travel to Canada for advice on things that have been forgotten back home, especially in the realms of dance and song. Clinging proudly to their traditional identity, the children, grandchildren and great-grandchildren of those first Scottish settlers continue to celebrate their heritage with mass social gatherings.

I have mixed feelings about events which advertise with slogans such as, 'Be a Scot for a weekend.' A part of me thinks it's uncool but I also rise to the fly every time, especially when the pipes and drums begin. As I've got older, I've grown to like this stuff more and more. Sure, there are bits I don't much like, but that's the way it should be. You can take from it what you wish, whether it's caber tossing, hammer throwing, bagpipes or lasses dancing. About the

THE HIGHLAND CLEARANCES agricultural policy of the late 1700s, when wealthy landowners threw tenants off their land in order to replace them with sheep, caused the displacement of thousands of crofters.

Many of the crofters, with their cattle, were initially removed to barren land or sent to the coast to take up fishing, something they knew little or nothing about. They had been forced to leave their homes, their belongings, even their crops in the field. Homeless and facing the prospect of starvation many crofting families were willing migrants, many others were forcibly removed from their homes which were then burned to the ground. Thousands of Highlanders were put on ships and sent across the Atlantic, some to American tobacco-growing regions, such as the Carolinas, where they became indentured slaves. Thousands more poured into Canada, especially Nova Scotia and Ontario. In Winnipeg, Manitoba – where the first settlers were dissenting clanspeople from the Strath of Kildonan, near the village of Helmsdale in Sutherland – there is a statue called *Exiles* which depicts a family leaving their home. One year earlier a twin statue entitled *Emigrants* had been unveiled at Helmsdale.

Be a Scot for a weekend

dances, the only sad thing is that a lot of them came into being originally for men, the sword dance, for example, was intended for warriors preparing for battle. Now, girls wearing leather pumps re-enact them with dainty ballet steps and I really don't like it; then again, the girls do look grand in their tartan skirts. They clearly adore it and have a huge following... A healthy culture should constantly be changing, I suppose.

There are some things that don't seem right at gatherings such as these, though, the fairground, crazy golf and a beer tent, for a start. And there are stands selling kitsch Scottish knick-knacks, T-shirts, bumper stickers, even tartan umbrellas. What's that got to do with the culture? Then you'll find that the beer tent and the fairground and the stands are what keep the whole thing rolling along; that the success of the event actually owes more to the beer than it does to cultural tradition.

Melanie Laird, chair of the committee which organizes the New Brunswick games, showed me around. I'd expected the organizer of such an event to be a big, hairy highlander. As it turned out, she had less hair than I'd imagined but seemed very nice nonetheless, and in her tartan waistcoat too. Her ancestors came from the Orkneys, so she was known as the Orcadian Canadian and was wearing the Orkney tartan to prove it. I told her I'd once been bare-assed at the Standing Stones of Stenness but I'm not sure she believed me.

Melanie first became involved in the games when she started to

learn Gaelic in order to discover more about her heritage. I was jealous. I always wanted to learn Gaelic so that I could be funny in the language of my country, but I never got around to it. Melanie did. She'd also learned many Gaelic songs and she visited Scotland often – she seemed to have more relatives there than I did.

'Scottish people make up a great part of the population of New Brunswick. That inheritance is a large part of our culture,' Melanie explained. 'Then we have the French influence as well. When the music of Scotland and France blends with that of the First Nations, it is awesome – especially the drumming. Music brings cultures together.'

I met some grand lasses who'd won prizes for dancing and singing, and Bruce Gandy, a piper who played some wonderful *piobaireachd* (pronounced 'peeb-roch') music on his Great Highland Bagpipe – the best kept secret in Scotland. To me, this classical music of the pipes carries the soul of Scotland; especially the 'Lament for the Children', wordless poetry which makes the hairs on my arms stand to attention. Immensely powerful and written by a man who lost six of his seven children to cholera, the 'Lament' gets straight to your heart, whether you like it or not. You can't sneak away from this music. If you've got an emotional side to you, like me, you're doomed.

Bruce was a beautiful player, with great shoes which had big buckles sporting the Halifax coat of arms. I especially enjoyed watching him while he was playing because pipers walk like newts. They do a funny little slow walk with dodgy steps that helps them to keep balance. Needless to say, he won the *piobaireachd* competition at the games. Some of the judges were even moving their fingers in time to the pipes as they watched.

Piobaireachd does take a bit of getting used to; it's a bit like when you first hear Indian music, you think it doesn't belong to you but then you get into it. Or like when your mother used to talk to you about Brussels sprouts. (Personally, I never got around to the Brussels sprout.) The massed pipe bands are a bit military for me but once they start up, I love their noise too – I get all warm inside. When I was a child I lived right opposite a school where every Friday night the Peter's pipe band would practise, so I know all those tunes from my childhood, they are such a huge part of me. And I defy anyone not to walk in step to the marching bands. I've tried not to be in step as they've marched along in Edinburgh, but you just have to. It's one of those things.

Opposite: The pipes, they are a'calling

Proud clan members

Home of our hearts! our fathers' home! Land of the brave and free!
The sail is flashing through the foam, That bears us far from thee.

We seek a wild and distant shore, Beyond the Atlantic main;
We leave thee to return no more, Nor view thy cliffs again.

But may dishonour blight our fame, And quench our household fires,
When we, or ours, forget thy name, Green Island of our Sires!

Our native Land – our native Vale – A long, a last adieu!
Farewell to bonny Lynden-dale, And Scotland's mountains blue!

THOMAS PRINGLE (1789–1834)

Remembering Scotland as if it were a dead thing is such a New World trait: these immigrants and descendants of immigrants seem to need something old. What they sometimes forget is that there are plenty of old things that weren't good – like the fact that the clans were all tribes, basically; gangs who killed each other and stole from each other. Whenever strangers come up and tell me they are representing their clan, I nod and say, 'Oh, that's nice,' but I wonder how much they really know. All the bad things get forgotten at events like this. They come to Canada and it's all *Brigadoon*.

There was a gathering of the clans at the New Brunswick games and I watched people marching along: men with their flags and their lace-up shirts and a lot of little corpses hanging down the fronts of their kilts – their sporrans; women wearing long dresses and shawls as if they'd come straight from the Highland Clearances. There were Wallaces, and Campbells (who have to be watched round the clock, in my opinion) and MacLeans, to whom we had to salute. I love to think of all the little clan offices set up around the world for those interested in tracing their clan's history.

I used to sneer at modern-day highland games and clan gatherings but now I'm not so sure that it isn't just culture on the move. I don't think anything remains static except that which is dead. I think these events have simply adjusted to suit and if people believe this sort of thing makes them Scottish, that's just dandy by me. I don't know what makes me Scottish, except perhaps being born there.

* * *

"I SPOTTED ONE GUY WITH *a fat belly and a pointed beard and a distressing kilt that was mysteriously short, like a mini-kilt. He had one of those lace-up shirts like out of Robin Hood and I'm sure he thought he looked a million bucks. I just knew he'd be carrying a clan banner and, of course, he was.*

Seeing him reminded me of the rules of dressing in a kilt. You dress completely first – shoes, socks, the whole shamoo – and then the kilt goes on last as you wrap the length of cloth around your waist so that the pleats are at the back. Before you make the final tightening of the straps, buckles and guy ropes, you kneel on the ground and check that your kilt is 'kissing' the floor. That means it will be at the right length when you stand up.

When I was a boy not only did we not wear kilts, we frowned on people who did. We called them 'cold bums'. We used to shout: 'Kilty, Kilty, Cold Bum!' To this day, I am wary of people who wear kilts. They have to prove themselves to me. That sounds terribly arrogant, but I always think they're on the make, especially when they're not in Scotland. I always think, 'Oh, what's your game? Let's see what you are all about.' I am not totally sold on the kilt even though I have a few myself.

There is a new wave of patriotism in Scotland that will do good things to the kilt and make it worn more widely than just when people get married. There are now leather kilts, denim kilts and working men's kilts with pockets in them. I kind of like that trend, the end of the old culture of the kilt. I can happily live without flag-wavers and marchers; they give me the collywobbles but the kilt has a long way to go yet.

I do wear my kilt occasionally, when I'm in Scotland. I just put it on and go for a walk. I have an old military badger sporran, and a fox sporran which came with a note that assured me it was road kill. I even have a skunk sporran from Nova Scotia. I always wear knickers, though. That rough wool rubs the hell out of you.

The whole underwear thing comes from the military. The original kilt was a wonderful garment for a soldier – a huge piece of cloth which wrapped around you, the only remnant of it left is the plaid, the big curtain that hangs from your shoulder. A kilt could be turned into all sorts of useful things, like a house or a tent or a sleeping bag. It was far too heavy to fight in, though, and was held on with a belt so that when soldiers went into battle they just loosened the belt and stepped out of it to fight naked, in the Scottish military tradition. That's why soldiers never wore underwear.

There was a mirror on the floor of the guard house. You had to stand at ease so the officers could see up your kilt during inspection and you got punished for having underwear on. It wasn't a vulgar thing but, personally, I think the 'going commando' thing is a bit overrated, to say the least. I'm one of the knicker boys. ”

Talking of knickers, Y-fronts don't cut it in caber tossing. Calvin Klein means nothing. While 'Scottish Soldier' played in the background (another tune I knew well from my childhood) I watched some big hairy men toss cabers. The best was a guy with long underwear on, who was brilliant.

I've always thought that the sport of caber tossing shows how boring life must have been in highland villages. How dull must it have been for someone to say, 'I know what we'll do, let's throw a tree up in the air this afternoon'? Many think the point is to throw the tree in the air but it isn't. The idea is to get the balance right and toss the bum of it over the head of it until it's as close as you can get to a straight line or twelve o'clock. It isn't a question of strength, it is mostly balance and letting the forward motion of the caber dictate the flip.

I greatly enjoyed the Scottishness of the day when I had least expected to. Before I left the games behind me, I bumped into a guy called Sean who, funnily enough, ran the beer tent. He summed up for me the reason Scottish exiles cling to their heritage so:

'Our expression of Scottishness brings us back to some place deeper emotionally,' he told me. 'I think it's the anchor that many of us fix to our lives to bring us back down to earth. We all lead busy North American lives and on the weekends we need some sort of spiritual connection to our past. So we throw on our kilts, we listen to bagpipes and we experience our culture and something that runs deeper through us. All the worries of life go away. We don't work at our Scottishness; we just enjoy the heritage of it.'

I understood what he meant.

Tossing the caber, Canadian style

Cape Breton Island, Nova Scotia

THE CAPE BRETON FIDDLERS ARE world famous and I had especially looked forward to visiting this island to meet them. Once I arrived, I learned something that delighted me even more – that the Cajuns of Louisiana also came from this region. French settlers in the seventeenth century knew the area as Acadia (from the Greek term for the proverbial Land of Plenty) and they became known as Acadians, which later got translated to 'Cajun'. The British threw them out, as the British would want to do. After all, it seems to be our duty in life to go around throwing people out of places and chasing them off. But some of the French made their way back and subsequent generations have kept their traditions alive. Now their music and culture is mixed with that of the highland Scots and the combination makes a unique noise.

What I hadn't expected, as I listened to the music in a bar in the island's capital Sydney, was the almost jazzy kind of syncopated rag of the piano and fiddle together. The sound that came out of the instruments played by two extremely talented young women jarred on my ear at first. I thought it didn't work but then I got into it. There is something about the lilting side of the fiddle that's a bit like the bagpipes. It's got that same feature that

CAPE BRETON ISLAND experienced an influx of more than 50,000 Scots during the Highland Clearances. Their influence remains today. Gaelic is still the first language for many older people, and the place names, such as Inverness, Dingwall and New Glasgow, reflect the island's strong immigrant history.

This rocky island of some 140,000 souls, which was once, the geology tells us, joined with Norway and Scotland, was connected to the Nova Scotia mainland in 1955 by the Canso Causeway, an S-shaped road that extends for almost two miles. Previously the island could only be reached by ferry. Once rich in coal seams that were exploited until the 1980s, as was fishing, the island's economy now relies heavily on tourism including the promotion of whale watching and the scenic Cabot Trail through and around the Cape Breton Highlands.

Cape Breton Island, which was granted to Robert Gordon of Lochinvar by Charles I in 1631, is famous worldwide for its fiddle music, which was brought to Nova Scotia by Scottish immigrants, and ceilidhs are a popular tourist draw. It also has a small French population, who were evicted from Nova Scotia by the British in the eighteenth century.

A Cape Breton fiddler and her accompanist

makes you want to jump up and dance. The musicianship was so impressive.

I shouldn't have been so surprised, I've discovered over the years that anywhere where the winters are long the musical culture is in fantastic shape. When folk are locked indoors for long periods of time, unable to farm, they do other things – including practising music for months on end. What they come up with is usually quite extraordinary. There is always a kind of panic about the loss of this kind of culture but that panic is generally started by people sitting in libraries. Those who are actually part of the culture carry on fiddling and dancing while everyone else is talking about it disappearing.

The early Scottish immigrants who arrived on Cape Breton Island lived in near isolation until the Canso Causeway was built. Many dreaded its coming. There is always fear when you build something like that, such as the bridge that joins the Isle of Skye to the mainland or the Black Isle peninsula to Inverness. People think they're going to lose something or invoke bad spirits from the dark waters by going against what is natural.

I guess they do lose something, but they always gain something at the same time. You can't expect islanders to sit in little communities forever just because it's funky and cute or so that you can visit them and watch them playing the fiddle as if they're garden gnomes. They want to evolve. They want computers and a house and a family and a car and rock and roll and foreign holidays down to the Caribbean. That's what people in China want, too. They want a Swatch and an iPod. They don't want to be sitting around eating chow mein and singing the old songs. That's the way it crumbles; it always has and it always will. The far away grass is always greener and sometimes the far away dollars are greener as well.

What's happened in Cape Breton is that, despite the causeway, they have really hung on to their Scottishness, which has remained pure. They still speak Gaelic and they have maintained certain types of step-dancing and music which can be traced straight back to the times of the Highland Clearances. It must have given them such inner strength to have that one thing that belonged to them, when everything else had been taken away.

I did get the feeling there, though, that their situation was a bit like the poor old piano player and the *Titanic*. Their fishing is gone and their coal mining had gone, and not just 'gone', they chased it

Whale bones on the shore

away. There is a trap people often fall into where they complain about something as if it fell on them from the sky. But they did it themselves. They caught the fish and sold them. It's not like the fish ran away or big, bad other fishes came and overfished their waters. It's been the same with the coal mining and apparently the farming isn't doing all that well either. I got the distinct feeling that Cape Breton's best days are behind it.

Although to be fair, I've seen societies on the brink like that before, and something else often shows up, either tourism or a new kind of crop that someone wants that they never wanted before. The outstanding example was the kiwi fruit. The Australian farmers weren't doing very well and then they started to market the kiwi fruit, which used to be called the Chinese gooseberry. Suddenly the world wanted to eat it and there was a boom.

I think that's the way it has to be thought out for the future of farming. You can't just rely on your same crop to work forever. You have to think of something new and vibrant or your livelihood will fade away. Farmers need to invent a new cheese or just give an old cheese a new name, like the British do.

In Chéticamp, an Acadian fishing village on the Cabot Trail, they are still firmly rooted in the past and happy to be so. To celebrate the ancient French festival of Mi-Carême, a respite day in the middle of Lent, the locals dress up and wear carnival or Halloween-style masks and parade from house to house. They pretend to be the current president or Saddam Hussein or some other famous person and their hosts have to guess their true

Las Vegas

identities. The participants often change costumes up to three times a day and they carry on doing it for six days! When we were children in Scotland after the war, we used to dress up like Winston Churchill and Adolf Hitler, but there was a creepy factor to the Chéticamp festival that would have made my grandchildren cry; it was a bit like visiting the Village of the Damned.

The masks the revellers use each year have been put to another purpose by one Chéticamp resident, in a way that surprised and delighted me. Chester Delaney is a scarecrow maker. I'd never met a scarecrow maker before. I never thought there were such things; I just thought farmers hammered scarecrows together from brushes and old clothes. When I was younger, we used to invent jobs that guaranteed you'd never be employed and mine was 'spear sharpener'. I reckoned if I could register with the social security as a spear sharpener, I could be unemployed for the rest of my life, happily picking up a cheque. I never thought of registering as a scarecrow maker, which would have been ideal in the heart of Glasgow.

I'd assumed Chester's scarecrows would be the straightforward type to scare the birds away but there was something much darker to them than that. Chester showed me the ninety or so scarecrows he and his late father Joe had made over the past thirteen years, all lined up in a huge circle in a field. With their Mi-Carême masks and costumes, they looked like part of some Satanic ritual, dancing in Hell. It was kind of freaky. There was a row of politicians including Margaret Thatcher, Ronald Reagan and George 'Dubya' Bush, all life-size with false faces on top of thin bodies and shabby clothes. There was Alice Cooper, a 'Grandma' and the Queen. All had notices on them and names, including a witch called Pamela – which I don't think my wife would have approved of.

Some were named after locals, such as a dead miner called Wayne who now had a permanent memorial in scarecrow fashion. Another was a fisherman, his clothes flapping in the wind, and there was a steelworker with a poem pinned to his chest that reads: '*Shift work took me out the door, till Sidney Steel was no more.*' It became more bizarre by the yard.

A talented amateur fiddle player, Chester told me the scarecrows started when his father was a janitor at a local school and planted a small garden. A neighbour warned Joe that he'd need a scarecrow to frighten away the deer or they'd eat all his vegetables. He made two and put them up in the garden, and the next morning

Opposite: Chester Delaney and his scarecrows

discovered a bus parked outside with tourists taking photographs. Chester carried on the tradition after his father died. Almost a hundred scarecrows later, 'Joe's Scarecrows' are on the official tourist trail. Chester stands on a stage nearby, playing the fiddle and singing old French songs for his coachloads of bemused visitors.

Scarecrow-making is a kind of art form, and I was thrilled by it. I love art and I love going to galleries. What really pleases me is all the ultra-modern conceptual art by Tracey Emin and all those people. I am so delighted with the way that's going and I love the way it irritates the Establishment. I think what I liked most about Joe's scarecrows was that they weren't trying to teach me anything. Sometimes I get bored by artists trying to teach me something, as if they are from the index finger school of entertainment. I look at abstract art and think, 'What the hell is that supposed to be?' hoping that I'm not being conned.

Chester's place was a cross between a side show, an end-of-the-pier kind of attraction and art. It had a truth to it that I loved and which had a profound effect on me. It was like going to a graveyard and finding the dead still standing. Although the scarecrows had a kitsch, Disneyland feel to them, they were of real people – many of them friends of Chester's. That gave the whole thing a creepy feel but it also made a wonderful memorial – it was a lovely statement about friendship. I wanted to copy it. I'd like to have scarecrows all over my garden. I once wanted to make a table for eating out at in the garden in summer. I wanted to make it with mannequin's legs and I was going to put kilts on them, or football shorts, but that's as near as I ever got to doing something like this.

The more Acadian people I met the more I liked them. When I discovered that they had originally been peasant settlers – as opposed to the Quebec French colonists who were sent by their king, Henry IV – I immediately knew why I liked them. That peasant thing gets me every time; it appeals so much, even in food. Whenever I've been eating well, you know, like at some place with several Michelin stars or something, I begin to feel bad. Soon after, I have to have peasant food again.

I am the same with people. I have to mix more with peasant people after a while. That's what I liked most about this bit of the world. There was a happiness in the air, a continental happiness, which really appealed to me.

Before I left Chéticamp, Chester made a scarecrow in my

THE ACADIANS ARE directly descended from the French colonists who arrived in North America in the seventeenth century from all over France. They integrated well with the local Mikmaq Indians, learning from them how to fish and hunt.

By 1755, however, some 14,000 Acadians found themselves sandwiched between British and French territory. After years of attempted neutrality, they were finally deported from the region in an ethnic cleansing exercise known as the Great Expulsion, after they refused to swear allegiance to the British and fight against their fellow Frenchmen.

Their lands were confiscated, their villages razed and their families fragmented. Some returned to France, but the majority headed south, eventually settling in French-controlled Louisiana, where the local dialect morphed the term 'Acadian' to 'Cajun'. In the 1760s, when Louisiana was ceded to the British and Spanish, a few Acadians returned to New Brunswick to colonize the region all over again.

My scarecrow and I listen to Chester play

honour, complete with a beard and moustache, red shirt and white gloves. I was the happiest I'd been since I was in an episode of *Wurzel Gummidge*, playing a scarecrow called Boggle McNeep. When I was a child, my ambition was to be a tramp but now that I'm one of Chéticamp's famous scarecrows I feel that I have almost achieved that dream. I am, after all, a natural scarecrow.

Chester also played the fiddle for me and it was a joy. I love that Cajun way of playing the fiddle against your heart and singing at the same time. Chester's art is good. His life is good. He's a true, nice man. I loved what he stood for and I loved the type of person that he is. There's a great country song by John Denver called 'Some Days are Diamonds'. My day spent with Chester Delaney, his scarecrows, and his Acadian friends – dead and alive – was a diamond day that will stay with me for a very long time.

The Cabot Trail, Cape Breton Island

RIDING THE CABOT TRAIL ON a motorbike has to be one of the greatest bike experiences in the world. Riding it on a shiny green Harley-Davidson fulfilled a personal dream. It's a strange bike, the Harley. It sends out a funny message. In the sixties and seventies it used to be a rebellious symbol, with a Hell's Angel look about it, but these days, if you've got a Harley-Davidson you look as if you've opted for early retirement, taken the king's shilling and 'gone fishing'.

Driving along that winding coast road in my leathers and my black helmet, it was the size of the horizon which got me the most – that huge big lump of sky and the ocean. I passed pretty painted houses and little coves filled with bleached driftwood. There were even flowers that looked like thistles, so I felt most welcome. It was a lovely feeling rolling along in the open air, especially when I reached the top of the hills and saw the road dipping and winding ahead. There was an extraordinary rush as the air whistled past me. I felt as free as a bird, the engine throbbing beneath me – there is no other noise quite like it although, personally, I like the more hooligan noise of British bikes.

There are warning signs all along the road for moose, the largest member of the deer family but with distinctive, flat antlers. Apparently if you hit one head on it's like hitting a furniture truck. I had a moose burger to celebrate not hitting one and it was delicious. I wonder what the plural of moose is? I think it is moose. It can't be mice. Anyway, a moose is a nice big thing, a unique animal that looks like it has its testicles hanging from its Adam's apple.

THE CABOT TRAIL is named after the famous explorer John Cabot – better known in his Italian hometown as Giovanni Caboto – who arrived on Cape Breton Island in 1497, paving the way for its eventual settlement by Europeans, chiefly Scots, French, English and Irish.

A 185-mile long highway carved into the mountains, the trail snakes around Cape Breton's rugged northern shore, overlooking the Gulf of St Lawrence. Looping around, the trail eventually climbs up into the famous Highland National Park, which ranks among Canada's most scenic destinations.

Named as one of the top road trips of the world, the Cabot Trail is visited by almost half a million people every year. The Scottish scientist and inventor Alexander Graham Bell, who emigrated to Canada and became Cape Breton's most famous resident, once said, 'I have travelled around the globe. I have seen the Canadian and American Rockies, the Andes, the Alps and the Highlands of Scotland, but for simple beauty, Cape Breton outrivals them all.' He made his home in the picturesque harbour town of Baddeck on the Cabot Trail and was there at the time of the Halifax Explosion, helping to mobilize support for the victims.

Riding the Cabot Trail

So, the Cabot Trail was a treat. I don't know why they called him John Cabot when his name was Caboto. What's wrong with Caboto all of a sudden? That's a lovely name. The whole explorer thing is clouded in mystery anyway, with all the Italians, including Christopher Columbus, claiming they discovered the New World when the Vikings were apparently there before them, and then I read recently that the Chinese were there before everyone else. Most of them were looking for cod – that was the key to the whole thing. Cabot was looking for land to capitalize on and to explore while everyone else was chasing fish to Newfoundland. There is apparently an influx of British moving now to Nova Scotia and I must say I'm not amazed. It's a wonderful place, with all that incredible music and scenery, and the people are so brilliant. There is a lovely warm friendliness that shows itself in the music and the people's way of life. I would live there in a heartbeat.

NEWFOUNDLAND

St John's, Newfoundland

For the man sound in body and serene of mind there is no such thing as bad weather, every sky has its beauty, and storms which whip the blood do but make it pulse more vigorously.

GEORGE GISSING (1857–1903)

"IT IS THE serendipitous nature of travel that is everything to me, the stuff that brings a light to your eye. I like to be open to whatever happens and to enjoy chance encounters. Some of the best moments I've ever known have been when two human beings who've never met before collide and are delighted by what they find. When they part, they are full of a sense that they didn't just miss something good and true by walking by.

Another aspect of serendipity comes from the weather and the nature of the world around us. Wild weather especially can be spectacularly beautiful. It can do great things to your head and your clothes and your voice. It can change the whole texture of everything when you have to shout to be heard and people can really feel what you are experiencing, instead of seeing or reading about a guy behaving in a kind of beige fashion. The farther north I went, and the weirder and wilder and bleaker the scenery got, the happier I was. The weather in Newfoundland is a bit like in the north of Scotland, or like the south of Ireland, around Cork; every ten minutes there's some big lash of rain comes whipping at you and then half an hour later it's away. You take it or you leave it.

Opposite: The edge of the world

I wish British forecasters would stop calling it 'bad' weather because I am sure the word 'bad' has a profound psychological effect. It rains a lot in Britain. It always has and it always will. If that's 'bad', then we're doomed. It's not going to get good any time soon so a much better idea is to take your shoes off and walk in it. Get a hat, get a sexy raincoat, get gear that looks good in the rain and get out there among it. Often you look out of the window and it's bleak and you think, 'Oh God, it will be horrible,' but when you go out it's not nearly so bad.

The people in Newfoundland didn't seem to mind the weather one little bit. They make the most of it. They have wonderful, long, snowy winters and places that used to be lakes become highways, so they get on their skidoos and off they go to hunt and fish through the ice and it's lovely. ”

A busker in St John's

I'VE NEVER MET A NEWFIE I didn't like. They're a grand breed. I've met loads of them in other bits of Canada and they're always talking about Newfoundland, which they call 'The Rock', and how great it is. Now I know what they're on about – it's a fantastic place, not least for the accents. Some sound as if they come from the west of England, some sound Irish and some sound like they've come from Mars. They seem to be everything you want them to be – simple and complicated at the same time. They don't mind getting a little drunk either; in fact, they're quite famous for it. St John's boasts more bars per head than any city in North America.

This is a place that statisticians must love coming to: they list it as the poorest of all Canadian cities as well as the place with the most rain, the most snow and the most fog. St John's is also described as the oldest city in North America and there are signs around the town that lay claim to the oldest shop and the oldest street. It is also listed as the place which gives more to charity than any other Canadian city, despite its poverty. The best factoid is that they have more sex than anyone else. Now how can they possibly know that? The statisticians must send out questionnaires for people to fill in, so it's obviously a load of cobblers, no one tells the truth on questionnaires. Unless, St John's registers something on the Richter scale – the whole place vibrating at night as everybody is banging away?

I have been going to Canada since 1972 and Montreal used to be my favourite place, but after I'd been there only a few days,

St John's had become my new favourite. It has an atmosphere I can't really explain; something you kind of *feel* just walking along the street. I especially love the peculiar smell of the docks. I have since I was a boy in Glasgow. Docks smell of fish, obviously, but also of ropes, tar, wood and sawdust and – in Scotland – whisky because the crates would sometimes break. The combination makes up that unidentifiable smell that every dock has: they smell of foreign places and going on a voyage; they smell of being a man and growing up. It's a smell that's always appealed.

St John's has a lovely skyline, too; a great mixture of the old and the new, with a church and a castle. Up against the hill there were all these houses painted peculiar colours because, according to the locals, they just use whatever paint is lying around left over from the ships. This approach certainly beats all those concrete monstrosities that seem to be springing up everywhere else.

Painted houses, a curiosity of St John's

Best of all, St John's was a jolly place. Maybe it's because the majority of its people are descended from those in the West Country of England and from Southern Ireland. I have never experienced quite such a depth of warmth and friendliness and hospitality. Sometimes people live in a place that is so hard they have to be good to one another. Anyway, there's something going on there that's very good – a lot of music, a lot of drinking, a lot of dancing and, well, maybe they do have more sex than anyone else.

St John's used to be the largest whaling port in the world, before the demand for cod took over. When Cabot arrived in Newfoundland he said the fish were so bountiful you didn't even

A pearl among crab-fishing boats

need a net, you just threw a basket over the side. Now there's a lot of shrimp and legged, shelly creatures in the depths a hundred or so miles offshore. Those rugged men you see on television who are said to have the most dangerous job in the world hunt the waters around St John's for lobsters and snow crabs. It wouldn't be my choice of career. And the gulls? They're like golden eagles. My God, I've seen smaller dogs!

I watched some of the fishermen at work and it was quite different from the stereotypical image of the salty old dog sitting by the dock, smoking his pipe and talking about monsters in the wide blue yonder, or breaking into a sea shanty. These days, it's all fork-lift trucks and young men and intensive production. I don't think health and safety was much of an issue for these guys, either – one chap straddled an incoming net in such a way that he could have lost his family jewels in a jiffy; he'd have turned around and been a soprano. I couldn't help thinking that this way of life was going to go, too. The equipment gets more and more sophisticated and so they catch more, but they can't keep fishing at that density without consequences.

I've always felt sorry for the crabs, those spiders of the sea; more and more of them are going to get caught. I mean, it's not as if they're lying fifty feet deep on top of one another waiting to be caught. On the contrary, the poor crab is just carrying on as it has for millions of years – sitting at the bottom of the ocean, minding its own business, winking at the girls. Suddenly – whoosh, it's in St John's. There's got to be an end to it. From where I was standing, St John's didn't look to have a future, economically, but I met some oil men from Aberdeen who were there to help service a local rig so, maybe?

Tourism is booming now, too, with people buying second homes in Newfoundland and locals realizing that they actually live in Paradise and making the most of their surroundings. I don't know if that's a good or a bad thing, but the province is definitely going to change.

Everyone I met in St John's was very welcoming considering I was what they call a CFA – one of them that Come-From-Away. Bar owner Keith Vokey fixed that for me by performing the famous Screech-In ceremony to welcome me to his country. Keith had been screeching in visitors for sixteen years in a tradition started by his father. I had to don a yellow sou'wester hat and sniff (as I am teetotal) some potent Screech rum. Screech is Jamaican rum that used to be traded for salt fish in olden times, when the Newfie fishermen took their wares to the Caribbean. You're highly unlikely to find it in your local cocktail bar; you're more likely to find it in a camping shop for starting fires. Legend has it that when an American officer in the Second World War first downed a shot of

Keith Vokey shows me how to kiss the cod

it he emitted a blood-curdling scream, from which the rum later took its name.

As I knelt on the dockside, Keith dubbed me an honorary Newfoundlander, touching me on each shoulder with a wooden paddle, then I had to recite traditional Newfoundland phrases:

'Is you a true Newfoundlander?' Keith asked me. To which I had to respond, ''deed I is, me ol' cock, and long may yer big jib draw.'

Keith and his friends sang me some local songs and taught me some other Newfie expressions. Then I had to kiss a cod fish on the mouth before being handed a certificate proclaiming me an honorary Newfie and Member of the Royal Order of Screechers. The certificate reads:

'Let it be known that the bearer of this document, having sworn that he has: kissed the Cod, downed the Screech, and shouted: "Long may your big jib draw!" will be considered an Honorary Newfoundlander and will have all the privileges and benefits afforded to a traditional Newfoundlander while visiting our island.'

I felt very proud, even though they'd spelled my name wrong.

Cape Spear and Gander, Newfoundland

CAPE SPEAR (not to be confused with Cape Fear) claims to be the most easterly point of North America. It is far more easterly than New York or Boston or any of those places and, stuck out into the ocean, the cape is North America's first landfall. Its squat lighthouse looks out towards the next landfall – Ireland – and the whole

CAPE SPEAR WAS originally named Cabo de Esperança by the Portuguese, which means Cape of Hope, and the Portuguese name became translated, later, to Cape Spear. The cape has had a lighthouse since 1836, the second to be built in Newfoundland. Its first light came from a lighthouse on the island of Inchkeith in the Firth of Forth on the east coast of Scotland.

Now the oldest surviving lighthouse in Newfoundland, it forms part of a national historic site. It is fitted out just as it would have been for a lighthouse keeper and his family in the 1840s. A gun battery was built during the Second World War and fitted with two ten-inch guns to protect Allied convoys coming into St John's Harbour. A German U-boat fired torpedoes into the harbour in 1942, but caused no serious damage.

Cape Spear lighthouse

place had a majestic feel to it. I could just imagine settlers arriving there, heading for oil or gold, or work, or cattle. That has always been the way of the New World, I suppose: the fluidity of the population with their willingness to up sticks and seek better fortune.

My next stop was Gander, international crossroads for air traffic. Gander is one of those places that everyone has heard of and yet no one I have ever met has been there – like Crewe railway station. Whenever you're on a railway journey through central Britain, they often say, 'Change at Crewe', yet no one seems to stop to look around. Gander is the airline equivalent and used to be a major refuelling post in the days when aeroplanes couldn't carry enough to get them farther than the east coast. It is also the base from which more than 20,000 American and Canadian fighter planes stopped en route to the war in Europe.

Gander is the lifeboat of the North Atlantic. If you're in trouble out there, they'll come and get you, or this is where you'll head for. Even when you fly across the Atlantic these days, the pilot often says, 'We are now passing over Gander,' and a strange sigh of relief

Above left: Gander airport
Above right: Gander air traffic control

comes over you because you think, 'Oh, great. There's land again. We're not going to be floating about in the sea trying out that whistle and the inflatable jacket.'

The town that is famous for saving people has a four-day Festival of Flight each year. At a community breakfast, I joined in the celebrations of Gander's fiftieth anniversary as a municipality. It was a pleasure to be in a town that was younger than I was! In a community centre, I found 1,400 or so Ganderites enjoying traditional Newfoundland bologna cake, fish cakes and baked beans. It was served up by women wearing red hats who were apparently part of the Red Hat Society, a group of over-fifties women who don red hats of every shape, size and description, have fun and do good works. I wished I was a woman so I could join them. Although I didn't much fancy the fish cakes for breakfast (and I'm a man who's been known to ask for the wine list at breakfast!), I loved the idea that people came together, ate together, renewed old friendships or healed old arguments. I think the whole world should get up and have breakfast together. I would love it to happen in my own home town. I'd show up, have breakfast with everyone, have a bit of a laugh, a bit of a cry, go and see a parade, get drunk and go to bed. Nothing wrong with that.

The Gander parade later that day, which crawled through the town to the wailing of police sirens, was followed by fireworks watched by those who'd flown in from all over the world to take part in what was called the Come Home Year. I spotted two real Canadian Mounties in the parade wearing the killer uniforms they used to wear, the red jackets, black hats and boots, not what they wear now (dark blue with a yellow stripe). I didn't like the parade, which seemed a bit contrived. Gander had a bedraggled appearance and there wasn't even really a main street to parade along, so the route went past shops and the backs of houses, with the two Mounties trying to march in step even though there wasn't any music. It was all a bit bizarre.

I think the main problem with Gander is that it's a purpose-built town. Those places never really work in as much as they don't have age or atmosphere. In this case, the airport came first and it needed three hundred men to work there. Instead of having them live there for a week or two and go home, they built a town.

The trouble is that it looks as if it's been brought in by helicopter from Ikea or something; just set up with gas stations and fast food outlets and badly designed houses. There is always a kind of

FOLLOWING THE TERRORIST ATTACKS ON mainland America on 11 September 2001, when American airspace was closed, thirty-nine transatlantic flights were ordered to land at Gander. Some 6,500 passengers and crew were cared for by the townsfolk for several days until flights resumed.

In what they called Operation Yellow Ribbon, ordinary Ganderites stopped what they were doing and took these strangers into their homes to feed, house and entertain them. People who lived several hours outside town drove in to help, bringing soup and sandwiches, cakes and pies. The church, school and local Lions Club were used as makeshift dormitories. The town's ice rink was sequestered to store all the food they'd need – the biggest walk-in cooler in the country.

A planeload of terminally ill children whose dying wish was to visit Disneyworld, Florida, had also been diverted to Gander, so the townspeople threw a big party for them with clowns and cakes to try to make up for their cancelled visit. Kidney patients who needed dialysis were tended to and those whose religion meant they had to pray at sundown were given special places to worship. Passengers with relatives in New York were taken into private homes and allowed access to telephones and faxes to try to find out what had happened to their loved ones. Members of animal welfare groups even crawled into the planes' cargo holds to feed and water all the animals on the flights.

The majority of the town's 10,000 residents volunteered their services. Even afterwards, when the town offered to throw a party for the volunteers, they refused, claiming they did what they did out of goodwill and not for recognition. A book has been written about the Gander experience, called *The Day the World Came to Town*, and a film is in the pipeline.

A typical Gander street

nothing feel to new towns and although Gander had such nice people living there, their town had that kind of soullessness about it, which I wasn't so keen on.

As an act of hospitality, Gander's experience that day has never been repeated anywhere in the world. Imagine 6,000 people dropping in for dinner! In a world in which there is so much rotten news all the time, it is delightful to point out that people are capable of such goodness.

When I asked David Brake, a retired school principal and Gander politician, what happened after 9/11, he answered with pride:

'We're world famous. The Americans especially were very appreciative of what this town did for thousands of people that came here. Everyone was cooking food, driving people around, taking people into their homes, showing them the sights. They even took them fishing.'

Special relationships developed, and some of the stranded passengers have returned since for their holidays. One American couple even came back to hold a day of thanks, for which they supplied all the food and drink and invited everyone who'd helped. David claimed the legendary Newfie hospitality dates back to the tough days of British rule, when people could be hanged for stealing a loaf of bread. Religion took a hold for the same reason. There were other motivations, too, he told me.

'Because it was such a harsh climate and so hard to live, people were starving to death. We helped each other out. During the Second World War, Newfoundlanders were among the first to volunteer for duty because they'd have starved if they'd stayed at home.'

Before taking me fishing, David gave me what he called 'a good scoff' with caribou soup, made from a reindeer he'd shot himself and trout 'fit for a king'. He added, 'in fact the king isn't getting them – you're going to have them! Then we've got roast beef sandwiches and my wife Sherry has some homemade baked buns and strawberry tarts and lemon cake…' I drew the line at the Newfoundland Black Horse beer, but the caribou soup was to die for. It almost turned me into Davy Crockett.

David took me on the back of his quad bike down a long gravel road fringed with fir trees. The Gander River is the principal river of north-east Newfoundland, fished for wild Atlantic salmon and brook trout by the Europeans since the mid-1700s. He waded out into the peaty water but I – in my tam-o'-shanter complete with red pom-pom – stood closer to the bank. We both cast our lines while enjoying the beautiful coldness of the day. David told me that fishing is free on this stretch of the Gander, unlike Scotland where it is ridiculously expensive.

Fishing to me has a lovely meditative quality to it. There is something mesmerizing about the water, and the casting and the rhythm of it all. I love the weight of the water around my legs, as it

Riding the trail with David Brake

tightens. David said that a day fishing was a day added to your life, and I think he must be right.

It is a mystery why sometimes the fish bite and sometimes they don't. Whenever I am with a film crew, the chances are I won't catch anything. Meanwhile, my host usually gives me the old line, 'Should have been here yesterday. They were jumping out of the water and biting our faces!' or, 'We were pulling them out of our waders!' That's exactly what happened with David, who told me wryly that he must have pulled the last two salmon out of the river a few weeks earlier.

'My God, what is it with Newfoundlanders?' I asked him. 'First, you chased the cod away and now we just ate the last fish in the country!'

* * *

"NOT KNOWING IF you're going to catch a fish is part of the joy of the whole fishing thing, as well as being out in the wilderness. There's something so basic about just you and the wind in the trees, plus the little ancillary noises like things plopping in and out of the water, birdsong, and little animals squeaking and scratching. I love the rattles among the pebbles.

Waiting for a nibble

Being so close to nature makes you feel lovely, enjoying your own company. When you're on your own, you're never actually alone, there's always action around you. Nice smells. A gentle breeze. You feel like a citizen of the world – less sophisticated, less 'officed'.

People say to me, 'You must get some ideas from your fishing?' I've never had an idea in my life from my fishing. To me, fishing is for the opposite reason. I get a lot of nothing when I'm fishing. That's what's so delightful because it shuts out the whole world and helps me forget about all the nonsense.

I don't like killing the fish I catch either. I like letting them go so that they should live to fight another day. I know other people feel differently. I was in Belize fishing once, staying at a fishing lodge. Some guys asked the guide why he put the fish back and didn't eat them. He replied, 'Because it's a sport. Do you take part in any sport yourself?' One of them said he played golf, so the guide asked, 'When you've finished a round, do you eat the ball?' I never heard it put quite so succinctly before. I'm still stuck with this image of someone eating a golf ball. ”

David told me that in the early 1900s the local people used to pull fifty-pound salmon out of the Gander and shoot caribou with fifty points on their 'racks', or antlers. Now they're lucky if they get a fish half that size, or a thirty-pointer. Humans aren't the only ones hunting here. Newfoundland has one of the healthiest populations of black bears in North America, some of which grow to 700 pounds. One winter, David and a friend were out in a cabin in the middle of nowhere, much farther north, when they were attacked by bears.

'Three of them were trying to break their way into our cabin. Luckily enough we had a shotgun. We didn't shoot at them, but we might have had to if they had kept on. We were firing over their heads and that keeps them at bay.

'One of the bears ripped the seat off my skidoo. You gotta carry oil to mix with your gas to keep the engine from freezing. He actually chewed up the oilcan and drank part of the fuel!'

David took his hunting seriously, so much so that he cooks and eats the heart of every animal he kills. He claimed it was an old Inuit tradition and that a hunter takes the power of an animal

The last fish in Newfoundland?

when he eats its heart. I had to take his word for it that a caribou heart stuffed with scallops and shrimp was delicious.

I liked David. He was a happy man with a happy home and a happy family. He was one of those people just glad to be alive. I also liked the people of Gander, who were awful nice folk. They find it very easy to communicate which is a lovely thing, a very Irish thing, in fact. People just swan up and talk to you like they've known you all their life. It takes you by surprise, and being a townie you get a bit suspicious at first, thinking, 'What's your game?' but it's the real thing and although it takes a bit of getting used to, it's well worth it.

St Anthony and L'Anse aux Meadows, Newfoundland

WHEN I WAS A BOY I learned that St Anthony was the patron saint of things lost and that if you ever lost anything you prayed to St Anthony and he found them for you. I don't remember him ever finding anything, but when I found myself a lost soul in a cold place called St Anthony, I couldn't help but think of him.

On the northernmost tip of Newfoundland, north of St Anthony, is L'Anse aux Meadows, an archaeological and World Heritage site once known as Jellyfish Bay. This part of Newfoundland is as wild and as beautiful as anywhere on the earth but when the weather's bad, it's all dreich and dreary, as they say in Scotland. It had the kind of drizzle that seeps into your bones like guilt. Scotch mist, some people call it. Like wet fog. You feel it doing your skin the world of good. It is the same weather as you get up in the northern isles in Scotland, where conditions can become Arctic overnight. You mustn't go there in your khaki shorts and prance about like you're in the tropics because it can suddenly change.

This area has a stunning landscape in a lonely, weird, windswept sort of way. Beyond is Baffin Island and the coast of Labrador. This was the last place people would stop before heading north to freeze. They'll come again, though, this time to use it as a holiday resort or to buy second homes. They'll treat it nice and come every weekend with their yachts and summer craft. The whole culture will change radically almost overnight, in much the same way the Viking history of the area has changed. It is all part of the natural process.

The Vikings who settled in L'Anse aux Meadows 1,000 years ago had a look, stayed about five years, thought better of it and buggered off. They didn't hang around. I thought they would have been after fish but it seems they were after trees, because they came from Iceland where there were none, and they'd settled in Greenland, where there was a shortage of them. So, they wanted food and wood and they only lived in L'Anse aux Meadows for a

IN THE ANCIENT manuscripts known as the Norse sagas, written on vellum between the twelfth and fourteenth centuries, a place called Vinland was mentioned, colonized by Leif 'the Lucky' Erikson, son of the feared warrior Erik the Red. Much later, the Vinland Map – which came to light in the 1950s and is currently in Yale University – was pronounced to be a fifteenth-century mappa mundi, redrawn from an original created 200 years earlier. The map's authenticity is now in some doubt, but nonetheless it depicts a large island west of Greenland in the Atlantic.

Everyone wondered where Vinland was until 1961 when a couple of Norwegian archaeologists arrived in Newfoundland, determined to prove that the Vikings were the first in North America, 400 years ahead of Christopher Columbus. They excavated and found eight wooden houses covered in sod turfs (including a longhouse), slave quarters and a forge. The Vikings originally called the place Vinland (meaning 'wine land') because they thought they'd found wine berries or grapes, but what they had found instead were cranberries, which – they discovered to their disappointment – made poor wine.

Re-enacting the Viking way of life

while, eating whale and seal and fish, killing the natives and often each other.

They smelted bog iron in the smithy, which is remarkable science for 1,000 years ago. It was the first time iron was produced in North America. But they used it to make a hundred nails to fix up the boats and get the hell out of there. With that weather, who would blame them? The discovery that they'd even been there was all down to a local fisherman called Dexter, who first told the Norwegian archaeologist couple about some lumpy ground and mounds north of St Anthony that weren't explained. The thing that amazes me is that they covered it all up again once they'd finished their archaeology. They put it back the way they found it, and I kind of like it – the way they left it.

You wouldn't know the Vikings hadn't stayed long in Newfoundland from the theme park they've created at L'Anse aux Meadows; it's got Viking jewellery on sale and people dressed up as Vikings in pointy-toed boots, wandering around a rebuilt Norse settlement. These former fishermen and women spend their days pretending to be the invaders who once lived there; the husbands and wives, chieftains, even their slaves. They re-enact the Viking way of life right down to stitching cloth with whale bone and smelting iron in the forge.

That sort of place is a bit too touristy for me. I don't like to frown on it when so much effort had gone into it – and some of what they have done is lovely – but I always feel that if you want to know what life is like in a place then ask the ordinary people – the Inuit eating whale blubber, or Chester Delaney making scarecrows – not someone dressed as a Viking. I understand they need to make a living to pay the rent – any port in a storm and all that – and I realize that tourism has become this region's lifeblood since they lost the fish. But it's kind of weird, and I don't think I've ever seen the equivalent of that particular set-up anywhere else. The Vikings were there for about ten minutes, whereas the indigenous Indians were there for thousands of years before that, but no one ever wants to be them.

A heavily bearded ex-fisherman who called himself Chieftain Bjorn the Beautiful, but whose real name was Michael Sexton, showed me around and introduced me to his wife, Thora the Battleaxe: 'She's sharp and deadly and puts the fear of God into any man.' In his orangey-red robe, hat and Viking belt, he gave me a tour of their weapons' house, with axes and swords, 'good for hacking people's legs off', and then we got into a light-hearted argument over whether the Vikings were better warriors than the Scots.

Bjorn the Beautiful and Thora the Battleaxe show me around

Living in the past

'We leathered you at the Battle of Largs,' I assured him. 'We Scots set you on your way... we chased the Romans, we chased the Vikings, we chased the English. We just chase people, that's all we do.'

Bjorn countered, 'Maybe, but Largs was only one battle.' He accused us Scots of hiding behind Roman walls. (They talk a good game, those Vikings.)

'The Romans built those walls because they were scared of us,' I contradicted. 'They were the ones hiding behind them. They left us where we were.'

The walls of the cozy Vinland houses were six feet thick and the turf on the roof acted as insulation, which they needed to have in this wild and lonely place. Fires burned in stone ember pits to keep out the cold and the wet. Some of the roofs sprouted flowers and were very pretty. The buildings were reminiscent of the blackhouses of Scotland. Those Vikings probably copied us.

Bjorn was well read on Norse history and recited some old poetry and texts which spoke of how the Vikings washed themselves regularly and changed their clothes and combed their hair in order to attract women. Those savages! What I loved the most was that they had such great names, like Magnus Bare Legs and Killer Stare and Vermin the Slender. I am so jealous of such names. I would love to have been in a band called Vermin the Slender.

The Vikings were a remarkable people and astonishing sailors to have regularly crossed such rough and dangerous seas in their shallow keel-less ships. They must have found the weather so rough once they did settle at L'Anse aux Meadows. I can just imagine them looking across the sea, wishing they were back in Greenland or Iceland, hammering away, making their own nails to sail their boat back. God, we have it easy, don't we?

Having visited Vinland, I could see why people travelled from miles around to reinforce the idea that maybe they were of Viking stock. People like to be Vikings. They love the picturesque side of their history. It allows them to say, 'Well, actually, we're not just an immigrant population, we are all Vikings at heart.' There's something very brave hearted about that, being a descendant of the hairy Vikings with their axe-carrying image. I guess the immigrant status is so shaky that people want something to cling to, a bedrock. They cling to religion, or to the old culture. Some kids even cling to gang culture just to get strength, an anchor in their lives. The more I travelled in this part of the world, the more

I came to understand the need for a past that these people all seem to share.

Quirpon Island, Newfoundland

WHENEVER I HEAR a place is famous for whale watching, I think 'Uh-oh'. I'm sure all the whales think, 'Right, let's dive' as soon as a whale-watching boat approaches. It's just like fishing. As soon as you claim somewhere is a great salmon river, you can cast and cast until the water's foaming and not get one fish. These creatures make up their own minds.

Quirpon Island (pronounced like 'harpoon') is the most northerly tip of Newfoundland and the last bit of civilization before the wild blue yonder. I stayed next door to the old lighthouse, in a house done up in the style of the 1920s, which was when it was built. A lot of these houses seem to enjoy looking rundown: quaint and lean and shabby, they hang about waiting for people to come and paint them. Most are worth a buck fifty now. In five years' time they will be worth half a million.

The lighthouse on Quirpon Island

From there, I went out in a boat to search for the humpback, orca and minke whales that swim in those waters. Truth is, I would have made a lousy whaler. I never see them until the last second, while others spot them miles off, spouting. I wouldn't notice them 'til the tail flipped over my boat. It's good to keep your eyes focused on wherever the whale might be, though, because it makes you forget that your stomach is coming out of your ear. Suddenly, my full Newfoundland breakfast didn't seem such a good idea. I'm okay on those kinds of boats as long as I'm away from the diesel. People talk about looking at the horizon and recommend all sorts of things to avoid seasickness but the worst for me is the combination of diesel and dead fish. After that, I can feel my inner organs coming down my nose.

I managed not to be sick this time, and when I did finally spot some pilot whales in the distance, I was very pleased. It's such a privilege to see something that size, living in its own wets.

A noble profile

I am always blown away by whales and dolphins, and deer and moose and anything big. To think that these creatures just wake up in the morning and go about their lives being that big. Often in Scotland I will be driving up to my house through the glen and I will see monster red deer with antlers, five feet high at the shoulder, a huge chunk of meat and horns and hair, standing by the side of the road. I think: 'How do you do that? How did you get so big and strong just grubbing around in the dirt?' It baffles the life out of me.

Icebergs aren't as moody as whales. They don't dive and hide. From Quirpon Island we went up in a six-seater plane over what is known as Iceberg Alley to get up close and personal with some icebergs. The ones we were hunting would have been calved from the same glacier that produced the iceberg that hit the *Titanic.* I was ridiculously excited, chiefly because I'd seen icebergs before. When I went to Baffin Island to film a programme called *Scot in the Arctic*, I was on first name terms with one at a place called Grise Fjord, the most northerly inhabited place in the world. I camped on a frozen sea for several days and the iceberg was my next door neighbour. It was the loveliest thing.

People are bottling the water from icebergs now – 15,000-year-old glacial water. I don't know how it tastes or how it looks in a bottle, but I'd love to have a go. I know that 'my' iceberg – which is how I came to think of it – tasted wonderful. I'd chip off some ice, melt it in a little pan over a gas ring, and make my dinner with it. It was the most glamorous water tank I have ever had. I don't know why I should get so excited about a big lump of ice. They exist for so many years, they float down from a glacier in Greenland towards Labrador and then the current takes them. They can be very dangerous if you're too close when they suddenly collapse, especially when they're a mile wide, or the size of Delaware. The farther south they go towards the Grand Banks the smaller and smaller they get, until they break up into bits. Once they do start to break up, they tumble over in their own space and form fantastic shapes called 'bergy bits' and 'growlers' before melting in the warmer waters. Bergy bits and growlers: I love those names.

Icebergs are made up of fresh water and then the salt water freezes around them. But the iceberg remains on its own, with a freshwater moat right around it. As the tide ebbs and flows beneath it, the iceberg rises up and down, scraping the sides of the rest of

the frozen sea. At Grise Fjord, I'd be lying alone in my tent and hear the iceberg groaning and scraping all night long. The Inuit told me that the spirits of their ancestors travelled inside icebergs, coming back to see them every spring. I'd complain, 'Well, your granddad was grumbling a bit last night,' and they'd laugh. In the end they named the iceberg after me, which was really nice.

After a few days of staring at my namesake up there, though, I started to see the Inuit ancestors in its facets. Not in a Disneyland kind of way, but I swear I could make out the white shapes of people standing around in a circle inside. An iceberg is like a big crystal, with different lights and shades. Looking into one is like looking into a fire as a kid and seeing faces and caves in the flames and the embers. I spotted one guy with a pixie hood that was kind of pointy at the back. I also saw a big face that looked a bit like Jesus, or at least a man with a beard and a crown of thorns. The television people who were filming me then thought I had lost the plot. By the time we got to Newfoundland to look at another iceberg, I couldn't believe my eyes. There were the ancestors again, this time in the crystal-blue veins of the beast – men with pointed hoods, like the Inuit wear, and a man who looked a bit like Max Wall. Once again, most of the people around me couldn't see it, but when we had filmed it, Tim the cameraman said he saw it too. I could have danced a wild jig.

Opposite: Pondering the perfect slide

* * *

"*EVERYONE THINKS ICEBERGS are white, and like ice cream all the way through, but they're not white at all, they're blue, the most spectacular turquoise aquamarine blue, like the late Paul Newman's eyes. It's like a huge piece of sensational jewellery gliding majestically along. They are so alien in their surroundings; a bit like seeing a polar bear in the middle of Sauchiehall Street, but they have such presence, such enormous power; a drama all their own.*

I'd like to tow one up the Clyde or the Thames or the Tyne or the Mersey and let all the kids see it. In a decent world we should all be allowed to slide down one. They're just made for sliding down, especially on the inside where there's bound to be a big pool at the bottom of a wonderful slide you can land in with a splosh!"

The pilot of our plane allowed me to take the controls for a while over Iceberg Alley, something I've never done before. I've sat up-front, and I've been in a glider, but no one ever said, 'Carry on. Have a go.' I paid little regard to whether it was safe or not. I didn't want to wonder what might happen. Health and safety is ruining the world – which is why children these days go out cycling looking like medieval knights. I say, let them go out in a T-shirt and skin their elbow. They won't do it twice.

I thought Jim, the pilot, was kidding me at first when he offered to let me fly. Then I thought maybe he was working the plane with his feet like a dual-controlled car or something. But he wasn't, and when he told me to turn it to the left or the right my heart sang a wee song. Georges Simenon, the Belgian novelist, once used an expression that I use a lot: in answer to a love letter he'd received, he wrote, '*I received your letter yesterday and I had a little party in my heart.*' Every now and again I have a party in my heart and flying that plane over that great lump of ice was one of those moments.

A wee party in my heart

At Quirpon Island, I had climbed from the helipad – installed for visitors who prefer to skip the boat journey and keep their breakfast – to the top of the lighthouse with its 360-degree view. Standing there looking out to sea impressed the hell out of me. To see the Atlantic spread before you like that, you suddenly get an idea of the sheer size of this monstrous piece of water. All that space enforces a kind of humility on you and makes you realize how puny you are. More amazing even than that was the thought of how far I had yet to go, north and west, on this incredible journey. I'd hardly even started, and there was all that wilderness yet to come.

All that wilderness yet to come

PART TWO

Sunshine is delicious, rain is refreshing, wind braces us up, snow is exhilarating; there is really no such thing as bad weather, only different kinds of good weather.

John Ruskin (1819–1900)

NUNAVUT

Iqaluit, Baffin Island, Nunavut

The wonderful thing about snow is that when it falls it covers everything up and makes even the ugliest place look beautiful. To arrive in the capital of the Inuit territory of Nunavut on the southern coast of Baffin Island when the climate is not so accommodating is to be confronted with a very different perspective.

If I had expected a picturesque snow-covered landscape in the home of some of the proudest hunting people in the world, I was to be disappointed. Collected at Iqaluit's yellow-painted airport by local undertaker Bryan Pearson in his sleek black Cadillac hearse, all my expectations of what it would be like coming to the edge of the world soon melted away. As Bryan so succinctly put it: 'There are three major issues here and they all start with a "D" – Dogs, Dust and the Dump.'

Iqaluit is a dust bowl for several weeks each summer, and the snow which used to stay on the surrounding mountains all year long now melts to an incongruous green for much of the year. Dried by a northerly wind, the dust that is exposed gets into people's clothes, homes, their electronic equipment, everything. The skidoos, abandoned vehicles and all the paraphernalia of living in a snowy climate sit around looking tired and shabby. In Bryan's words, 'It's a fucking mess.'

Bryan Pearson is a Liverpudlian who left home as a teenager for a life in the merchant navy and ended up unemployed in Montreal

Opposite: Dogs, Dust and the Dump

IQALUIT WAS NO MORE THAN a prime fishing spot for the Inuit until it was identified in the 1950s by the Americans as one of the sixty-three sites for radar stations forming part of the Distant Early Warning Line, or DEW Line.

When the Soviets began to match American missile technology during the height of the Cold War, it was decided that the two existing lines of radar stations across North America – the Pinetree Line (from Newfoundland to Vancouver Island) and the Mid-Canada Line (along the 55th parallel) – were no longer sufficient. The new DEW Line ran roughly 6,214 miles (along the length of the 69th parallel, 200 miles south of the Arctic Circle, from Alaska to Baffin Island, and included stations in Greenland, Iceland and the Faroe Islands.

More than 25,000 Canadians were employed to build and install the radar stations, an engineering and construction triumph in the most hostile of environments. By 1958, the DEW Line was key in the new NORAD (North American Aerospace Defense Command) scheme for joint continental air defence, but within a few years – as technology outpaced their capabilities – the radar stations were deemed useless and several were abandoned, including the one at Iqaluit.

Almost thirty years later those still functioning were upgraded and incorporated into the North Warning System, but by 1990 and the end of the Cold War, the stations were handed over to the Canadians, sparking a controversy over who would pay for the clean-up of large amounts of hazardous waste they'd caused.

Bryan Pearson chauffeurs me in his hearse

almost sixty years ago. He saw an advertisement for a job in Nunavut and jumped at it.

'When I first came here in 1956 it was an American military base. They were in the process of building the DEW Line. In those days that was all hush-hush. We didn't even know where we were going. They put us in aeroplanes and flew us all bloody night to this place. We slept in tents in the winter. We were pioneers, freezing our asses off. It was a challenge.'

Bryan started working as a dishwasher (affectionately known as a 'pearl diver'). Then the baker got fired, so they appointed him because he'd worked in a bakery as a kid in Liverpool putting the crosses on hot cross buns. He has done most jobs in Iqaluit since then. He set up a company making pre-fabricated buildings, he was mayor for sixteen years, he runs the cinema, owns a bed and breakfast, broadcasts the local radio station and, twelve years ago, became the town's undertaker.

'When you live in a place like this,' he explained, 'you've got to make a living and do whatever you can put your hand to. There were no politicians, no council. People didn't even vote.'

Before he took on the role of undertaker, prisoners from the local jail were detailed to bury the dead. Then someone complained that it was an infringement of their civil rights.

'The dead used to get a plywood overcoat and a ride to the cemetery in the back of a truck,' said Bryan. 'Now we give them

Opposite: The DEW Line golf balls

some dignity because we have a hearse and proper coffins, which I have manufactured and flown in from Montreal. I don't prepare the bodies or anything; I can't stand that. I can't even look at them. I receive them in a bag and I put the bag in the coffin.'

Bryan told me that the town is running out of ground in which to bury people. Cremation is not an option because of the expense. It had never crossed my mind before how much petrol it must take to burn a body, or how out of the question that is in a place where fuel prices are so high. I don't know what we're going to do if the rest of the world is faced with that too. Maybe we'll have to start burning people the way Hindus do – by making a wood pyre and setting it alight.

There is no shortage of customers for Bryan, as Iqaluit has a high rate of suicide and a lot of deaths from drugs and drink-related problems. Drugs are widely available – anything from marijuana to ecstasy to cocaine – and Bryan claimed that most of the town's movie-goers regularly arrive at his cinema stoned. I can remember doing that myself with *2001: A Space Odyssey.*

An opera fanatic, Bryan flies frequently to New York to see performances at the Metropolitan Opera House. A complicated man, learned and self-taught, he reminded me of a lot of people I grew up with in the shipyards in Glasgow: well-read, educated but curmudgeonly. People like that all have this grumpiness because they're bright. They can see things turning to shit all around them but no one much listens to them. Bryan was very sure of himself and had one foot firmly in the present and another firmly in the past. They seemed to be arguing with each other, which I liked about him.

IQALUIT WAS, until 1987, known as Frobisher Bay after Martin Frobisher. A swashbuckling sixteenth-century British explorer, admiral and privateer, Frobisher travelled three times to the New World in search of the Northwest Passage and a route to China.

On his first visit, he set out with three tiny ships, one of which was lost in a storm. The second defected back to England. Having landed at Baffin Island in the third vessel, *Gabriel*, the Inuit kidnapped half of his crew, so he collected some mineral samples, took a hostage and sailed home. Having had his samples examined, the Yorkshireman believed he'd discovered a low-grade gold ore, so he returned with several hundred Cornish miners and Elizabeth I's blessing, to set up the Cathay Company and a fort from which to mine the ore. He sent more than 1,000 tons home to England for smelting. After further analysis, however, British experts finally agreed that the ore was hornblende, a type of 'fool's gold', useful only for repairing roads.

Frobisher went on to fight the Spanish under Sir Francis Drake, and eventually died from his wounds in a battle off the Spanish coast in 1594. The bay on which Iqaluit stands still bears his name. The capital of Canada's newest territory, Nunavut – which is the size of western Europe with fewer than 30,000 people living in it – reverted to its original Inuit name meaning 'the place of many fish' in 1987.

Frobisher was convinced he'd found the route to China when he first arrived on Baffin Island because the locals looked so Asian with that high-cheekbone Mongolian appearance the Inuit have. Then he found the black rock with twinkling glittery bits inside it, and being no slouch, he shot back to England, stopping only to grab a local in his kayak on the way. He gave the poor Inuit guy as a present to Elizabeth I, who toured him around as a little showpiece, making him throw his spear and do some tricks, until he died of the flu. Isn't that the saddest thing?

Frobisher wouldn't recognize the place now, with its houses on stilts that look like abandoned fridges and its fibreglass municipal

buildings that resemble above-ground swimming pools. The schools don't even have windows (why bother with windows when it's almost always dark?). There is wealth in Iqaluit beyond any fool's gold, though. In 1993 the Canadian government settled a land claim with the Inuit to the tune of five billion dollars. As half of Iqaluit's 6,000 residents also earn good salaries working for the government, everything from house prices to the cost of importing goods is sky-high. The rent for a three-bedroom apartment is approximately thirty-five hundred dollars a month and some of the bigger houses sell for several hundred thousand dollars apiece.

All basic provisions arrive in Iqaluit by air or sea. The ships use the same method of unloading containers onto barges as Frobisher used when he first arrived there in 1576. There used to be a dock, built by the Americans in the 1960s, but the tides (some of the highest in the world at forty-five feet) and the winter ice – which can be nine feet thick in the winter – soon destroyed it. The empty containers sit around, abandoned or used for storage by the Inuit, along with scrap vehicles, used electrical goods and any other old junk that is too expensive to get rid of.

'The biggest problem we have here is waste disposal,' admitted Bryan, 'although the dump was a great place to go foraging. The Americans threw millions of tons of stuff away – vehicles and engines and bulldozers. Now they've stopped burning everything and they're just accumulating instead, crushing all the metal and shipping it to Montreal to sell to the Chinese.'

One dump was full of everything from half-frozen dead dogs to plastics, tyres, animal skins and vehicles – things the people of Iqaluit are no longer allowed to burn because of pollution. They can't bury it because of the permafrost, so the mountain of crap just gets bigger and uglier. In the old days, they used to take it out and leave it on the ice until it sank into the sea, something they are no longer allowed to do. It's all very well saying 'Don't float it or burn it', but I think before you shout that you should have a plan B. I haven't got any answers, but something has to be done.

Another big problem in Iqaluit is dogs. When the Inuit first arrived with the American military fifty years ago, they let their dog teams loose. The dogs soon bred and became a problem.

'When I was mayor,' Bryan said, 'I appointed dog officers because we had vicious, hungry huskies, which are very primitive creatures, running around and scaring the hell out of people. Now the Inuit want compensation from those who shot their dogs.'

Few of the houses in Iqaluit are on mains water because of the extreme temperatures, so fresh water is delivered by tanker every day. Sewage is taken away by a separate truck to a treatment plant. It used to be quite different.

'Prior to that, we had a very sophisticated system,' Bryan explained with a smile. 'They were called honey-buckets. We just used to throw our sewage in the bay.

'At the annual spring festival we still have the honey-bucket flinging competition where you fling your bucket into a forty-five gallon container. There is also a seal-skinning competition, harpoon throwing, and the Mouth Pull where two men sit facing each other and pull on each other's mouths. The first one to let go is the winner.'

There was one other competition Bryan told me about which I have to see before I die. It is called the Ear Carry in which heavy weights are attached to men's ears by pieces of string. The one that can carry the most weight wins. Brilliant.

Iqaluit has no public transport, so one of the most lucrative businesses in town is the taxi industry – especially when the

temperature is forty below and there are hundred mile an hour winds. The town has more taxis per head than New York. I have no idea how the taxi drivers find anywhere though, because the streets have no names and the town only gave the houses numbers a few years ago. The property at the farthest end of town was designated No. 1, and the one at the other end was No. 3,260 or something. People mostly give directions to someone's house by describing it as a few doors down from someone else's, which is fine if you know who everyone is but a nightmare if you're from out of town.

Bryan showed me a Canadian base for jet fighters, set up since 9/11, and a sixty-nine million dollar hospital with hardly any doctors or nurses – 'we can't recruit them'. There was also an eight-million dollar French school with just a handful of students, an Arctic college and the Fort Knox liquor store, which was broken into more than any other building in town. The two prisons were what Bryan called 'a growth industry'. Most of the inmates were in for being drunk and disorderly, which was very popular when I was growing up too. Iqaluit's jails tended to fill up when the weather turned, he said: 'If you do something bad, you may as well do it in the winter and get free lodgings and three meals a day.' Whenever they become overcrowded, inmates are flown fifteen hundred miles west to the region's former capital, Yellowknife – the same distance as between London and Cairo.

He showed me the Pan Am building, once used by the now defunct airline as a stopover hotel, crew-change hub and refuelling depot. 'All sorts of interesting people used to come through here,' Bryan said.

'There were two flights a day and I used to meet them all, to sell carvings to the passengers. I remember the actor Robert Mitchum came off a Trans World Airlines flight one night, drunk as a skunk – a big man too – and spent five hundred dollars in our store. We had never seen so much money; it was incredible. The Shah of Iran was here, too. He was travelling to Tehran.'

Many of the Inuit who live in Iqaluit, even those who work for the government, still hunt for their food – mainly char fish, seal and walrus, as well as the occasional beluga whale, which is full of nutrients and considered a delicacy. They are allowed to hunt for up to a hundred whales a year. During the hunting season in the summer months, the Inuit often relocate from their houses to tents on the beach to be near to their boats.

It's great when people put tents up behind their homes and go camping instead of living in their houses. I love that. It seems a great idea to me. I was a townie in their midst and the things that made them happy were unknown to me. Everything took me by surprise. What was also great was the nine-hole golf course Bryan showed me, made with old carpets laid on the tundra. They used to play on sea ice, dyed green with food colouring. They even have golf carts. We Scots really started something with this game; the only one played on earth without a referee. No one blows a whistle. They don't need to. In Scotland, we're a nation of gentlemen.

Bryan blamed the town's high suicide rate and drink and drugs problems on the fast pace of change for the Inuit. 'These people lived an extremely primitive lifestyle for the last four or five thousand years only to be suddenly thrust into the twentieth century with a bang. When I came here, maybe two of them spoke English, and now they're all working for the government.'

* * *

SUICIDE IS THE worst thing that can happen in a family because everyone blames themselves. I've had it happen – friends of mine have killed themselves in the past. You always think, 'My God! If I'd only phoned. If I'd only gone round. If I'd only have shown more compassion. If only, if only, if only…'

I'm no social worker but I think what happens is that the Inuit get an education and then the penny drops and they realize that despite all they've learned, they're probably going to remain in Nunavut forever. I think they must reach a certain period in their lives when they think, 'I'm not going to make it south. I'm not going to the big time.' People then have to make choices.

They settle down, sometimes very happily and accept their lot saying, 'This is me. I am happy. I'm going to marry and bring my kids up here.' Others get depressed and start to drink or take drugs to create a false reality; the rest kind of naturally follows. They think that if they're ever going to be someone they have to get away otherwise they'll just have to look at those buildings every day.

When I was young, Sweden had the highest suicide rates; then it swung to Japan, with all the young people who felt they were underachievers. Now it seems to be the poor Inuit who have one of the highest rates. That is very sad indeed.

Bryan claimed the Inuit elders had done a remarkable job at keeping their community cohesive in such times of change: 'They are very aware. Long before scientists started talking about global warming – before the words even meant anything to anyone – they were the first to say that changes were happening and that our weather patterns weren't the same. I would love to learn just one eighth of what they have forgotten.'

I met Adameei Itorcheek, a successful young businessman who introduced the Internet to Iqaluit and was at the forefront of wireless technology. Adameei told me that his mother arrived with a dog team in the sixties and is now an elder. He went on to become one of the town's success stories, having worked in the fire service and been a paramedic too. He'd travelled the world over and had such a powerful optimism. A wealthy man, working for the government, he nevertheless had one foot very definitely in the Old World. His belief in the elders warmed my heart.

'Those that first came here were the ones willing to be open to new ways,' he said. 'Their generation came pretty close to starvation and they came here because the government brought them in to put their children in the schools.'

Adameei was one of the negotiators who settled the 1999 Nunavut Land Claims Agreement with the Canadian government, 'without a shot being fired'. The agreement created the territory of

WHEN THE CANADIAN GOVERNMENT BEGAN to investigate the life of the Inuit who lived far in the north of its country, officials couldn't easily pronounce the names of those they came across. So, in 1940 they issued each of them with a leather dog tag, giving everyone a number prefixed with letters signifying their location (such as E for East), their community, and the order in which they had appeared in the census.

The Inuit were encouraged to take easily pronounceable Christian names, so that they became known as something like 'Eddie E7-139' or 'Mary W8-1542'. They were then expected to remember their numbers, those of their neighbours and all the regional codes as well. Many Inuit grew up with this system, believing it to be the norm for white men until they travelled to cities and discovered that they had been treated differently.

In 1969 Project Surname was set up to replace the numerical system with one that gave the Inuit names directly relating to each of their kinship lines. The numbers were gradually phased out, although many still keep their dog tags and think of themselves by the only 'names' they'd ever known.

Nunavut (which means 'our land') and gave the Inuit autonomy over it.

'We are now the generation that questions and challenges. We say, "Hey, wait a minute, let's be realistic about how decisions affect us."'

Adameei told me that the EU ban on hunting polar bears and on the sale of seal products helped the local bear population expand from 5,000 when he was a child to an estimated 25,000 in modern times, a number which had impacted hugely on the reduction of the seal population on which, for food and skins, many Inuit still rely for survival.

He said it usually takes the federal government ten years to listen to the elders. 'When the Americans first came, their engineers asked us which direction the winds came from and we told them, "North. Our prevailing winds are north." But they built the runway east-west. It goes north-south now.'

Adameei was one of the last generation to be given a dog tag, in one of those bright, colonial schemes to treat the Inuit as if they didn't exist. It makes you ashamed that the British Empire was part of it. He was known as 'Adam E7–2256' until Project Surname. He joked that he was going to rename his street 'Project Surname Survivor Road'.

'Today's Inuit are survivors,' he said. 'This area has always been a melting pot for different cultures and different philosophies going back to Frobisher. People say half the Inuit work and half don't but by whose definition are we gauging work? I know quite a few hunters who don't make any money off the government but they sustain themselves as they have always done.'

Adameei is optimistic about the future as long as the Inuit care for their elders, nurture their kids and maintain sustainable hunting for future generations:

'We need to look at where we came from and where we are going. We need to keep making changes because if we stay in one spot, it's not going to do us any good. Our elders didn't do that; if the hunting was no good, they moved on. We, too, are constantly evolving.'

I liked that these people constantly harked back to the elders. It surprised me, but I thought it was healthy. I liked, too, that most of the children were bilingual in a place where their culture and their language are so closely linked. English is the language of power, the language of information and technology, and I could see why the kids were drawn to it but I loved that they still spoke Inuit at home.

Tookie Pootoogook, an elderly Inuit, was sitting next to me as we watched some old Inuit films at the Iqaluit Museum. They were mostly images of his family and friends from long ago. There was his grandfather and his great uncle, plus many other friends and relatives, standing in the snow outside their igloos, all dressed in fur. The old man sitting beside me was wearing a baseball cap and sweatshirt. As he watched the films, he sighed and shook his head, saying, 'They're dead, all dead now.'

What struck me the most about the film was how happy the people looked – and how comfortable, standing around in the snow in their traditional sealskin clothes and hooded garments with leggings, talking and laughing, playing with their dog teams. The women wore fur parkas and carried their babies in the hoods, all warm and comfortable, their faces looking out. I would love to have known them. They knew who and exactly what they were back then. Their lives were so different to the Inuit way of life now.

Seeing those long-dead Inuit in that snowy situation moved me deeply, especially Tookie, remembering it all so well and watching a time when his life was something else. Later, I was told that he lives at the Salvation Army hostel and visits the museum every week to watch his past, which can't be good for him. I don't know what he does there. I should imagine he gently weeps. His whole world has changed radically; from the way of the dogsled to the

Tookie Pootoogook

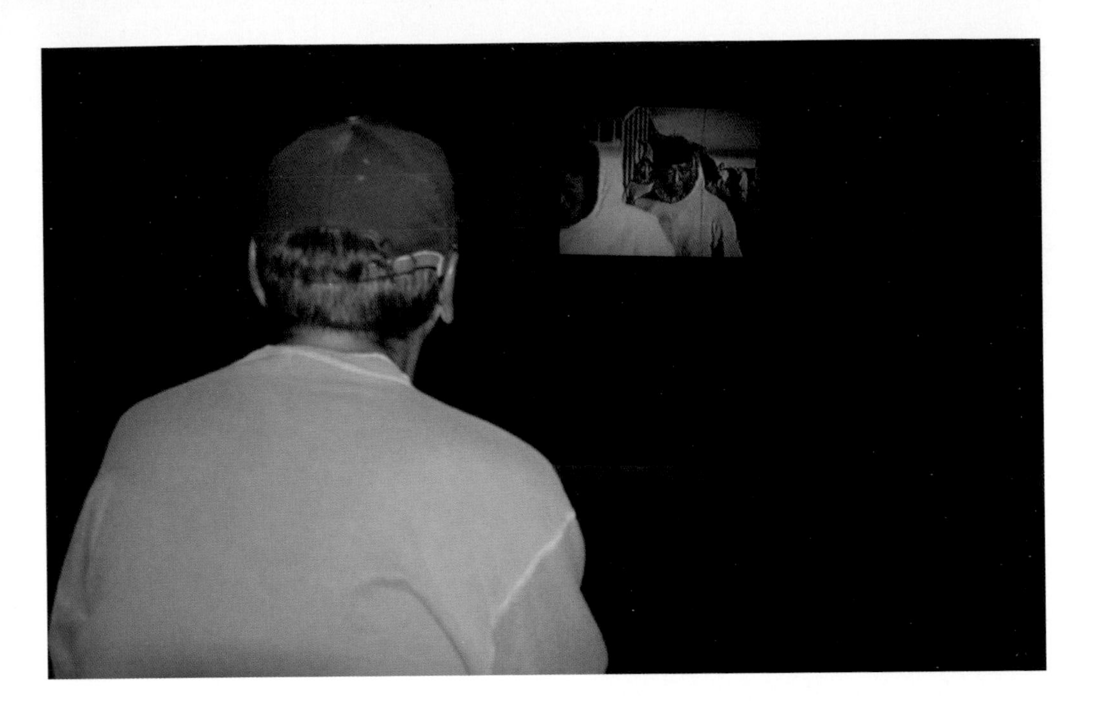

Tookie watches old movies

Internet, prefabs and fast food. Tookie seemed completely unsure what his role in the modern world might be, and his uncertainty, I think, is representative of the Inuit in this region in general. I think many of them were unsure of what to do. His face will always haunt me and seeing him there like that made a wee hole in my heart.

* * *

"AS I EMERGED from the museum and looked around Iqaluit, it felt like a very different world from that society of snow-dwellers I'd just been watching. Iqaluit was not at all Home Sweet Home, nor a place its people seemed to be in control of. It looked scruffy and knackered and raggedy-arsed, with crap lying all over the place. Mainly, there was no snow and snow kind of defines the Inuit. I don't say they need winter to survive but everything they do great is in the snow.

Snow is a great forgiver of untidiness. Even the skidoos outside the houses looked as if they were rotting – I got the feeling that they were just waiting for winter to come so they could really come to life. (It's a good name, isn't it, skidoo? It's better than ski-mobile, or whatever they called them. I'm old enough to remember when skidoo was a normal word. If you were leaving a place quickly, you'd say, 'Let's skidoo.')

Maybe I was just a Scottish Glasgow townie enjoying the luxury of imagining the Inuit doing what they do rather well. I am often guilty of lashing out at things I don't understand, especially when I'm out of my depth in other people's cultures. But when you see people like that, in a place where it's all dust, and with those sheds and buildings that look as though they've arrived in a parcel, there is something not right about it.

I spotted a husky dog creeping around the rubbish dump and that summed it all up for me. That husky should have been barking and woofing, charging through the snow with a sealskin collar, not sniffing at the rubbish. He didn't even know he was a metaphor. ”

Iqaluit's Arctic Survival Store gave me a brief taste of the old life, with its Georgian doors and great sense of an age of exploration. Kitting myself out for the impending wilderness of the real north I bought some polar bear deterrent. Every home should have some, don't you think? I asked the owner how far the bear had to be away for it to be effective.

'A metre and a half,' he replied.

'I'm dead,' I said. 'If a bear gets that close, I might as well spray myself.'

THE HUDSON'S BAY COMPANY IS one of the oldest companies in the world and was, for a time, the ruling body in North America. Once the largest landowner in the world, it was founded in 1670 to fund exploration for the fur trade, which was its chief commercial concern.

Started by two French traders and a consortium of Boston businessmen backed by the English Navy, the company was given a charter by King Charles II as 'The Governor and Company of Adventurers of England trading into Hudson's Bay'. Under that charter, the company was required to give two black beaver pelts and two elk skins to any visiting member of the British royal family, a tradition which continued until 1970 when the Queen was presented with two live beavers, which she donated to Winnipeg zoo.

The company's monopoly in the seventeenth and eighteenth centuries gave it control of more than a million and a half square miles of modern-day Canada and North America, chiefly south and west of Hudson Bay. Setting up a network of ubiquitous red-roofed trading posts at forts across the continent, the trappers and traders who worked for the company soon wrenched control of the fur trade from the French by negotiating new deals with Native Americans, giving them woollen blankets, metal tools and hunting implements in return for skins and furs. The trading forts, especially the company's headquarters at York Factory, Manitoba, were the subject of fierce battles between the French and the English during their war at the end of the seventeenth century, until York Factory was finally ceded to the British in 1713.

When the fur trade went into decline the company diversified into whale oil and the sale of supplies to the thousands of settlers encouraged to move to North America by European nations eager to lay claim to the New World. In 1821 the company merged with the North West Company of Montreal, giving it trading control over even larger areas of land between the Atlantic and Pacific Oceans and nearly all trading operations in the Pacific Northwest.

During the mid-nineteenth century, trappers extended the company's control into Oregon and northern California, around the same time as it began to print its own paper money, printed in London in denominations of English pounds. But by 1870 the trade monopoly was abolished and all trade in North America was made open to any entrepreneur. On the company's 300th anniversary in 1970, its international headquarters were relocated from London to Winnipeg, Manitoba and then later to Toronto, Ontario. The only part of the company's trading post business still operating today is in the North American department stores The Bay, Fields, Home Outfitters and Zellers. It also operates finance branches dealing with mortgages, personal insurance and credit cards, as well as car rental, bookstores, cinemas, oil companies and food outlets. In 2008, the company was bought by NRDC Equity Partners, parent company of the Fortunoff and Lord & Taylor department stores, and became a multinational corporation.

I hoped that a gun or flares would be more of a deterrent, so I asked him to show me some. He had bangers and rocket launchers and all manner of kit. Pegged to a frame was a big seal skin, with holes where the flippers had been. It takes six skins to make a parka, apparently, depending on the size.

Hanging up on a wall was a wolf skin for sale for a thousand dollars. The owner of the store assured me there was nothing better: 'The snow doesn't stick to the fur.' White fox skins were cheaper at four hundred and fifty dollars each, as were the hides of silver and red foxes. I've never worn any wolf but I have a sporran that is a fox and people give me real brain damage about it. I keep telling them it came from a road kill but they never believe me. God knows what would happen if I turned up with a wolf. I would have demonstrations in my honour. It's a different kind of society where I come from.

Nicole Pauze, a sixty-something great-grandmother and one of Iqaluit's eighty taxi drivers, drove me around the town. Nicole, with her bright orange hair, was such a happy individual. Originally from near Montreal, she had wanted to see the world and ended up in Iqaluit. If I wanted to see the world I'd have gone to Monte Carlo or somewhere, but maybe you do see the world in Iqaluit after all.

Nicole Pauze, seal taxi driver

'I wanted to see who these people were who were living at the other end of the world and what it looked like,' she explained.

'I find it very interesting. I love them very much and the weather is fantastic. It's dry even in the winter time and it doesn't chill you to the bone like I heard British weather does.'

Iqaluit is Nicole's home now. She found she fitted perfectly and has earned a great deal of respect. That's got a lot to do with it, I think; the fact that she isn't nothing. That means something in a smaller society like this – that you're someone and that you count. If you're a taxi driver everyone knows who you are, they know you're good at what you do and suddenly you're a person of substance in the community. That gives you proof every day that you exist. I used to worry about that when I was a kid – that I would live and die and no one would notice I'd been there. It wasn't a desire to be famous, it was just a desire to be noticed; that people would notice that I'd been there, and had left a footprint.

Nicole took me on the Road to Nowhere, which even had its own blue and white road sign. When your children come home at night and you ask, 'Where were you?' and they say, 'Oh, nowhere', that's where they've been. One of the world's mysteries has been solved at a stroke.

The Road to Nowhere

The Road to Nowhere used to be a dusty road leading to a sand pit where trucks would pick up sand to throw down for the roads. Now it's a paved road to somewhere – to a brand new part of town, a couple of years old, known as Uptown or The Other Part of Nowhere. Apart from being popular with courting couples, the road now leads to the town's most expensive houses which retail at around five hundred thousand dollars, with addresses like '40, Nowhere'.

I asked Nicole who would buy them.

'Government people,' she replied.

'But if you had that much money, why would you want to live here?' I asked. Her answer was simple:

'You make money here, you keep your money. There is no other way to spend it. So then you can afford to travel around the world and go other places, something that maybe you wouldn't be able to do when you are living down south.'

Nicole told me that the house I was staying in had recently sold for seven hundred and fifty thousand dollars. I had no idea I was living so high on the hog!

Nicole's most troublesome passengers are usually the women of the town who, she said, behave 'like the queen of the castle', especially when they've been drinking. She recently had to ban seals from her cab:

'Someone put a dead one in the back when I wasn't paying attention. It wasn't frozen and seal meat has a very strong smell. It took me a week to wash my car with all kinds of product to take care of the awful smell. So now before someone puts some meat in my car I make sure that it's frozen.'

Nicole clearly loved Iqaluit, but the place was too weird for me. It was neither fish nor fowl. It wasn't Inuit and it wasn't southern white. It wasn't anything. It had a feeling of being a temporary, impermanent place. I know there are people who've been born there but it didn't look like it to me. It seemed like everything could be swept away tomorrow, folded up and taken away, and there would be nothing there.

Maybe that will be what happens when the Northwest Passage thaws and everyone moves in for the oil and gas and iron ore. People will want to own it and they'll try to do deals with the Inuit government, who are going to be under pressure again. They've been under pressure before – from the loonies in Washington and Moscow during the Cold War. Now there is going to be even more

VAST QUANTITIES OF petroleum were discovered in Nunavut in the 1970s but exploration was then halted due to high transportation and extraction costs. The Nunavut Land Claims Agreement, which gave the Inuit legal right to 135,000 square miles of land, also included potentially lucrative mineral rights.

As North America begins to run out of resources and the changes in weather patterns make the Arctic more accessible, further exploration for oil, natural gas and minerals is already underway. Early estimates claim that Nunavut may be able to account for up to twenty-five per cent of Canada's oil and gas needs. Existing gold and diamond mines are also being developed further. Other mines harvest lead, zinc, copper and nickel.

Large quantities of high-grade iron ore have also been discovered on Baffin Island and are being explored for future use by the Japanese automotive industry. Petroleum production is a major industry in Canada, with the highest density of wells being drilled in Alberta. British Columbia, Saskatchewan and Manitoba also have wells. Petro-Canada, one of the four main players in the Canadian oil industry, has extensive interests in Nunavut. The other key oil companies are Husky Energy, Imperial Oil and Suncor Energy.

pressure from the oil people and those who want to own the land. It just seems to be never ending, that quest for oil and gas.

I do think that owning Nunavut has done the Inuit a great deal of good, however. They get a lot of personal satisfaction from owning their land. I hope it works out fantastically well for them. I can see everyone keeping their eye on the place and they're going to have to be awfully clever to fight these bastards who are going to come in and take whole swathes of the surface of the earth away and leave big holes, a kind of industrial rape – but we'll see what happens.

* * *

"I'VE BEEN IN some horrible places and thought, 'How the hell can anyone live here?' Then I realized that someone probably drove through my little home town once and said, 'God, look at these people! How can they live in this place?'

Your home is your home. It's got nothing to do with what it looks like or what star rating it gets from anyone who's passing through. As they say in Scotland, 'East, west, hame is best.' You hear people waxing lyrical and singing songs like 'Take Me Back To—' wherever, and you've been there and you say, 'What? You want to go back there? Are you daft?' But home has got this power over you. You can feel it coming through your shoes. I know I am home again when it comes right up my legs.

The farther I travel, the more I miss my bed and the personal things I haven't had in years – little bits of food, little Scottish sausages and other items I suddenly get a longing for. All immigrants are like that. You meet Scottish guys in Toronto or Vancouver, Sydney or Melbourne and you ask what they miss the most and they never say, 'Oh, I miss the heather on the hills and the sound of bagpipes as the sun's going down.' They say, 'I miss Irn-Bru and square-slice sausage and brown sauce.' Like them, I miss those tiny luxurious things that make your life worth living, especially food.

No matter where you live (and I've lived in various places – London, Los Angeles and New York), there is always a moment when you're on the plane and someone says, 'Where are you going?' and you say, 'Home.' But you are leaving your home town, the place where you were brought up. The first time you say it, you think, 'Oh my God! I'm in Glasgow but I said I'm going home!' It takes a real bite out of you. It feels as if you've let someone down or said something treasonous. But home is where the mortgage is. That's just a fact of life. It's not where you hang your hat – it's where you pay your debt. Your home is where your bed is. It's where your shoes are. ”

Rebecca Veevee is an Inuit TV chef and comedienne who is trying to get her people to spurn the Western fast food they have adopted in recent years and go back to cooking traditional dishes like caribou, seal and whale. There is a high level of diabetes among the Inuit and Rebecca blames it on the junk everyone seems to eat these days.

Before I met her, I had visions of that shit that appears on British daytime television with assorted chefs and celebrities farting about for half an hour, chopping onions and talking crap. On my way to her tiny kitchen where Rebecca's show is recorded, I thought, 'Oh God! Have I come to this?' I needn't have worried. Rebecca was a joy. Standing watching while she was being filmed, I rejoiced as she sang while she cooked and enthusiastically thanked her blender. She made burgers with wild caribou, egg and onion which were the best ever, and maktauq soup from beluga whale which tasted a bit like squid – it was slightly rubbery at first but as soon as you chewed it became this other thing and was delicious with veggies and some noodles.

Rebecca was a genius. Hers was sensationally good food made well. You know that Buddhist thing – if you put love into it, love

TV chef Rebecca Veevee cooks caribou

comes out of it. That's something I learned a long time ago and Rebecca had it in spades. We had a lovely time together and instantly liked each other, she really had the Force.

Some people shine and some don't. You see a lion in the zoo and he's kind of matt, looking around his cage and farting, but you go and see a lion in the wild, with no water, nothing, and it has a shine; a barely perceptible sheen. You see that in healthy people too. Their skin shines in the sun; there is a gleam from them. When they are sick or in a place they don't belong, people go matt. The shine goes away.

Rebecca was just where she belonged, singing and doing a dance as she cooked. This wasn't showbusiness. It wasn't even daytime television as we know it. This was the real deal.

Auyuittuq National Park, Pangnirtung, Nunavut

THE LANDSCAPE OF this national park carved by the last ice age two million years ago was sensational. Holy Mother of God, I felt like I was in *Lord of the Rings*. This was a miraculously wonderful place, so pristine, and yet they only had something like 600 visitors a year.

Before I even got to the heart of it, I had to trek miles up a valley towards the mountains. In the retelling it will be much more. It'll stretch to twenty-five or thirty miles, who knows? Then there is the

AUYUITTUQ NATIONAL PARK, on the Cumberland Peninsula of Baffin Island, comprises twenty-one thousand square kilometres of some of the most beautiful Arctic wilderness. In the Inuit language, Auyuittuq means 'the land that never melts'. They are thinking of renaming it Auliqtuq which means 'the land that never used to melt'.

Glaciers, fjords and ice fields dominate the spartan landscape on which scant vegetation grows. Few creatures live there, only twelve known species including lemmings, hares, Arctic foxes and polar bears. Established as a park in 1976, the region's most famous mountain is Mount Asgard, which featured in the opening stunt of the James Bond movie, *The Spy Who Loved Me*. The nearest town is Pangnirtung (known as 'Pang') on the coast of a fjord with a population of around fifteen hundred. It was established as a trading post by the Hudson's Bay Company in 1921 and now operates a successful turbot fishery.

Above: One more river to cross
Below: The Wringing of the Socks

story of how I broke my stick. In truth, I snapped it in the river between two boulders, but in legend it could have been in a polar bear fight or I could have wrestled with a walrus. Perhaps I went to put my foot on a stone in the river and the stone looked up at me with two wild and vicious eyes. I could see the tusks sticking down. I had to thrust with all my weight to save the rest of the lads – although I was on my own, you understand…

That trek along the ancient riverbed was brilliant. I loved the way the clouds hung below the mountains at the end of the glen. (Well, strictly speaking it was called a fjord in those parts, but it's a glen where I come from.) This was superb country, although I found some of the stony riverbeds tricky to navigate. I've seen enough rivers to last me the rest of my days. I will never again be able to listen to Jimmy Cliff singing 'One More River to Cross'. Despite trying to look elegant and cool, I ended up on my arse in one of them and gave my feet a soaking. Pulling my boots off, I engaged in an old Scots custom – The Wringing of the Socks.

This was true wilderness and one of the most unspoiled, unexplored, spectacular places on earth. I could hear the tributes as I crossed it:

'Connolly of the Great Outdoors, explorer and hiker, scared of nothing, boldly stepped into the wilderness, caring not for life or limb. A bear jumped out from behind a rock but he had his trusty aerosol with him. No bear dared come within ten feet.'

There was a lodge in which visitors could sign a book and there were all the usual type of comments, including one from a Scotsman who wrote that he couldn't wait to take his first dump north of the Arctic Circle. Trust a Scot.

There was one really moving entry, about a fella called Philip Robinson who was killed on Mount Thor, which apparently has the tallest vertical face in the world and people come from all over just to climb it. His friends had built a cairn for him and they carried it up the mountain in a sort of pilgrimage. One wrote: '*This has been the hardest, most important journey I've ever done. Blood, sweat and tears, the weight of stone on our backs for a man I love. We set out … on a glorious day Sunday … We camped at the glacier river … the night was windy, terrifying next morning, felt bleak grey and empty without you. I wanted to hate that moment. I wanted to hate Thor in that moment. I wanted it to crumble and dissolve so that no one could ever climb there again.*'

What a memorial.

PHILIP ROBINSON WAS a Parks Canada ranger who died on duty in the summer of 2006. Aged twenty-six, he was abseiling with a group of nine American climbers when he slipped and fell six hundred metres.

Pauline Scott, a communications officer for Parks Canada, said later, 'Philip was amazing. He connected to everyone. He was one of those larger than life people.' His father, Brian, said he hoped to lead the rest of his life the way his son had taught him.

Mount Thor, also known as Thor Peak, boasts the world's greatest purely vertical drop at 1,250 metres (4,101 feet) of sheer granite, angled at 105 degrees. Philip Robinson's death occurred during the world record attempt for the longest rappel or abseil from Mount Thor. Despite the tragedy, the team managed to break the world record in his name.

We camped out for the night just beyond Windy Lake. I was north of the official green marker that defines the point that the Arctic Circle crosses this barren rocky landscape carved out by glaciers. It runs 66°30'N of the Equator. It was certainly freezing.

Arctic Circle marker

I must have a hot gene in me, though, because I was as warm as toast even though it was bitterly cold up there. I did offer to share my tent with a member of my shivering crew (who were huddled together in a hut), partly because I was scared a bear might come, and if it did, and there were two of us, it would improve my chances to fifty-fifty. If a bear had come in, I'd have switched on my bear aerosol and inhaled deeply. I certainly wasn't planning on aiming it at the bear. I went to bed that night with the goodnight prayer of my old granny in my mind:

> Goodnight my dear and sweet repose. Lie on your back and you won't squash your nose.

Waking up the next morning and looking around me was astonishing. The silence and the solitude were overwhelming. The far north brings with it a peculiar kind of quietness; and I find it's a lovely thing. I don't know why, I don't particularly get profound thoughts, I just get nothing. It's a big, big, emptiness – and it's awfully good for me. On top of Mount Asgard I could see the Penny Ice Cap (named after the Scottish whaling captain and explorer William Penny) and nearby was the Turner Glacier which is a remnant of the Ice Age. There's also a large glacier lake fed by three waterfalls, and a hole in the glacier like a tunnel with water screaming out of it. That is so weird but it's extraordinary to behold.

The sad thing, though, is what is happening to the place with global warming. It's a disaster; you can feel it in the air. Where the permafrost is melting and becoming temporary frost (they'll have to change the name, it doesn't 'perma' any more) there are avalanches happening every five seconds. Not like Alpine avalanches, because there is so little snow, maybe just fifty rocks tumbling down a hill into the water. But as I sat there it happened right before my eyes and it was scary. I'd never seen that kind of erosion before. Erosion is something that happens over centuries where I come from.

And there were huge horizontal cracks in the glacier that lay dripping from the top of the hill. The walls were really thick apart from where the cracks were but the experts say it will only last about another year. I am just a stupid big hairy townie and no instant expert simply because I have walked across the place, but it looked to me as if it was going to collapse tomorrow. When it does, it's going to make a bloody freezing tsunami coming down that valley. It's going to be hell. And there were two of them – another glacier farther up was in the exact same shape.

The best way to see this amazing landscape is from the air and when I flew over the glacier in a helicopter, I could see that I'd been wrong. Those walls that I was worried about were like Jericho; they're not coming down any time soon. The glacier, which looked like a huge white river coming down the valley, was as solid as a rock when we landed the helicopter at the confluence of three other glaciers. I even got out onto it for a while, it was like being on another planet. I was quite nervous at first because I could hear the glacier tinkling away, as it melted beneath my feet, but I wasn't really scared because it was such a jolly noise – it would be good to put to music, the way they do with whale song.

There were puddles on the top when I broke into the ice with my heels. I wondered how thick the ice was. It might have been a mile but it felt like four inches to me. I thought, 'If I fall in here, they're not going to find me for twenty years. I'll eventually emerge up the river eighty feet long and two inches wide.' Luckily, I didn't fall in and I am now on first name terms with a glacier. We got on just dandy. Then I was flown to the top of the mountain and set down

A moving river of ice

Opposite top: On top of the world
Opposite bottom: Glaciers like ice cream

so I could get a panoramic view – me, a little pink thing on the top of the world. It was a breathtaking place to be, even if I felt a little like Captain Oates from Scott's South Pole expedition who said, 'I am just going outside and may be some time', never to be seen again.

It was like being in the middle of something galactic, like the Milky Way. Not many human beings have been where I was that day. I got a real sense of what's happening in the world on top of that mountain; it became glaringly apparent to me. It's the kind of experience you tell people about: 'Listen, I did a thing once. I've seen something remarkable.' What is it people say? That they touched the face of God? I didn't do that but I saw it with my own eyes from the top of a mountain.

I was sitting on the edge of something enormous and it was breathtaking, not only in its size and scope, but also in the enormity of the ignorance of the human race. What do you do with something that big? The glaciers are melting. What should we be doing? Because recycling your garbage isn't going to do it.

The thing that really dawned on me was how the whole glacier thing works. They're hanging over the mountains like a big drip of cream, as if they're oozing into the valley, but actually they're retreating up the hill back up to where they came from: the top of the hill will be the last to go. How weird is that? The glaciers are melting and retreating and I could see it so clearly from up there; I could see where it had been and where it's going. It is on the move and all the recycling in the world isn't going to stop it.

* * *

" AS SOON AS *people become celebrities they start lecturing the public as if they know what they're bloody talking about. I have had it with people eleven years of age on* Blue Peter *lecturing me. Fuck off! I don't want to become one of those bores who talks about the environment and recycling and all that other junk that seems to make people feel guilty as if they caused it, which is total bollocks. I went to Catholic school where they told me God was dead and apparently it was my fault. I hate this blame culture. Shit happens, deal with it. That's my standpoint, but I don't think it will take off as a religion.*

Everybody cries 'Disaster!' but they're so busy running

about looking for who's fault it is that nobody's thinking what we can do about it. Meanwhile, the game is being played before their eyes. All the people I talked to in Nunavut seemed to have an optimistic outlook. In a bizarre kind of way they were looking forward to minerals being found because everybody is going to get a bit of a handout from the government from it. Once the snow melts completely they might be just standing in Paradise. If that national park is anything to go by, holy bloody moly, that's Paradise okay. I've never seen anything like it.

There is a massive change happening but the world is going to win. The Inuit people are determined to deal with climate change; they won't be defeated by it. Most of them will find a way round it. They'll find a way to fish; they'll find a way to mine whatever treasures were unavailable to them when the snow was there. They'll have a look at what's there once the snow has gone.

There are no trees in the national park now but there will be. In Scotland they call it 'crow-planted'; the crows eat the seeds, shit and a tree grows. As more ground becomes exposed by melting snow and ice and then trees grow and make the ground firm, there will evolve another place. Similarly, the people will change; they'll have to, or move.

The future is frightening if you want it to be, but it's also awe-inspiring. I was changed by what I saw that day on the mountain top; it was my chance to witness something unbelievably grand. I was looking at the beginning of the world, not the end. The world wins out every time – when it explodes, when it floods, when it freezes, when it melts, it wins. There is a massive change happening and it's going to be unbelievably interesting to watch. ”

The Inuit in nearby Pangnirtung didn't seem to be that bothered about the effects of climate change. They were more concerned with making a buck, trying to keep body and soul together and paying the rent. As most of them seem to be on welfare, their chief worry was trying to get their kids educated and fed. It is guys like me who have the time to lie around and wonder about nature.

The children seemed well fed and happy. They were all playing

out in the dusty streets or driving their motorbikes and quad bikes like loonies. They laughed a lot and were very friendly. Much of the town's social life revolves around fast-food joints such as Kentucky Fried Chicken and Pizza Hut. At one end of the town kids were eating junk and doing wheelies, while at the other end the elders spotted a whale in the bay. The two sides of the whole Inuit way of life came together really neatly.

Happy kids

Once again, though, I was saddened to see that their town, which is bang in the middle of all this sensational beauty, was a bit of a dump. I personally wouldn't like to live there. Having said that, I haven't been invited to and I am sure the people of Pangnirtung don't give a toss whether I would like to live in their town or not. The houses reminded me of garden sheds. There was a lot of rubbish lying around – old boats, vehicles, bits of wood. It seemed to me that most indigenous people who move into a city create an untidy environment because they've had a history of dropping things behind them. Until recently the things they dropped were organic and biodegraded, so it didn't matter. But plastic bags and old motorcycles and bicycles and skidoos don't just disappear, they take forever to rot. I'm not sure that white people are any more

Skidoos waiting for snow

caring, they are just neater and tidier and have got that side of things together, so that it's a matter of 'out of sight out of mind'. I don't know what the Inuit should do about that, or even if they should do anything. I get confused as to what's patronizing and what isn't. But I know what crap is and what isn't, and if the sea and the land are full of crap then something should be done about it, no matter who put it there or why.

Not that the Inuit don't have a connection with the landscape surrounding them. One valley leading to the mountains was 'named' after the grandfather of Billy, the warden who had escorted me through Auyuittuq National Park. But because his grandfather had been given a number not a name back then, so the valley had a number too. These extraordinarily strong, poetic people, who are as honest as the day is long, seemed to find the history of their naming rather funny but I didn't find it the least bit funny. To think that the Inuit had been taken to the cleaners for centuries incensed me.

The whalers came to take the whales and the seals. They raped the place until they were fed up and the whales went away. Then the whalers walked away. Then the government stepped in to take away the Inuit names and steal the children from their families to educate them separately. It makes me so damn angry that it was done in your name or the name of your grandfather or great-grandfather. The fact that the Inuit are not upset about it quells the fire a little. As does the fact that the Canadian Government has

Simeonie Keenainak plays Scottish whaling music

since apologized and made amends. They're a good government; they seem to be deeply sincere in most of the things they do and I like that about them. Maybe it's the Scottish influence?

I walked to the outskirts of town to sit on a rock in the backyard of Simeonie Keenainak, one of the town's greatest musicians. A former Mountie and sea captain, he had been playing the accordion for fifty years. The music he plays harks back to the time of the Scottish whalers, who also imported booze, bannock biscuits and sexually transmitted diseases.

'There have always been accordion players in these small communities,' Simeonie told me. 'They learned from the Scottish whalers years back. I used to hear the music when I was a child and I taught myself.'

As we sat on his porch, inhaling the smell of seal cooking in the kitchen, I listened; there was a lovely homely, available feel to his music. He was off walrus-hunting the following day, two hundred miles north. He told me walrus had a taste like blue cheese, especially after it has rotted in the ground for a month in traditional Inuit style. I loved watching Simeonie as he played the accordion he'd bought from the Hudson's Bay Company in the 1970s. Two of his tunes, 'Good Memories' and 'Beluga Water', sounded so Scottish but they weren't Scottish at all, they were his own compositions influenced by the past, which I found breathtaking. I played them back later in my hotel room so I could learn them on my banjo.

CANADA WAS FIRST traversed and mapped in 1789 by a Scotsman called Alexander Mackenzie, who was born on the Isle of Lewis in the Outer Hebrides then, at the age of ten, moved with his family to America. Working as a fur trader for the North West Company, Mackenzie set out by canoe to try to find the Northwest Passage to the Pacific Ocean. He discovered a river in the Northwest Territories, the longest in Canada, that he called Disappointment River because it flowed north to the Arctic and not to Alaska as he had hoped. It was later named after him.

Five years later, he made the attempt again, navigating dangerous rapids in canoes and the most hostile of environments on foot. Encouraging his men with rum, he eventually crossed North America from Quebec to Bella Coola, British Columbia, thereby completing the first recorded transcontinental crossing twelve years before Lewis and Clark, the more famous explorers, achieved that goal farther south.

Knighted by George III in 1802, Mackenzie served in the Canadian Government until his return to Scotland in his fifties. He died soon after of kidney disease and is buried on the Black Isle in the north-east of Scotland.

Simeonie told me that when he was a child, he and his parents would make the occasional journey into 'Pang' for provisions: 'My dad used to come for ammunition for his rifle, for tea and tobacco, flour, sugar and other things.' When young Simeonie saw his first white man, a Hudson's Bay manager, he hid behind his mother's legs. 'I thought he was the ugliest thing I'd ever seen in my life!' Simeonie told me. I've heard this before from people who seem to think we're a weird-looking bunch. That Hudson's Bay man must have been a relative of mine.

I went on to meet Ken Davidson, the town's leading bone collector and owner of the red-roofed Hudson's Bay store which dates back hundreds of years. There is also an old blubber station in town where the Hudson's Bay men would haul the whales to skin them, reduce the blubber to oil and export it all over the world. That was a huge industry until the whales took the hint and buggered off.

Ken buys walrus tusks, whale bone, polar bear skins and animal hides to sell to traders the world over. He was doing what Hudson's Bay men had been doing for centuries. One enormous walrus tusk he had was worth up to four thousand dollars. He showed me the skin of a ten-feet tall polar bear with the all-important claws still attached, shot by a local woman hunter the previous year. What really flabbergasted me, though, was a walrus penis bone. It was thirty inches long. Ken explained:

'When I told my wife I'd bought a walrus penis, she turned all red in the face. She asked, "Did you buy it for us, or for the store?" I said, "For the store, of course!" That was so funny.'

I had met some polar bear hunters up in Grise Fjord who showed me the penis bone from a polar bear. I didn't know animals had a bone in their penis until then. I read about it since and discovered that there are a very few animals who don't: The hyena doesn't and we don't, so we humans are lumped in with a bloody hyena. If animals have a bone in their penis there's no need for Viagra, all except for us and the hyena – an ugly pair of bastards stuck on the face of the earth. The blue or grey whale has an enormous penis, ten feet long or something but you would expect that. You'll never guess who has the biggest? It's the barnacle. A barnacle penis is ten times the size of itself and it can come out of the shell and go looking for the female. Yes, it can nip out for the night, have a go and come back later, while the barnacle sits in watching telly.

Ken Davidson and his walrus penis bone

Igloolik, Nunavut

THERE IS STILL a kind of pioneering feel about arriving at airports this far north. With no roads and no other means of getting in or out, you develop a real sense of adventure just getting somewhere. And there are no toilets on the small planes you travel on here, so I took an empty drinks bottle, just in case. Looking at its narrow neck, I realized a jam jar might have been better; some would say a goldfish bowl.

Whenever you arrive somewhere as remote as Igloolik you are given a proper welcome. Most travellers have never been that far north before and most go either because they're driven by a dream or because they've a job to do, so the people who already live there really turn it on for visitors.

What's also kind of exciting about being at the edge of the world is the element of the unknown. You forget how primitive the conditions are or how quickly you can be in a place where you feel very, very alone. There are big mountains and deep water and slippery stones that bring their own element of adventurism and carry with them that little tremble. You leave the comparative

safety of your room and a mile or so later there are bears, and things creeping about both in the sea and on the land, that can eat you with their big long teeth and claws. You're on the menu for all sorts of things that think human beings are delicious. This is a place where things really do go 'Grrr' in the night.

Up in the north, you're kind of doomed unless you realize who and what you are. If you're going hunting, you can't pretend that you know things that you don't because the fog's going to come down or the wind is going to blow up or the waves are going to get big or the snow is going to trap you, and you're going to find out pretty damned sharpish if you're a man or a boy. If you're a bit of a wuss then you're going to go down with all hands. You can get into serious trouble in such inhospitable terrain.

Even the most seasoned travellers think, 'I hope I'm okay here.' And that's because, even if you're with sensible people who really know what they're doing, sometimes you are very far away from help – if you break a leg or something – so you just hope in your heart that everything goes according to plan. I think they are different kinds of guys from us, these people who live pretty much on the edge. And this is the edge. Okay? Make no mistake about it.

Once you have been to the high north, though, it draws you back. Africa is like that as well – during the days of the British Empire some people who'd lived there experienced a thing they called *mal d'Afrique*, which was a longing to go back; apparently India is the same. The north, especially the Arctic, has the same pull. I think it's the silence.

* * *

"WHEN I WAS *in the Arctic once before, the silence was so profound that I could hear my heart beat when I was lying in my sleeping bag. If I moved my stomach I could hear all the contents slopping and flopping around like the tide coming in and out inside me.*

Such silence is a remarkable thing. It drives you inside your brain. You're not on acquaintance with your brain a lot of the time because you're so distracted by everything around you. You don't think about who you are and your place in life or where you fit. In silence and aloneness like that you're driven to think about yourself and it is no bad thing.

I used to wonder if I was happy. People often ask, 'Are you happy?' and I'd always wondered. Then I read The Practice of Contentment *by the Dalai Lama and it brought about quite a change in me. I discovered that if you swap the word 'happy' for the word 'content' you might find that you are happy after all, and I did. We've all been sold this image of what happiness is and I think Western society mistakes laughing for happy. You think if you're not laughing you're not happy, but that's not always true.*

Those were the sorts of things I discovered when I was up there; those subtle realizations. Happiness is not about fame or success or riches, it's about who loves you and who you love. There are no distractions this far north, except for the odd iceberg and that's the same distraction every day. As you go farther south, the distractions are staggering from the second you wake up; some people even wake up with a radio making noise and telling them things. You find yourself having to write everything down because otherwise you're going to forget it.

Even driving to work you're bombarded by all these

different messages – hoardings, neon lights, radio. Everyone is trying to make you think of other things: buy their goods or get a loan or consolidate your debt or buy Esso, buy Shell – blah blah blah. There's McDonald's hamburgers and KFC. Drink beer. 'Here is the news: There is a flood in Peru. The Russians are attacking the Georgians…' Buy BP. Eat another hamburger. By the time you've gone half an hour, you've forgotten where you're bloody going and you find yourself thinking, 'My God! Where am I?' Then you must remember to post those letters or pay the so-and-so bill, and the number of times you forget because you're under such unbelievable pressure to think about other things that have nothing to damned do with you.

Up in the Arctic, you don't have that. The place lets your brain alone. That gigantic space brings its own solace and quietude. You may be uncomfortable with it at first; you find that you sleep badly because it's so silent. But once you get used to it, you long for it again. ”

I had so many preconceived notions about what some of the places I'd be visiting would be like just by their names – Goose Bay, Yellowknife, Medicine Hat. When I got there and they weren't at all like I'd imagined, I was surprised.

Igloolik was one of those places. Were there igloos or did they do a lot of licking? I couldn't wait to find out. The name actually means 'there is an igloo here'. The town is way above the tree line, on land that is as flat as a pancake. It must be seriously whipped by winds. The geographical centre of Nunavut, Igloolik is famous for

Inuit boulder sculptures

being the territory's most traditional town: its people speak the oldest form of the Inuktitut language and stick to the old ways more than the rest of the territory. For many years, they wouldn't even allow television.

Of course the kids there now are all into hip-hop, which causes a bit of disruption between them and the elders. It's the oldest story in the world – the old ones want it to stay the same and the young ones want it to change.

There was a rural feel to the place, and wandering around the town I was amazed how neat and tidy it was compared to the other communities I'd been in. You would think it had been vacuumed that morning. Maybe it's because the stuff they leave lying all over the place is more picturesque than the city guys' stuff. That taught me not to jump to conclusions. The people of Igloolik had got their act together, perhaps because there is no booze allowed in town at all – I don't know if that was a government decision or a decision taken by the elders.

Mind you, there isn't much of anything else either because, as with all these northern communities, everything has to be flown in which makes everything expensive. The supermarket was almost empty apart from a few caribou and fox hides for sale. Food was frozen and pricey. A bottle of shampoo cost me seventeen dollars, just to wash my flowing locks so admired by millions the world over.

The most modern building in town was a white, mushroom-shaped thing that looked like a flying saucer that had just landed. It is, in fact, the polar bear research institute. I think the most research the local people do into polar bears is get them in their sights, kill them and sell their skins.

The polar bear research station dominates the town

A grave complete with toy polar bear

The town's graveyard is terrifyingly near the rubbish dump. They put the dead people at the top of the hill, and the dead things at the bottom. In the early days the Inuit didn't bother burying people, they would just put them on an ice floe and send them off to be disposed of in the sea. Now the graves are built up from the ground like cairns because the gravediggers can only get down to about three feet through the permafrost. I was hoping there would be some personal messages written on the simple wooden crosses but there were just names and numbers along with some plastic flowers stuffed into Coke cans.

You find artificial flowers more and more in graveyards and it's really weird to see the colours all blooming in the wintry landscape. I can understand using artificial flowers where fresh flowers must cost a fortune, but it gives me a shudder. I often think people must put them to make it look as if they visited more often than they do.

There were a couple of teenagers' graves, but the average age of those who'd died was sixty. Funnily enough, there were lots of little teddy bears on the graves, even on those of older people. At first I thought that they had adopted a Western habit but then I realized that they weren't teddy bears at all, they were polar bears. I was getting my cultures all mixed up.

I have felt for many years that we should be much more acquainted with the dead, as are the Inuit, for example, and especially in a place such as Igloolik where everywhere you go in town you look up and see the crosses looking down on those still alive. We shouldn't be so frightened of death. We should be able to handle it the way those with older traditions always have; they're closer to it. When loved ones die, they prepare themselves, they don't shove death away. It seems to me that as people get older in the West we hide them in homes as if there's something wrong with them, when ageing and death are the most inevitable things on this earth and they're not going to go away any time soon.

Abraham Ulayuruluf was born in an igloo in 1936. Now he lives in a modern house with double glazing and cable television. He is one of Igloolik's youngest elders, all of whom have a crucial role in preserving the language, teaching hunting skills and providing a link with the past. Abraham was a little man with big, strong hands and a ready laugh. With his smiling eyes and enormous spectacles,

THE WORLD'S LARGEST predator on land, the polar bear – whose Inuit name is *nanook* – can reach weights of more than fifteen hundred pounds and almost ten feet in length. *Ursus maritimus*, its Latin name, lives mostly on seal meat, which it hunts for on the sea ice in and around the Arctic Ocean. First identified and named by the eighteenth-century British explorer Constantine John Phipps, the polar bear is officially an endangered species, with an estimated twenty-five thousand left worldwide.

With its highly developed sense of smell, a polar bear can detect a seal up to a mile away. It also has good eyesight and hearing. Its multiple layers of white-to-yellowing fur grow on a layer of blubber almost four inches thick and the pads on its paws are especially adapted to give it traction on the ice. Excellent swimmers, polar bears have been spotted swimming in their doggy-paddle style several hundred miles from land.

Largely solitary and not as territorial as their grizzly brothers, the polar bear will sooner run than fight. The Inuit often use dogs to distract a bear until they can shoot it. Once killed, almost every part of the animal is used, from the meat to the oil to the sinews. Only the liver is thrown away because it contains near fatal doses of vitamin A. Western hunters have, in the past, been responsible for the deaths of an estimated 1,500 polar bears a year – sometimes shot from helicopters.

The 1973 International Agreement on the Conservation of Polar Bears introduced hunting quotas for the first time. In 2000 it was extended to include indigenous hunters. Sport hunting in Canada is still allowed, with hunters often paying as much as thirty-five thousand dollars per bear. Since May 2008, however, no hunter is allowed to take any trophies home, and bears can only be shot during certain periods and in limited numbers. Nunavut accounts for some eighty per cent of polar bear deaths by hunting, with some five hundred shot each year.

Abraham, my new best friend

he had a wonderful laugh that sounded like a glacier melting. It was music to my ears. Best of all, he seemed very happy and positive about the future.

I asked Abraham about his average day as an elder and he pointed to an ordinary little chair, the kind you wouldn't think twice about in a jumble sale, where he sits in his fringed kaftan and receives people. He was very accepting of his position as an elder and ready to share his wisdom with anyone who came to ask him things. He answers them, often with jokes and stories. He had an amazing collection of badges that visitors had given him over the years, most of which he'd pinned to his traditional blue Inuit hat. As he travelled around Nunavut, others added to his collection. He even had a badge with a picture of our own dear queen. His hat really was a thing of beauty, sitting on his head like a crown.

Abraham took me, with his son-in-law Solen, to Igloolik Point, jumping into his boat like a greyhound out of a trap. He was as fit as a flea. We set off laughing and smiling and talking of the old explorers. Sailing through a small crop of icebergs, I felt like an explorer myself. At one point, through his son-in-law, he asked in a very clear little voice, 'How old are you?' When I told him I was sixty-five, he said, 'I am seventy-two.' We both burst out laughing for reasons neither of us knew. Maybe we were just laughing that we'd lasted the pace.

En route to Igloolik Point

Abraham filled my heart with joy. He would touch me every now and again and at one point he said the most beautiful thing to me: 'I feel as if we've been friends for a long time.' Later, he said, 'You are my friend,' and I thought, 'I am indeed, and you are mine.' I am immensely proud of that. Although Abraham and I didn't even speak the same language, we communicated through laughing. I can't imagine anything better.

On the way to the point Abraham told me about hunting walruses and polar bears (which he said were delicious and I believed him). Sometimes Inuit dogs frighten a bear so much that it panics and freezes so that the hunter can actually run up and kill it with a knife. When I looked at the size of Abraham and thought of him killing a polar bear with a knife, I was amazed. Before the Inuit had guns, he said, they used to kill a walrus by spearing it and putting a spike in the ice so that it couldn't get to the surface to breathe and would start to suffocate. When it finally came up, panicking for air, they would stab it with a special tool. Abraham rejoiced in how much he liked the liver of the walrus. The liver, he insisted, was his favourite.

Igloolik Point is a peninsula on which there is a ceremonial circle for Inuit elders, who used to gather there to sit and eat. The ground was littered with discarded walrus and whale bones. Under the old Inuit belief system of shamanism, this was the place where the shaman or priest used to invoke demons to ward off evil spirits. I had half-expected Abraham to still believe in demonology but he didn't. He spoke of demons as a thing of the past, not as if they existed today. He liked the old stories but accepted them as mythology and I liked him more for that.

Abraham told me that when the ugly white men first came to Baffin Island they weren't welcomed by the early natives – they turned them away. Then the expedition led by English rear admiral and Arctic explorer Sir William Parry arrived in 1822 and he and his team were iced in. At first, Inuit and explorer all seemed to get on well but then there was trouble over women and other matters until, eventually, there was a fight over an Inuit wife and a shovel, of all things. The shaman was asked to do something about it. He cast his magic, the ice melted, and the white men left the following day. Either someone had had a word in the captain's ear about what was likely to happen if they stayed, or the magic worked. Extraordinary times.

In Inuit mythology white men are considered to be the result of a union between Inuit women and dogs, because they were such dog-like creatures. The myth goes, that the elders floated eight of these dog-men on an ice floe, left to fend for themselves because they were so repulsive. When white explorers arrived years later, the Inuit believed they must be the children of those dog-like creatures, looking for their mothers. We must be a pretty ugly bunch when it comes to how other people see us, which is really interesting because I think we take ourselves as the standard and everyone else as looking weird. We think we are what handsome is; that we are beautiful and the rest are all something different. We don't realize that everyone else is thinking that about themselves too, and that some people find us repulsive and strange-looking, and they think we smell pretty weird as well.

* * *

> " *THERE IS A lovely thing about old men like Abraham who calmly accept being old, along with the wisdom that comes with age. Being with him reminded me very much of old men I knew when I was a boy. I used to love going to the public park where old guys would play dominoes and cribbage, smoking their pipes and scraping out the thick tobacco from them with their pocket knives.*

I remember one of them telling me that he was an Old Contemptible and explaining what that was. He had a badge with 'VR' for Victoria Regina on it and he said Kaiser Wilhelm had called the British 'a contemptible little army' so they'd rejoiced at being known as the 'Old Contemptibles' ever since. I loved those old men. They had little picture cards that you got with cigarettes and they'd show them to me. They had that lovely calm wisdom of men who had been in wars. Abraham had that, too – the wisdom of a man who'd fought walruses and whales and polar bears and seals and survived.

I think that our relationship with age has changed. The old men I remember have disappeared and been replaced by ones who use Grecian 2000 and take all sorts of tablets and pills. People are not content to act their age any more, although acting your age is about as sensible as acting your street number. People say to me, 'What do other sixty-five-year-olds think of the clothes you wear and the way you behave and how you live?' I reply, 'I haven't a clue. I don't hang around with sixty-five-year-olds.'

The older I get the more difficult I find it is to tell how old anyone is anyway. I used to be an expert. I used to get it within months sometimes. I was eerily good at it, but now I'm out by decades. I couldn't tell a twenty-five-year-old from a thirty-seven-year-old if I had a gun to my head. They look the same to me. It's not a failing; it's a blessing. As is the fact that the concept of ugliness disappears as you get older. It shows itself up for what it is, which is nothing. I used to say on stage that getting old is like getting drunk – everyone gets better looking, and it's a fact. Suddenly when you're older you understand what ugliness is – just an attitude. There is no such thing as physical ugliness.

I find the Abrahams of this world beautiful to look at. I love gazing on the faces of old men and old women, especially their skin. The crinklier someone gets, the more beautiful they become. Keith Richards has a head start on us all. I think he gets more beautiful by the hour. He's like a carving of a man in granite.

I think one of the reasons we lost our respect for older people is that they were so belligerent after the Second World War. Rock 'n' roll started it really. Our elders became so anti-rock 'n' roll that they created this huge divide between youth and age. Before then, there was always some respect. Then it declined. My generation took an immense amount of stick about our hair, music and clothes. It seemed everything we did was wrong. It was wrong to be a teddy boy. It was wrong to be a rocker. It was wrong to be a hippy. 'Your music sucks. Your behaviour sucks. Your attitude to sex is wrong, wrong, wrong.'

Older people had been through so much war and depression that freedom was a difficult pill to swallow. They'd say, 'I didn't fight in two wars to see my children with green hair, poncing around with skirts up to their waists and see-through blouses. Everyone is gay all of a sudden and men wear make-up. What the hell is going on? That's not the freedom I fought for!' But freedom is freedom is freedom and I think it only served to irritate young people more and more until a chasm developed. Especially in Europe, where there was real disillusionment with religion and morality (although I believe young people have every bit as much morality as older people). They saw their parents and grandparents as sheep who'd blindly accepted the word of those who presumed to know better, but didn't.

So now you don't get wee old men any more because no one from the generation that grew up with all of that is in a hurry to become one. Why should anyone be in a hurry to look old, or be shepherded to the beige section of the shop by middle-aged idiots who should know better? Who wants to wear grey clothing just because they're a certain age? Not me. ”

Near to the ceremonial circle at Igloolik Point was the grave of a sailor from Parry's ship, who didn't make it home. The sailor's name was Alexander Elder and he died in the spring of 1823. Poor old Alexander. He was thirty-six years of age and his grave said he was a Greenland mate. I read that a Greenland mate was an expert ice sailor who based himself in Greenland and hired himself out to expeditions such as Parry's. I found mention of Alexander Elder in Captain G. F. Lyon's private journal, which is a diary of the ship, the HMS *Hecla*, at the time:

'Greenland mate departed this life after the confinement of a few days, his complaint was a confirmed dropsy which had considerably swelled his whole body and limbs. The poor man suffered considerable and severe pain from the oppression on his

Alexander Elder's grave

chest, which on examination after death was found to contain six pints of water … a party were employed digging his grave but after many hours' labour and breaking ten pick axes were unable, on account of the frozen state of the earth, to penetrate deeper than three feet.'

I love that – the British dependence on doing the right thing. His mates broke ten pick axes just to get Mr Elder three feet down.

Historians think he came from either Northumberland in the north of England or from Scotland. Elder is a good strong Scottish name, but there's no shortage of good Scottish names in Northumberland either, so I don't know where he came from. When the sailors were all chased away by the shaman because they were messing around with the women, they left without Alexander. And there he remains.

Someone stole his white tombstone years ago and took it hundreds of miles away to Pond Inlet – hoping to maybe trade it for money or tobacco or alcohol but no one was interested. They dumped the stone in a ditch where a missionary later found it. He tried to have it transported back to Igloolik but came upon a huge problem because no one would take it, due to the old superstition against carrying a tombstone on a ship. Eventually he had it sent back overland by dog sleds. They split the tombstone down the middle like a sandwich and carried it in two bits. So now the bold Alexander rests in peace again, his tombstone once more intact, in that lonely, windswept bit of the world very far from Scotland or Northumberland or wherever it was he came from. I really felt for him lying there. He'd spent his whole short life in the cold, travelling around navigating the ice, and now he lies in a cold field with no break from the wind, in a place where people can steal your tombstone and not give a bugger.

* * *

"I MISS MY SHOES WHEN I'm away. Shoes are one of those things you don't travel with many of. They're cumbersome and heavy so you usually only take two pairs, probably some sneakers and some sandals. But whenever I'm away I think about the rest of my shoes. I've got maybe a hundred pairs in various places and I wonder about where they all are.

I once had a pair of patent leather brogues with a kind of leopardskin part that looked a bit like Dalmatian. They were to die for. The patent leather had that kind of oily colour change thing and the fur fabric was regarded as pretty bad taste by most people, but I adored them. Then someone stole them from my house. There was a party, and afterwards my shoes were gone, and a coat of mine. That must have been twenty years ago and I still wonder where they are. I wonder if someone is walking about in them. I've never seen an equivalent pair.

The other thing I miss is my Davy Crockett hat. That went missing at Heathrow airport. I was going to play polo on an elephant in Nepal and I thought my Davy Crockett hat was the very gear to wear. But when I got to Delhi, my bag never showed up. I was very well compensated by the airline but my hat was in my bag. It was made for me in Dublin by a friend and I miss it so much. I always wore it when I was away fishing and I've tried so many hats since but the joy of it has never returned."

You've probably noticed over the years that I'm a bit of a dandy and a well-turned-out chap. So getting a new sealskin suit (my last was made for me in Grise Fjord) seemed like a natural thing to do, although it is not the kind of thing to be seen wearing in Sauchiehall Street on a Friday night.

The Inuit take a great pride in making traditional clothes for hunters, as they have done for centuries. Seamstress Atuat Akkitirq learned how to sew animal skins from watching her mother, who watched her own mother before her. Each woman started sewing at around eleven years old. In the stark white interior of her modern house, Atuat offered me a selection of materials, including sealskin for my new hairy suit and boots, and all sorts of caribou for my socks and gloves. Her grandson is a hunter and gets her all the skins she needs. Each one was pegged out on a wooden frame – I could still see the holes where the ones she offered me had been stretched – just as you still see skins on frames outside people's houses all over Nunavut territory.

Once the meat has been cut away and used, Atuat scrapes each skin of hair and blubber with a sharp blade and then soaks it in water for a couple of weeks to soften it up. She chews the hide between her teeth or tramples it beneath her feet to soften it further until it can be rolled up. It was an incredible thing to watch, that hard sealskin softening before my eyes with her saliva and chewing. I thought it would need water or oil but it didn't; it just needed hard work, folding and chewing, folding and chewing. I was tired just watching her and my teeth started to feel painful. All that chewing had worn her teeth down, almost to a point. It is an extraordinary process.

Atuat told me that the young women of Igloolik don't like the taste or the smell of chewing animal skins and refuse to deal with them in the traditional way. They prefer to beat and pound them into submission. I think the effect on their teeth might be a factor. There is far less demand for the clothing these days as synthetic fabrics have become more widely available, but Atuat said her son and grandson still proudly wear her suits, and that others want them once they see how beautiful they are and realize how well they stand up against the weather.

As she measured me with a tape, she chattered away in Inuktitut. I was sure she was saying what a he-man I was. I could imagine her speculating how such a huge muscley creature as me would be capable of killing many caribou and seals. I think she saw me as a walrus killer who could strangle a caribou in one squeeze. I chattered back to her in English. I only hoped she got the part about me wanting eighteen-inch vents and French seams.

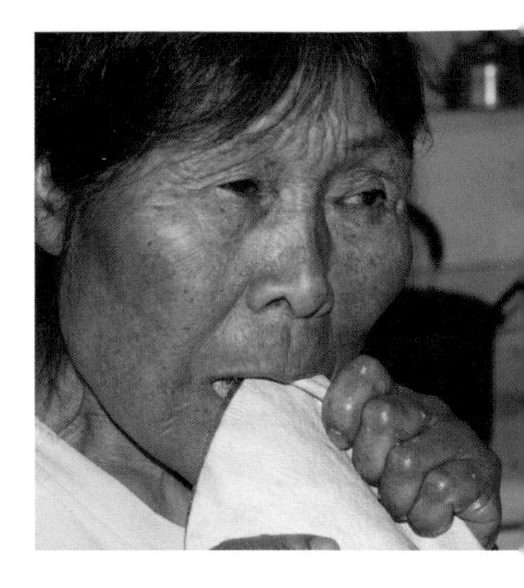

Top: Atuat wearing her teeth to a point
Above: What the best-dressed hunter is sporting

She measured my feet for some boots using the kitchen floor tiles as a gauge. The soles would be made from the skin of a bearded seal and the softer upper from that of a ringed seal. Atuat did such incredible work; she was such a clever woman. The boots she showed me were so beautifully handstitched I could hardly see the seams around the moccasin edges. When I went for my final fitting, I was amazed. The clothes she had made me were a fantastic fit. I pulled on layer upon layer – caribou socks followed by seal boots and the sealskin suit with a hood. I'd never had so many clothes on in my life! I was as comfortable as if I was in bed. I've always felt that before a little hunting, a visit to the tailor's is required and I cut a fine dash in what the well-dressed young man in Igloolik was wearing that season. This was a collector's piece, ideal for those evening strolls through Glasgow, even if I did smell like cod liver oil. Suitably acquitted I could go and kill something furry for no reason at all, other than to eat it raw. Or maybe I could just frighten an animal to death by jumping out from behind a tree, dressed in my suit…

* * *

" PEOPLE SHOULD SEE *Inuit handiwork – they are pieces of art by genuine and very profound artists. The suit Atuat made me should go into a museum. I know some find sealskin unattractive but you have to let your biases stand aside and not go all Heather Mills.*

There's a difference between the urban complainer and the Inuit, who know what they're doing because they've been doing it for thousands of years in an honest and open way and with very good reason. I wouldn't happily wear my sealskin suit in public; it's not the kind of thing I would even buy. I actually find it kind of cruel and fraudulent to do that, but as far as the Inuit are concerned I am really tired of protestors telling these people how to live. I have a great desire to shout 'Shut up!' at the top of my voice when people start protesting about others, or throwing paint over their clothes. If they threw paint over my clothes, I would be the last person they ever threw paint over. Live and let live.

I don't like the whale industry at all and I'm delighted that it's kind of stopped, although I know it hasn't completely stopped – Japan and Norway seem to constantly want it

Marvelling at some colossal whale's bones

started again. I realize all the arguments about keeping the balance, and the seals and so on; I just don't like the thought of people killing those magnificent creatures. What I don't have a problem with is the Inuit doing it. They've been hunting whales for centuries and they eat it, they wear it and they use it for all sorts of different reasons. It's been the way of life for them for so long and I don't have one second's problem with that.

When I saw some whale bones on the beach and realized the size of those monsters of the deep, it rammed it home to me what a breed of men and women they are, those little men who go out in sealskin boats and take on in combat such a colossal creature – the poor big thing. The trouble is it doesn't know it could squash them just like that. The whale is just another one of these animals that suffers from being delicious – like chicken. ”

If you're anything like me and you've watched the Olympic Games and wondered how anything synchronized got in, then I think I have the answer. When I was in Iqaluit, Bryan Pearson had

Watching a demonstration of the Alaskan High Kick

told me about some Inuit games that were devised years ago to keep warm and stay active. In Igloolik, a couple of teenagers, Damian Tulugarjuk and Silas Qulaut, were happy to demonstrate some of them for me on the veranda of Silas's home.

His Alaskan High Kick was remarkable to behold. The target was a small block of wood dangling seven feet up on a thread. Running at it and then leaping into the air like a mad man, both feet extended before him, Silas managed to hit the wood every time. Then he did it holding one foot with his hand and kicking with the other. It was like yoga made into a sport.

He could also jump up to four feet eleven inches from a kneeling start while wearing just thick woolly socks. He'd won medals for it at the Inuit Games – a second place for the Alaskan High Kick and a gold medal for other types of kicking. I asked him if he'd ever considered playing for a Scottish football team. I'm sure they'd have him tomorrow. These remarkable young men also demonstrated the Head Pull, lying on their stomachs with strips of material tied around their skulls, pulling each other's heads in opposite directions. Then the Mouth Pull, the silliest game I ever saw, and painful too – each one with their arms around the other's shoulders, fingers hooked in the corner of each other's mouth.

'I heard stories from the elders that they used to rip their mouths open playing this,' Silas told me. I wasn't at all surprised.

There was the Aeroplane, where one guy stood stiffly and the other spun him around, which was quite extraordinary to behold. The funniest thing about it was that on that very day, at home in Scotland, my local highland games were being held. I couldn't help thinking how weird it seemed to me that guys did a bit of mouth pulling or high kicking or head pulling while back in Scotland there were people running about throwing trees into the air. Truth is, there was nothing weird about any of it. People have been in competition for centuries doing the silliest of things, or at least they seem silly from the outside until you see the dedication they put into it. Knowing we are capable of wonderful silliness makes me very proud to be a human being. When you consider that there are people all over the world shooting each other and dropping bombs on each other, they would be much more gainfully occupied trying to kick a piece of wood or doing a bit of mouth wrestling.

> Songs are thoughts, sung out with the breath when people are moved by great forces and ordinary speech no longer suffices. Man is moved just like the ice floe sailing here and there out in the current. His thoughts are driven by a flowing force when he feels joy, when he feels fear, when he feels sorrow. Thoughts can wash over him like a flood, making his breath come in gasps and his heart throb … And then it will happen that we, who think we are small, will feel still smaller. And we will fear to use words. When the words we want to use shoot up of themselves – we get a new song.
>
> ORPINGALIK, INUIT SHAMAN (1923)

Out on a chilly promontory overlooking the harbour I met two other people who were excellent at their chosen sport. Rhoda Kunuk and Mary Taukie, teachers at the Igloolik pre-school, showed me the basics of Inuit throat singing. Being an old folky, this was a real treat for me. I'd heard of throat singing, an oral tradition also known as *piqqusiraarniq* and *katajjaq*. Inuit history is rarely written down so in the old days this was the way news passed from one to the other, by song and story. Usually two women sing facing each other, staring into each other's eyes, almost mouth to mouth. Sometimes there are words and sometimes there are just deep grunting sounds in the throat, but either way, it is sensational to hear.

These two were taught by their elders and are now teaching the next generation.

Throat singing

'It was a sort of game started by the women while the men were away hunting,' Rhoda explained with a smile. 'I'm the leader and Mary follows. She copies every little thing I do so it takes a lot of hearing too. We take turns and whoever laughs first stops.'

The song always ends when they break down giggling, which is the way they have always done it. Making each other laugh isn't intentional but they kind of get off on it.

I was blown away by the sound those women made. It was so rock 'n' roll and had such a modern feel to it. I'd love to hear them as a rhythm section in a band, or take them to a folk festival in Scotland where they'd take the wind right out of everyone else's sails. I'd never heard anything like it in my life. One song called 'The Dog Team', which also had strange dog noises in it, was one of the most beautiful, original things I'd ever heard. Rhoda told me it was created by a girl to inspire her dog team to become successful.

I don't recall being so incredibly moved by a new music in many a long year. Their enjoyment factor was so deep and real, and honest too. One of them had a bairn wriggling about in the hood of her parka, like the Inuit women of old. He woke up halfway through and popped his head out to listen or maybe to join in. I can't say enough about how much I loved the syncopation and the rhythm of throat singing and the lovely female noise. I am going to get some recordings and play it as I drive along the road. It's so exciting to find something you like that you've never heard in your

An extra voice hidden in a hood

life before. It was heart-stoppingly good; like the first time I heard Buddy Holly or bluegrass or Hank Williams or Earl Scruggs. It was just the same – my skin went funny and the hairs on my arms tingled, the way that greatness makes you feel.

Like when you see the Taj Mahal for the first time or you see a new type of painting that you've never experienced. It's a lightning bolt to your heart.

The Inuktitut language is almost impenetrable to me. I don't understand a syllable and it doesn't relate to anything I've ever heard before, even though the Inuit gave us the words 'kayak' and 'anorak'. The written language is worse; it looks like a geometry exercise. I was completely dependent on interpreters in Nunavut so I decided to enrol in a class in Inuktitut at the pre-school and see if I could learn anything.

Teacher Eunice Uyarak told me that European missionaries first taught the Inuit to write and speak in English so that they could study the bible. Thankfully, Inuktitut was still the first language of Igloolik. I asked if she thought that would change as English was now the first language of the Internet but she seemed to have great faith in Inuktitut surviving. She said that computer programmes were being translated from English for that reason, which is a great idea. She explained that there was an old Inuktitut hunter language and a more modern version, along with hundreds of different dialects. It was incredibly complicated and Igloolik's children were taught in a sort of sing-song chant. It's amazing that schools all over the world make the same noise: they're learning basically the same thing, using a little international song. If you're ever passing a school it warms your heart to hear them.

School's improved since I was a lad. God, when I think of those bloody nightmares who taught me. In Igloolik children actually went to school to have a good time. The atmosphere was so nice between the kids and the teachers. I tried to join in the singing as best I could and managed to pick up a few basic words, which had a surprisingly Welsh lilt about them, with the double 'l'.

I had been feeling very foreign in Nunavut. I felt like an interloper and an intruder and it wasn't a pleasant feeling. I was uncomfortable in the climate. But there is something deep down that links us all – words and sounds. Mrs Uyarak taught me how to spell my name, which I'm proud to say I finally mastered. It was the first time I'd got something right in the classroom in many years. Then I found music that linked and touched us and realized I had that in common with those children and those throat singers, and it was a lovely feeling for the future.

There were plenty of other examples of Igloolik trying very hard to hang on to the old ways. Its people, who have a joy and a friendship and a closeness, also have a genuine love of the old ways for all the right reasons – because they're worth hanging on to. I think we're in the middle of the death throes of the traditional ways. Parts will survive, the way they always do all over the world, despite the encroachment of contemporary Western society. You go up the Amazon river, or any remote place, and find a tribe and wonder if they've seen white men before, and they come sauntering through the trees wearing Yamaha T-shirts. The modern world is so powerfully pervasive and so attractive to people who are not a part of it. An iPod or a mobile phone is a miracle to someone who lives in a jungly or an Arctic place. It's just so seductive and it will win every time.

The good bits of the old ways will stay, though. The throat music will stay because it's a joy to do and a joy to listen to. It has no reason to disappear. The sealskin clothes will disappear, because manmade fibres are cheaper and lighter, but those are good reasons not bad reasons. Everything worthwhile changes. Languages that don't change die, like Latin. Gaelic is dying because it's not changing and English is in a constant state of change as new words are added and old ones subtracted. If you don't change, you die. I think the best of the old bits will survive; I don't know about the Mouth Pull, though.

Next week's lecture is: 'Evolution – My Part in its Downfall'.

* * *

"I HAVE FLOWN SO MUCH *in my life that anyone who's daft enough to ask me about my tips for travelling will get a stream of information from me about what you should wear when you're flying:*

Always wear cotton. Especially cotton underwear. As a matter of fact, always wear cotton underwear anyway. Don't wear anything manmade when you're flying. You could explode if you wear nylon. It will choke you to death, especially on those private cozy-wozy aeroplanes where you're more scrunched up than you are normally. So, make sure your underwear is good and there's lots of room in your pants.

Don't drink too much or you'll be peeing like a racehorse. Ignore all this nonsense about eight glasses of water a day. Since when did we ever drink that much water? We're not camels. I didn't drink that much beer when I was drinking! If you've got an aisle seat, drink all the water you like and charge up and down to the loo. Otherwise, you'll be clambering over people and they don't like it.

A hint, a wee special present for you, is my advice to take a fresh pair of socks. You'll be absolutely stunned, especially if you're on a long journey, at how much better it makes you feel just before the plane lands. When you get up to brush your teeth or powder your nose or whatever you want to do, change your socks with a nice fresh pair and you'll be flabbergasted at the buzz you get from it. A seasoned traveller told me that many years ago. It sounds like nothing. Try it. You will thank me.

Someone once told me if you put brown paper in the sole of your shoe, you won't get jet lag. I've had friends who've tried it and said it is nonsense. It was an Irishman who told me in the first place, so he may have been taking the piss. Nothing will help you with jet lag. It has no plan. There is no shape to it. One time you'll do a journey and will suffer horrendously then you'll do the same journey six months later and get none. Jet lag is a sneaky thing."

Pond Inlet, Nunavut

ON THE WAY TO POND INLET, we touched down at the tiny Inuit hamlet of Clyde River. Coming from the River Clyde myself, it was a nice stop to make. The first sight that greeted me, apart from the fog which obscured the Cordillera Mountains, was a sign warning hunters only to shoot male polar bears. There were two photographs supposed to illustrate the difference between male and female bears but I could see no difference whatsoever. I am sure the same negative was used for both.

On we flew to Pond Inlet, the most unlikely sounding Arctic town on earth. One of the most northerly points of my journey, it was the gateway to the Northwest Passage. Pond Inlet looked to me like a carbon copy of Igloolik, with its drab grey buildings like packing cases. They even had the same government building, which they must buy in bulk. Perhaps they sell them in six packs?

A boat comes to Pond Inlet once a year and delivers everything from food to spin dryers to flat-screen televisions, and that's it,

their only chance 'til the next year. They have to order a certain amount to get it on the ship. I met one man who was delirious with joy to get a year's worth of nappies for his baby. That's what I call living on the edge. I think the rest of this world have done this area both great favours and great harm. I think we often bring a kind of pseudo-culture and pseudo-religion everywhere we go. We presume that our ways are better than theirs and kind of enforce them on people, or certainly we have done in the past. But it has to be remembered that we also bring good things, such as medicine and items that make life a little easier – electrical goods, tools, four-

POND INLET WAS given its name by Sir John Ross, the Scottish explorer and rear admiral, who came from Stranraer and joined the Royal Navy in 1786 aged just nine. Sent by the Admiralty in 1818 to find the Northwest Passage, his first mission failed largely because he was plagued by mirages of mountains on the horizon. He returned a decade later in a steamship, only to be stranded with his crew for four years, surrounded by pack ice beyond Lancaster Sound. They only survived by abandoning their vessel, walking to another shipwreck, and eventually sailing away in its longboats once the ice melted.

Ross had followed in the footsteps of the seventeenth-century explorer William Baffin (after whom Baffin Island is named), whose early observations of the tides and position of the Hudson and Davis Straits continued to be drawn on for many years by countless sailors. Ross named Pond Inlet in honour of Englishman John Pond, who was at the time Royal Astronomer and Superintendent of the Nautical Almanac.

Huskies hungry for meat

wheel drives. Outsiders might prefer to see dog teams hauling goods but the local guy doesn't.

Walking around town, I spotted some walrus carcasses on the beach and they were just huge. I'd hate to be chased by a walrus. There were lots of husky-type sled dogs sniffing around and putting the wind up me with their yowling and howling. They're a bit too wolfy for my liking. The Inuit throw them chunks of seal to eat, sometimes frozen so that they have to lick it to make it edible. None of that lying by the fire for them. There was one huge hairy dog like a St Bernard crossed with a Newfoundland who was a beauty. When I saw him lying on a big bit of plywood, all tied up, I said, 'Hello, big hairy fella,' and he looked up as if to say, 'Who are you calling big hairy fella?' He had the best expression; a big Glasgow face. 'Who are you talking to?'

The chief purpose of my trip to Pond Inlet was to go hunting for 'country food' with a traditional Inuit family – David Suqslak, his wife Maggie Qanguq (carrying her baby, May, in the hood of her parka), and sons Curtis and little Eric who, at the age of five, had already shot his first seal. I wasn't sure exactly what we would be hunting for – maybe some Arctic char, a seal or a walrus; I guess anything that is free and nutritious in a place where a cabbage has to be flown thousands of miles and costs seven dollars.

Pond Inlet is said to be an amazing place to see the illusive narwhal. I knew I could be in deep trouble over this because the narwhal is my daughter Scarlett's favourite animal. The only problem is that it is one of the Inuit's favourites too – whenever possible, they love to kill them and eat their fleshy foreheads. If David were to fix one in his gun sights, I hoped to nudge his arm at the crucial moment otherwise my daughter would never forgive me.

I'm not a hunting man myself. I like to go fishing but I don't hunt, nevertheless it was a great privilege to be with hunter-gatherers who still live as they have lived for thousands of years. These people aren't hunting for fun. They're not tiptoeing over the moors to bag a few grouse for a laugh. They're hunting for food and skins and they use every part of the animal. There is something spectacularly good and right about what they do; hunting is such an essential part of their ancient culture.

THE NARWHAL IS a rarely seen Arctic mammal that only swims in waters north of latitude 70°N. A species of white whale, whose sister is the beluga, narwhals can grow up to sixteen feet long and weigh almost two tons.

The distinctive feature of the narwhal is its single, spiralling, white tusk, which can reach lengths of ten feet, growing out of its large bulbous head. It was originally thought the tusk evolved for the narwhal to break through the Arctic ice, but more recent studies have linked it to echo-sonar function and as a sophisticated sensory organ capable of analyzing the constituents and temperature of the water.

In Viking days, a cup made from such a tusk was said to protect its drinker from poison. In medieval times, the narwhal tusks that arrived in Europe were marketed as the magic horns of unicorns and could be sold for many times their weight in gold. Elizabeth I was presented with a jewel-encrusted narwhal tusk said to be worth the same as a castle. Later, when Arctic explorers discovered the 'unicorn of the sea' for themselves, the value of narwhal tusks dropped to more realistic levels.

In Inuit mythology, the narwhal was created when a woman using a harpoon to catch a beluga whale fell into the sea and became twisted around the harpoon and the beluga. Also known as the moon whale, it is almost completely cylindrical in shape. The creature, whose name means 'corpse whale' in Old Norse, has blue-grey skin with brown or white blotches, which resembles the pigmentation of a corpse. Each mammal can live up to fifty years and they are among the most social of whales, travelling together in pods of up to twenty. Their diet consists mainly of squid, shrimp, cod and other sea-life; they have also been known to eat small seals. There are thought to be around forty thousand narwhals left on the planet, more than half of which live in Canadian waters. Their chief predators are man, killer whales, polar bears and walruses. A scientific study last year listed them as potentially the most vulnerable to climate change.

David still hunted with his pack of dogs. His son Curtis, a keen user of the Internet, was more into Facebook. He liked to buy Western goods on auction sites, too, and have them sent to him through the mail. He spoke English fluently and yet there he was, out hunting with his father every weekend, so there was this great divide between them that somehow didn't interfere with what each of them did.

I read an article by a local Inuit girl who'd become a vegetarian. Her family nearly disowned her because they had lived almost exclusively on meat for centuries. They couldn't grow anything fresh for many months of the year in the cold Arctic climate, so her sudden vegetarianism was regarded as scarily weird. Plus there is the whole food culture in Inuit societies of sharing meat whenever you have it. If you are successful in hunting a seal or a walrus, you divide it between your neighbours. You don't hide it, sneak bits and pretend you don't have any meat in the house. It's a very democratic system, designed so that everyone gets to eat, even those who can't hunt. To have a vegetarian in their midst must have seemed such an insult. The Inuit don't really understand food fads yet, but they will.

Seals' eyeballs are delicious, apparently. Maggie, David's wife, told me she'd had some for breakfast that morning. I took her word for it. No one said what seals' eyeballs reminded them of – probably chicken, everything reminds people of chicken, doesn't it? I lived in terror of being offered an eyeball and looking bad-mannered by turning it down. I saw someone on television once saying that cockroaches tasted of apple and I thought, 'I'll take your word for it, pal.' I've never eaten anything like that. I don't even like anything that wobbles, except jelly. Even that wobbly jelloid stuff you get inside pork pies makes me puke. I think all wobbly food should be outlawed.

The landscape around Pond Inlet is spectacular. If they ever needed a reason to live there, the Inuit just have to look around them at where the mountains fall down and meet the horizon and the glaciers seem to come right out of the sky. One local told me that the main glacier above them had receded a hundred yards since the 1940s, so it wasn't in a hurry to go anywhere.

The icebergs in the fjord were great, too. We saw one that looked just like a Viking ship, another that resembled a moccasin and a third that was like an old art deco radio with rounded shoulders. The best was the one that looked like the White House, perched

Opposite top: Stunned by the scenery
Opposite bottom: Out in the boat with David

Family outing

on a barge. Icebergs are huge great noble things sitting in the water but when you get up in the morning they've sailed away on the tide, it's as if they were never there. That never fails to surprise me.

We camped out on the ice – me looking like an escaped convict in a bright orange suit. I didn't wear my fabulous sealskin suit with the caribou boots after all. I was going to, but I checked everyone else and no one was wearing theirs and I didn't want to look like a Charlie. Plus Eric, David's five-year-old son, told me it wasn't 'cool'. That did it. I took the sealskin gloves as a symbolic gesture and I must say I'm glad I did. They were delightful, with their fabby woolly lining. I soon wished I had the whole thing on. We set up the tents on a remote beach – not the spot I, as a dedicated follower of Baden-Powell, would have chosen. It was cold and I had wet gloves which began to smell like a seal. There comes a time in every man's life when he should swear never to go camping again – sure proof that he's learned the good life. It doesn't seem to have happened to me yet.

Maggie was in charge of starters and successfully reeled in a few fish to fry on an open fire. We boys had to go out and get the main course. Seal hunting arouses strong emotions, so it's maybe worth saying that they are not an endangered species. At last count, there were more than five million seals in Arctic waters, and they were all giving us a wide berth. Early the next morning out on the boat, David and his sons spotted some seals after a while, although I couldn't see any at first. As with whale watching, I am always the last. David told me to look for shadows in the water.

The first seal I spotted dived in off the ice and as each mammal can stay down for twenty minutes, I think it was saying 'Bugger!' to the hunt. David took a few pot-shots, but missed. I quickly realized that this was the real deal. Any seal that had the temerity to stick its head above the water after that was going to pay the ultimate price. A friend on another boat nearby radioed whenever he spotted seals and David also had a hydrophone, or underwater microphone, to listen for creatures beneath the boat. 'A narwhal makes a ticking noise,' he told me. I put the headphones on hoping to hear whale songs or seal whistling or narwhals clicking or octopuses farting, but all I could hear was dribbling water, like a little boy peeing, so we kept looking.

One expression I've never understood is, 'keep your eyes peeled'. Keep your eyes peeled for a seal? How do you peel your eyes? I wonder where that comes from? The peeling the eyes thing seemed to work, though. Thank God, I kept a little penknife for that very purpose. I gave my eyes a quick peel and two seals showed up. Before I'd barely blinked, David had shot one; a female ring seal. David assured me the females tasted better than the males. She looked so much like a person, it felt like killing a mermaid or something. Not at all like killing a fish.

I felt guilty and uncomfortable taking any part, which was absolutely silly of me. Hunting seals is part of the Inuit culture; I guess it's just not part of mine. The sheer size of it in the water and the way it struggled at the side of the boat as it was being gaffed; it was just so obviously a mammal. But as they say of nature, it's 'red in tooth and claw'.

Once the seal was in the boat, it didn't look its best. I touched its skin and it was kind of wobbly. It looked fat and jolly; as if it should still be swimming around. The death of a creature is very strange, even a little trout or something. I don't usually kill the fish I catch but if I do and eat it for my breakfast there is still a terrible feeling of guilt about taking the life away from it. If you live in the Inuit climate and you've descended from people who have lived in it for

Top: Enjoying raw seal
Above: Eyeballs ready for the plucking

A dead mermaid?

thousands of years, then it's a different story altogether. We are two different creatures with a completely different ethical stance. Ours is not to judge. David wasn't the slightest bit uncomfortable about the demise of the seal. He was delighted to see the creature and so were his family who found great comfort in it. They were looking forward to eating it raw when they got it back to the campsite, which is exactly what they did – eyes and all. An hour or so after we'd returned from the hunt and while the others were still feasting in a circle of blood-stained ground, a cry went up that some narwhal had been spotted out to sea. Thinking of my daughter, and abandoning the spaghetti I was secretly enjoying, I went to have a look.

The narwhals were surprisingly close. There were about six of them all gambolling, or whatever it is that narwhals do. They were joshing around in the water looking delightful. All of a sudden there was the most almighty bang. One of the Inuit fired at them and they all dived at the same time like a single animal. It was the most shocking thing because I hadn't seen the gun and I hadn't

expected it. The show was over. Their little display of jollity had come to an end with the most violent noise.

It was a very good day for me that day. I learned a lot about myself. I thought I had changed since I was last in the Arctic, but I hadn't. I was still a big bleeding heart hippy liberal. I thought I'd become all Inuit and full of bloodlust out on the ice there, but I hadn't and I didn't really understand their way of life at all. I am all for them being allowed to kill their quota of animals and carry on as they have done for centuries, but that day really brought it home to me that the Inuit and I are completely foreign to each other. We're not joined at the hip at all. I love their foreignness and I love them, but I'd thought I was getting close and I wasn't. I hadn't even scratched the surface.

It was a real reminder of how the world actually works. Some people shoot things and some people go to the butcher's and buy things. I'm the guy who goes to the butcher's, and I think it is as simple as that. I felt kind of foolish – like a big silly townie dressed up which, of course, I am most of my life.

Above: Shooting at the narwhal
Below: Stranger in a strange land

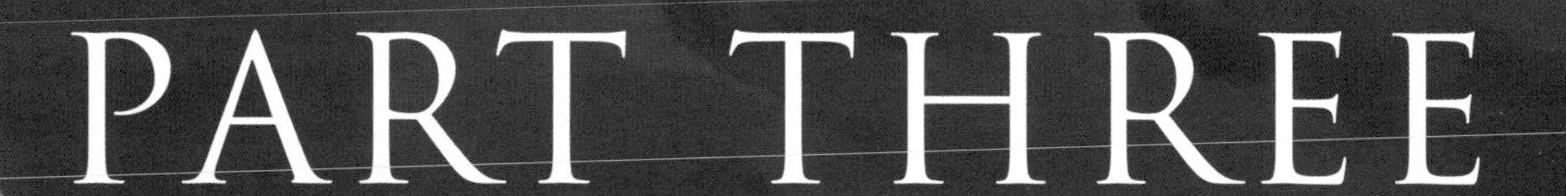

PART THREE

Adventure… exists only in the mind of the man who pursues it.

As soon as his fingers have grazed it, it vanishes to appear much farther off, in another form, at the limits of the imagination.

Pierre Mac Orlan (1882–1970)

NORTH POLE
YOU ARE HERE
2882-M
SOUTH POLE
IQALUIT-802-M
LONDON - 6831-M
COLUMBIA-7155-M
LAS-VAGAS - 2792-M

NUNAVUT

Resolute, Cornwallis Island, Nunavut

NOT ONLY IS Resolute one of the coldest inhabited places in the world with an average annual temperature of minus 16.4°C, it is also one of the smallest with just over 200 souls. Having been to this place on the very edge of the Northwest Passage, as far north as I would go on this journey, I can understand why.

Named Qausuittuq by the Inuit, which means 'the place with no dawn', Resolute was founded as a weather station and military airfield in 1947. It enjoys twenty-four hours of sunlight during the summer months and endures twenty-four hours of darkness in the winter. One of the first sights to greet me when we landed on the gravel runway at Resolute Bay Airport was an old Lancaster bomber, which is my favourite aeroplane, bar none. It was this that

Opposite: A long way from home
Below: Resolute from the air

Crashed Lancaster bomber

won the war for Britain in my opinion. Actually, it's a toss-up between the Lancaster and the Spitfire but, with a gun to my head, I'd choose the Lancaster.

My father worked on Lancasters during the Second World War and told me that when a flight took off loaded to go and bomb some place, the ground would shake. That's what I always think of when I see a Lancaster – the humming drone it made, the ground shaking with its four engines, and that lovely big square tail. Those young pilots and rear gunners were brave men; they were like medieval jousters. They were the last people to go to war for a really good reason. The world was going to be dominated by a nutter and they went and they fought and they won in this frighteningly beautiful but ghastly thing. It must have struck terror into the hearts of those poor Germans huddled in their houses below.

The Lancaster at Resolute had crashed just short of the runway during a weather report run in 1950. There's no known reason for the crash but, personally, I think they looked out of the cockpit, saw Resolute and lost the will to live. They just let the plane hit the deck; death was a much better choice – although thankfully no one died and just one person was injured. It certainly makes a strange sight at the end of the runway, especially as it is so remarkably well preserved. You would think people would have come and taken it away and used bits of it for garden sheds, but then again they don't have garden sheds in Resolute. They don't have gardens. Bugger all grows in that horrible, empty, windswept place.

Resolute has no reason to be anything or to pretend to be anything other than what it is – a warehouse station. I guess it's going to become a base for those who will come and dig for oil and all the other goodies under the ground in Nunavut. Soon, there is going to be a superhighway up there because of the political disharmony between the West and the Islamic world. They'll be drilling in Canada like there's no tomorrow. I get the feeling that a

RESOLUTE AND RESOLUTE BAY WERE named after the nineteenth-century ship HMS *Resolute*, which in 1852 was one of the earliest in a series of vessels sent by the British to try to discover the fate of John Franklin's expedition to the Northwest Passage.

An experienced Arctic explorer and Royal Navy officer, Franklin had set off in two reinforced steam-powered ships, the *Erebus* and the *Terror*, six years earlier. Having become icebound in Victoria Strait near King William Island, Franklin and his crew of over 120 men were never seen again, despite having two state-of-the-art vessels and carrying enough provisions for up to five years.

After extensive investigations by more than thirty separate search parties (fuelled by a £40,000 reward), the graves of three of the Franklin crewmen were eventually discovered on Beechey Island where the two vessels had first overwintered. Notes from the crew claimed that Franklin died a year after the ice locked them in, and that the surviving crew had set off to find help. In 1854, local Inuits told visiting sailors that forty of the remaining Franklin party had died on their trek to find civilization. Forensic tests on those whose bodies were found showed that they may have succumbed to botulism and lead poisoning from poorly constructed cans of food, or possibly contamination of the onboard water system. Diseases such as pneumonia and tuberculosis had also been a factor.

During *Resolute*'s 1852 search for evidence of the Franklin expedition, she too became stuck in pack ice, this time floating east off Viscount Melville Sound. With heating and strengthened timbers, the vessel – whose figurehead was a polar bear – was designed to withstand such conditions for years if necessary but was abandoned by the captain and crew after one year (for which he was later court-martialled). Three years on, *Resolute* was discovered by an American whaler more than 1,200 miles from where she'd been left. Freed from the drifting ice, she was taken to Connecticut and eventually returned to Britain and presented to Queen Victoria in 1856 as a 'token of peace'.

When the vessel was finally broken up in 1879, the British Government ordered that a desk be made from her timbers and presented to the then US president, Rutherford B. Hayes, in thanks for the ship's return. It remains in the Oval Office of the White House.

A desolate windswept town

new gold rush is about to happen. Everybody's getting ready to make some money and there's no human warmth in it. It's all about taking; there's no giving going on. And the town is so ugly with its sheds and industrial plant and dumps everywhere; it's a kind of shame.

Aside from the tale of the Franklin expedition and those who lost their lives trying to discover what had happened to Franklin and his men, the town of Resolute and its surrounding area has another awful side to its story. A large group of Inuit from northern Quebec were forced to move there, and to other similar locations, in 1953 to establish sovereignty for Canada.

A crime was committed against those people, who were abandoned to the elements. What happened to them was every bit as bad as the crimes committed against American Indians, Aboriginals, Maoris and indigenous South Africans. When you think about people behaving like that, it is sinful. I can't imagine the Canadian Government would be allowed to do that today – move people around just for political reasons and abandon them.

It must have been so miserable being made to live on that desolate stone in the sea.

I visited the Inuit cemetery in Resolute and it was full of the graves of the poor buggers who'd been forcibly relocated. There were a lot of babies, and many older people who didn't live very long at all. One man born in 1964 died twenty-six years later in 1990. The tombstone for another poor soul, who only lived six days, said he was born at Resolute Bay on 20 May 1962 and died on 26 May. Another tombstone was inscribed: '*Over the years you've given your best, now it's time to relax and take that well-earned rest. May the coming years bring you every contentment. I wish you a happy retirement.*' It must be some kind of joke. A happy retirement? In that graveyard? With the wind whipping past? My God!

A couple of miles outside of Resolute there is a remarkable sight – a partially restored Thule settlement. The Thule people were the ancestors of today's Inuit. They don't actually mind being called Eskimos, by the way, although I'd always thought they found it offensive. They just kind of resent that it's other people's name for them when their own name for themselves is Inuit.

Graves of the Inuit

THE INUIT FORCIBLY RELOCATED FROM Port Harrison in northern Quebec, solely to establish Canadian sovereignty during the Cold War, were promised land, new houses and plenty of wild food to hunt. The authorities assured them that they could return home within a year if they were unhappy.

When they arrived in the High Arctic, however, they discovered only a few buildings and a harsh landscape completely different from the one they had known – it supported little game and there was not enough snow to build their traditional buildings. The strange hours of daylight were also completely alien to these Inuit people. Pleading to be repatriated, they were told that the offer had been rescinded. They were forced to remain and suffer terrible privations, living on a diet of beluga whale during the migration season and government handouts the rest of the year. Many died, and a great number of those who survived suffered variously from alcoholism and depression. Some of the women resorted to prostitution.

Forty years after these once happy Inuit were sent north, a government inquiry called the relocation programme 'one of the worst human rights violations in the history of Canada'. Those Inuit who were still alive were paid C$10 million in compensation. The official inquiry shocked the Canadian people and led directly to the setting up of the Nunavut territory six years later.

Thule whale-bone roof

The whale-bone roof on the restored Thule house was pretty nifty; a bit like an igloo without the snow. It reminded me of the ancient Pictish houses in Scotland, dug deep into the ground with a roof over the top; or the old American sod shanties the pioneers made, when they'd dig a hole and put a roof on it rather than labour around finding timber with which to build walls. The Thule used whale bone instead, which was probably their only material 1,000 years ago. They were amazing hunters of whales, and the first people to travel from Alaska to Greenland using the Northwest Passage as it was then.

I read in some historical literature that between the years 1400 and 1650, the temperature dropped so much that everything froze up and the bigger whales stopped swimming to those seas. Funnily enough, the books don't say why the climate changed then and they don't blame anyone for it either. They don't say it was thanks to the desperate overuse of camp fires or wood stoves or people firing spears into the air. I don't think there was much recycling going on in the fifteenth century, or people sifting through their garbage. They didn't have the same blame culture then. The temperature just changed and everybody got on with it. The Thule people took to hunting more for walrus and seal and caribou, like the Inuit of today.

The first residents of Resolute, the Thule liked it enough to stick around and build some houses. Personally I prefer Whitley Bay, but that's just a matter of taste. Even grass finds it hard to grow there. What a wonderfully hardy people they must have been. I sat in one of their homes for a minute and imagined myself waiting for the wife to come back with a bit of whale for my dinner. Perhaps a bit of vertebrae? I was getting rather knowledgeable about my whale bits. A man's home is his castle, I've always said. That place was fixed up perfectly; a good style for someone with D-I-Y skills. Young people hoping to get onto the housing ladder shouldn't go to those fly-by-night house-builder types, they should think whale bone and a shovel and a fishing net.

Exploring this ancient dwelling further, I discovered that it had an inhabitant – a lemming; a wee, hairy, mousey affair. What a splendid little man he was. What a beautiful creature, a delight, with his lovely shiny coat. I didn't flinch when he appeared. Wildlife doesn't scare me at all. I stood my ground and he retreated. I have always cared deeply about the lemming's reputation. People think that lemmings commit mass suicide, but they don't. The myth was repeated in a Disney film called *White Wilderness* in the fifties, which made everyone believe it to be true but it is total nonsense and the unfortunate lemmings have been considered suicidal ever since.

THULE HAD BEEN a name given to an island far to the north in literature dating back to 300 BC. The ancient Europeans believed it to be part of Iceland or Greenland. The Scottish Gaelic for Iceland is 'Innis Tile', which means Isle of the Thule.

The Latin term *ultima Thule* means any place located beyond the borders of the known world. Thule has also come to be considered as a Nordic version of the lost city of Atlantis, populated by those with superhuman powers.

When a municipality in northern Greenland was named Thule in deference to the many centuries of mythology about the island, its inhabitants became the Thule people, direct ancestors of the Inuit Greenlanders.

Whenever you read about the Northwest Passage or talk to anyone about it, one name keeps coming up – Sir John Franklin and the last of his three Arctic explorations, which was a complete failure. The British knew the Northwest Passage wasn't a realistic or viable trade route to Russia and China, and that even if a route through could be discovered it would only be open once or twice a year, and even that couldn't be guaranteed because of the ice. But they owned

Sir John Franklin

more land than any other nation in the world and they wanted still more, for the Empire. On top of that, they desired power and sovereignty over lucrative trade routes in this remote part of the world so they sent Sir John Franklin to look for the Passage in two ships with officers and men who would never be seen again.

Franklin is always made out to have been a bit of a lad: he'd fought at the Battle of Trafalgar under Lord Nelson, he'd explored the coast of Australia with the British explorer Matthew Flinders (who was his uncle) and he'd been governor of Tasmania (then called Van Diemen's Land). Having completed two overland Arctic explorations and decided that everyone was going too far north for the Northwest Passage, he chose to try further south and that was his undoing.

When you think of those voyages made by explorers on old bits of sailing vessel and steamship, your heart does go out to them. They didn't have radios, they didn't have radar and they didn't have much of anything to tell them anything. There was no wildlife and no birds to take direction by. They didn't know where they were half the time or what was looming up at them through the fog and the mist – maybe an iceberg or a big bit of rock. They only had latitude, they didn't even have proper longitude yet and they were away for years and years at a time. The Franklin crew spent their first winter in the Arctic at a place called Beechey Island and they were there for ten months. Ten months! That's a hell of a winter.

Franklin, who was nearly sixty when he left London, filled the ships' holds with meat and 8,000 tins of food. The tins, soldered

Modern maps of the Northwest Passage

CANNIBALISM AMONG SURVIVORS of wars and disasters has been well documented over the centuries. Among the most famous are those who survived the sinking of the French ship *Medusa* in 1816. They boarded a raft and then started to eat each other or throw the weak overboard. Fifteen crew and passengers were eventually rescued from the four hundred who first set sail. In 1846, a group of settlers known as the Donner Party, who were heading for California, got caught in blizzards in the Sierra Nevada. Several resorted to cannibalism to survive.

In 1918, following the sinking of the American steam vessel *Dumaru* off the coast of Guam, survivors who took to the life rafts ended up feeding on the corpses of those who didn't survive. During the two World Wars, cannibalism became the only means of survival for some trapped during the Siege of Leningrad, by those in the Russian Gulags and by some Japanese captors of European prisoners of war. In 1972, after a Uruguayan aeroplane crashed in the Andes, many of the sixteen survivors ate the flesh of dead passengers in the seventy-two days before they were eventually discovered high in the snow-covered mountains.

badly with raw lead, may have been the cause of many deaths as lead would have leached into the food and severely weakened the men. Can you imagine? You're stuck in the ice for years. What the hell do you do? Where do you go? You can't go forward you can't go back. So you break out the silver and have a bit of nosh, not knowing you're poisoning yourself with the lead from tins. One of the upshots was that the crew went skew-wiff mentally (which is what lead poisoning does to you), and the whole journey ended up a total disaster.

Legend has it that some of the men survived for four or five years before they died way south of where their ships became trapped, having walked for miles over the frozen wastes. Those poor men. There are records of Inuit watching forty of them dragging lifeboats across the ice. They gave them some seal to eat. Later that year, the Inuit found thirty-five dead, many with bits missing where they'd been eaten, the news of which shocked Britain to the core; cannibalism was also suspected because of the knife-scarring on the bones that were found. But when they started wolfing into each other there was still plenty of food left so it looks like they all went bonkers. I don't think there's anything apart from murder that shocks people more than cannibalism. It's a very odd affair. It's the ultimate in desperation, isn't it? To eat another person.

The floating old folks' home

So many people gave their lives to this bleak Arctic region of the planet and I'm sure a lot of them gave up their sanity, too. I hoped I wouldn't lose mine on my own passage west which would be far less hazardous – eight days on a Russian scientific survey ship named *Akademik Ioffe.*

From Resolute Bay, our vessel would travel west and eventually south on a voyage that Franklin and so many like him had longed to complete. For the previous three years, the *Akademik Ioffe* has been able to ferry a handful of intrepid tourists on this most elusive of journeys, thanks to changes in the world's weather. Success was not a given, mind you, and the captain who showed me around the bridge still had to study the winds and ice charts and use the latest technology, such as GPS navigation and sonar equipment, to make sure that the ice wasn't closing in around us. If we got stuck, we'd have to summon an ice breaker because the vessel we were on was only a Class B ice-strengthened ship and couldn't push through solid ice. What was even more amazing was that a hundred-metre-long ship could be navigated by the twiddle of a computer button. I was tempted, when his back was turned, to head straight for an iceberg.

One of the first things I did having boarded that sturdy survey vessel, was to check the welding. My advice to you before you sail any distance in a ship is always check the welding. I am a welder – I know. I'm a comedian, of course, but I'm first and foremost a welder. I had a good look at the welding on that shallow draft, Russian-made boat with its strengthened hull and I must say there was some fine work. I felt very safe and sound.

During lifeboat drill, I met my fellow passengers (most of whom were surprisingly elderly). I couldn't help but be struck by the irony that while Franklin and all those who'd tried to find their way through the Northwest Passage had lost their lives trying to do it, I would be on a cruise ship in comparative ease, eating very nice food and wine with a bunch of old people.

Just in case, I carefully eyed them up to see who I'd eat first if things went horribly wrong.

I didn't want any stringy old stuff.

* * *

I FELT LIKE a foreigner among the people on that boat, an alien or a spaceman. We didn't live on the same planet, we didn't listen to the same music or keep the same company or do the same things. Reading might have united us, because my generation tend to read books as opposed to e-mails, but I think that was all that linked us.

Whenever I'm with people my own age, I don't feel as if I'm with like types. I prefer to be with people younger than me.

Maybe it is vanity. Everyone with a beard is vain. I preen and comb and condition my hair. I trim my eyebrows because they're so bushy they shove my glasses out and I can't see properly. I trim my moustache and think, 'God, that's the best looking beard!' I like a huge Moses beard best but I haven't done that for a while. My wife doesn't like it but it's my favourite.

I aspire to looking like a tramp; I set my sights very low. Handy hint number 179B: set your sights extremely low, and you'll be a happy person. I thought I looked great in my purple beard, especially when it was new – all dark and shiny. I thought, 'Feck! That looks amazing!' It wasn't showing off so much; sometimes you need proof that you exist because in today's world you can be beige in a jiffy.

So I choose my clothes carefully. I have a vast wardrobe for a guy who looks like a tramp. I have very good shoes and shirts and I collect them and I like them very much. I preen and primp and I'm not the least bit embarrassed about it, especially when I'm with people who are ten to twenty years younger than me.

The only exception is young women. I find I get bored very quickly with what they want to talk about. I can never understand older men having affairs with younger women. It's not a puritanical stance, but if I was going to have an affair it would be with someone my own age, who knows the world that I know.

I've often spoken to my wife Pamela about it. Once, though, she was really wounded by something I said. I'd read a magazine article about some star who had owned up to his wife that he'd had an affair and felt much better for it. I thought, 'You should keep that to yourself. All you've done is dumped your guilt on your wife. You might feel great but now she has the worry of feeling that she somehow wasn't enough for you in some respect. Since when was that fair?'

I was toying with all that when I met up with my wife after she'd visited a Matisse exhibition. I said, 'What do you think? I think he should carry information like that to the grave.' She looked at me and said, 'Are you trying to tell me something?' and then she started crying. She swears that it was Matisse that made her cry, not me, but I still think it was me and that kind of haunts me to this day. ”

Beechey Island, Nunavut

THERE ARE THREE graves from the Franklin expedition not far from the shore on Beechey Island, overlooking Erebus and Terror Bay. The simple markers for those who gave their lives are for Able Seaman John Hartnell, aged twenty-five; Royal Marine Private William Braine, thirty-one; and John Torrington, twenty, petty officer and leading stoker from the discovery ship HMS *Terror*. Hartnell and Torrington died during the January and Braine in April, 1846.

Torrington was the guy I couldn't help dwelling on the most. Someone had shown me a photograph of him earlier that day. It wasn't a very pleasant picture because it was taken shortly after he was exhumed in 1984 by scientists from a Canadian university. Having seen his face, I gained a kind of respect for him and a relationship with him that I wouldn't have had I not seen it. His white headstone reads: '*Sacred to the Memory of John Torrington who departed this life January AD1846 on board the* H.M. Terror *aged 20 years.*' It was odd to think that he was still lying beneath that, in the same position, his face just under the stones.

John Torrington, deceased

* * *

I NEVER TAKE photographs along with me when I'm away. I miss people. I miss my wife and kids, but I try not to think about that. I just get on with what I'm doing and deal with what is. When my computer's working, the picture on the screen is of my granddaughter and that's nice, but I don't take framed photographs and, quite frankly, I don't trust people who do. You go into any office and see the guy with a picture of his wife on the desk and I guarantee he'll be the randiest man in the room.

We have millions of pictures of when the kids were small and all that kind of jolly stuff but very few of my past. I've got no interest in the past at all. My past is very dark. I don't like it. I had a very unfortunate past – although some of it was brilliant and great fun. But the important bits were kind of dark and I tend not to dwell on it. So, I don't have many pictures of it and the ones I do have tend not to make me feel good.

I don't get angry any more; I just get kind of sad about the whole sorry state of affairs and lost opportunities. I'm okay. I'm cool with it. I look at photographs from my childhood and it's like a foreign country. It's like a dream place where I used to visit and I don't any more. ”

The scientists who conducted post-mortems found that Torrington had exceptionally high levels of lead in his blood, probably ingested from the food. He was a stoker from Manchester who shovelled the coal; a strong young man yet he'd died during the first winter. What a rotten death, to end life like that. The saddest thing about those young guys is that they would have been desperate to go on this famous expedition. Franklin would have been like the Neil Armstrong of his time, flying to the moon. The men who sailed with him would have been regarded as astronauts. I bet they applied for the job and only the best were chosen – a hundred and twenty-nine men. One young officer even wrote home to his family: '*I hope we get to stay over one winter. I hope we get iced in. I'd love to experience that.*' Be careful what you wish for, eh?

Poor Torrington. Poor all of them. I wonder what Torrington would say if he could see the visitors to his grave these days, the old ladies in kagools or men in orange suits, arriving in inflatable Zodiac boats, screaming up to where he's buried. When he arrived at Beechey Island all those years ago, he thought he was on an ultra-modern craft with its anti-icing devices and steam heating in the cabins, its retractable screw propellers driven by a London railways steam locomotive and special, iron-clad bow. They must have thought they were invincible.

There's an account of the behaviour of one of Franklin's captains, a man named Francis Crozier. An Irishman with a reputation for being a bit crazy, Crozier sailed his ship (*Terror*) between two big icebergs that were so close together that some of his men fainted. One went mad; the poor guy lost the plot completely.

The weirdest thing was that the Beechey Island gravesite looked exactly as it did when Franklin stood there the day they buried his men. I had this haunting feeling that time hadn't moved on there at all. A lot of things had withered and died everywhere else, but at Beechey Island it was as if they'd buried those men yesterday. There were the same mountains, land and water, exactly in the same position as they'd been back then. Usually there's a house or

a field or a farm or a factory or something that has changed; maybe a big chimney or a church, but out there, nothing had. The place is still just as windswept and horrible. Next to nothing grows. You're not welcome there unless you're moss.

The windswept graves of Beechey Island

I remember once I was in Nepal with Max Boyce, the Welsh comedian. There were some flags across a river, like pendants on a piece of rope, so Max asked our guide, 'What are they for?' The guide replied, 'To appease the moon.' Then Max said to me, 'My God, we're far from home.' Since then, I've felt that on many occasions, and I did again on that windswept barren rock. If dead men could speak, I'm sure the first sentence out of their mouths would be, 'My God, I'm far from home.'

The rest of the sailors, too, must have stood at Torrington's grave, freezing to death in their inadequate, rotting clothing, and wondered what was going to become of them. All hell was waiting for them just down the road and they didn't even know. The northern ice cap was growing in those days, so when winter fell the ice just came upon them as if it was attacking the ship. There are detailed accounts from a surgeon on one of the ships who wrote that ice would surge out of the sea like a hand reaching up. Pillars of white would come crashing through the surface. The most frightening thing was the noise. The ice would knock on the side of the ship, letting them know who was in charge. It must have been terrifying. Imagine looking out to sea, into a whiteout, with nowhere to go and the ice whacking your boat. It did them in eventually. Then the lead poisoning crept in and people started going a bit strange and paranoid. Holy macaroni! I wouldn't wish that on anyone. It's amazing the others lasted so long.

What a strange expedition theirs was. The ships carried a library with a thousand books. They had a carpentry shop, a blacksmith's and a shooting range for the marines to practise. They formed a theatrical company and used to give performances. Oh, how I'd love to have seen that. They were quite happy to sit out the winter, with all that grub, until spring came to melt the ice so that they could sail the Northwest Passage and be 'The Boys'. But the ice didn't melt. Not for years. They sent men on dog sleds to get help from a Hudson's Bay station but that was hundreds of miles away and they never returned.

You wouldn't believe what else they were carrying with them. They had lightning rods, brass curtain poles, a big heavy stove and twenty-six silver plates. Once they'd abandoned ship, the Inuit saw them dragging forty-foot lifeboats full of this junk across the ice. My God! They were crazy; a different type of people altogether.

The old stove left for Franklin in case he returned

Franklin doesn't sound all that bright to me, making the poor jerks from below decks trudge his candelabra and silver plates across the snow.

All the while they were missing, back in Britain there were songs and poems and stories of derring-do being written about 'bold Franklin in the Arctic'. People had already heard tales about the weird natives who lived in houses made of snow and ice. They'd seen drawings of walruses and polar bears. They couldn't wait for more news. The country was completely abuzz when Franklin and his men disappeared. The newspapers were chased to publish even more stories by Franklin's wife, Lady Jane, who volunteered to go on one of the ships sent to look for him. She was probably going to give her husband a hard time. 'Where do you think you've been to this time of night, loafing around the Peel Sound?'

She was always trying to raise money to fund search parties. Much came through public subscription but she put up a lot of it herself. In total more than £10 million was spent over the years trying to find Franklin's crew. That must be like a billion or something now. And all those people went to their deaths trying to find them. What a hell of a waste, all for the Empire. For years, no one knew what had happened to them but eventually the expedition's progress was traced from Beechey Island to Starvation Cove on the mainland, where the last survivors ended up eating each other. I can't blame them – I would do it myself.

At Beechey Island is an odd, cross-shaped cairn made of a hundred food cans with stones in them. It was obviously meant to be some sort of message but, over the years, people have emptied every single can and found nothing. Another cairn like it was discovered on a hill and torn to bits, too, but there was still no message. Nobody knows why they did that. Maybe they were halfway through building it and noticed a thaw happening and said, 'Let's go!' There was also a pair of cashmere gloves with a stone on them, weighing them down. The fact that someone went off without his gloves in that climate is very weird. It's all such a mystery.

One of the expeditions that came looking for them later built a little shelter for Franklin on Beechey Island in case he returned, which of course he never did because he'd been dead several years at that point. They thought he might be out doing something and if they missed him, he could live in the place they named Northumberland House until he was better. The bones of the house are still there, a skeletal outline of what it once was. It would

The mysterious cross-shaped tin-can cairn

The derelict cabin

have been all secure and watertight once, but the ravages of the weather and polar bears breaking in to look for food haven't left much of it standing. By the time I stepped over the threshold, the floor was littered with barrel staves and hoops, planks of old wood and the remnants of an old stove, but it still felt a great privilege to be there.

Elsewhere on Beechey Island were all sorts of memorials to the various explorers, doctors, sailors and adventurers who'd since given their lives, one way or another, in attempts to navigate the Northwest Passage. One, to a Desmond Henry Fogg, read: '*He contributed greatly to the north's growth and development and knew the feeling of independence, freedom and accomplishment. Against the broad black sky of night, for Des the stars will shine so bright. The Northland's Challenge he bravely met, for Des the glorious sun has set.*' Good on you, Des.

Despite Des's jolly little grave, there was an overwhelming feeling of sadness on Beechey Island. I couldn't stop thinking of those poor men from Franklin's expedition standing there and thinking, 'Oh my God, we'll never go home again.'

I can't imagine what that must have felt like. I've never found myself in that position and I hope I never do. Except of course when I was a bit drunk, I might have said, 'My God, I'll never get home again!' Different thing though, isn't it?

* * *

"THE MORE I followed in the footsteps of Franklin, the angrier I felt at the propaganda I'd been fed about him all my life. I was always led to believe that he and the rest of those explorers were heroes when, as far as I could see, they were a bunch of tossers. The touting of upper-class idiots as heroes has happened throughout British history and I am tired of it.

Franklin got it completely wrong. The ship that came to save them got it wrong and had to be rescued by the Americans. I refuse to treat these commanders like heroes. I think they were dithering, blithering idiots who killed a lot of good men. Rich, middle-class, arrogant pricks.

I had less and less respect for Franklin. He was fired from his governor's job in Tasmania for being inept. He had made a mess of an Arctic expedition just before his final one and only saved his arse by writing a book about it, in which he comes across as quite the hero who ate his own shoes to survive. That seems to be a great habit among Arctic guys – when you're starving, eat your shoes. Maybe they had edible shoes or something, I don't know. They have a word for people like that in Scotland – it's 'stumer'. It sounds like tumour but it means an amazingly stupid person who is a big bumbling idiot. This stumer went to the Arctic at the pressing of the authorities by his wife ('If you don't give him this job,' she said, 'he will die of disappointment'). Well he got the job and other people died, not quite of disappointment but of things a lot more painful. If he'd only gone north instead of south.

Roald Amundsen (the Norwegian explorer known as the first to traverse the Northwest Passage) at least had half a brain. He listened more and he spoke less. When he got to the Arctic, he said to himself, 'The Inuit obviously know their way around,' and he asked for their advice. He went in smaller boats, without the candelabra, and he didn't go round calling places Amundsen Strait or Amundsen this that and the other.

British explorers like Parry and Baffin, on the other hand, were too busy giving places names – as if they didn't already

have them. I hate the kind of arrogance that trod the world. They presumed that the names places already had were only for the native chaps. What did they know? If they'd only translated those names, they'd have found they meant things like Don't Come Here Bay, Desolation Point or Starvation Cove. They might have learned something.

Whenever I read history I think, 'What were the plumbers doing when the kings were all beating each other with big sticks?' Now I wonder what the average carpenter was doing while Franklin was on the upper decks eating rabbit by candlelight in his bow tie, making a total arse of the whole affair. Prancing about the Arctic with a silver dinner service, dressed as if he was going to dinner in Pall Mall.

The big mistake these people made was that they took Britain with them in their ships. Okay, so Franklin died, but he died alongside some smashing, innocent young men from Edinburgh and Glasgow and Manchester and Liverpool and London, just ordinary Joes. People didn't even know their names until some of their graves were found a hundred years later. But all you hear is Franklin this, Franklin that and Franklin the other. I find it tiresome, the officer class being applauded and his poor wife trying to find him, raising dough. They never found Franklin's body. The Inuit said they buried him in sand which turned to stone, which sounds like a cement block to me. I don't know why they'd do that, although I know why I would. Let's hope the lads set about him and had him for their tea. ”

Gjoa Haven, King William Island, Nunavut

ONE OF THE FIRST THINGS I saw when I arrived at Gjoa Haven was a native drum dance, which was brilliant. Just when I thought I was losing the will to live, trapped on the floating old folks' home, the Inuit saved me again.

A group of elderly ladies, dressed in traditional black and white fringed garments, stood in a hockey hall on a windswept knoll overlooking the harbour and sang in that incredibly moving way, that 'ay-ye-hay-a-hay' noise that sounds as if it's only got vowels.

GJOA HAVEN, whose Inuit name Uqsuqtuuq means 'plenty of fat' and refers to its abundance of seals and walruses, was described by Roald Amundsen as 'the finest little harbour in the world'. On King William Island, named after William IV by explorer John Ross, Gjoa Haven has welcomed visitors and explorers since the days of the tall ships.

Amundsen, who named Gjoa Haven after his seal-hunting sloop *Gjøa*, had developed a childhood passion for Arctic exploration after reading of the doomed Franklin expedition. In 1906, following three years trapped in ice (two at Gjoa Haven) he and his crew became the first to traverse the Northwest Passage between the Atlantic and Pacific oceans. His survival and that of his men was partly due to his adoption of the survival skills of the local Netsilik Inuit, whom he'd befriended and whose animal hides he wore instead of traditional woollen garments.

Unlike Franklin, who had been at Gjoa Haven before him, Amundsen learned how to use dog sleds, make traditional knives and spears, and hunt for wild food. Six years later, he used the same techniques (plus the gradual slaughter of his dog teams for fresh meat) to reach the South Pole. In 1925, he was in one of two aircraft that achieved the world record for flying farthest north, to 87°44'N. One of the planes was damaged beyond repair on landing, so all six crew had to squeeze into one small plane after a month of clearing snow for a runway on the fragmenting ice.

A year later, Amundsen made the first crossing of the Arctic in an airship. In 1928, while on a search and rescue mission for a second airship attempt over the North Pole, his flying boat was lost in fog north of Bear Island, Norway. His body was never found. He was fifty-five years old.

They also performed some great throat music. The theme of the song, they told me, was how, in a place with no landmarks, you get somewhere to hunt and how you get back, which in terrain like that is everything. The landscape there was as barren as any I had seen; there were about three blades of grass every hundred yards.

Opposite: Making bannock

The music was dead clever, especially the guy working a one-handed drum, which was flat and thin. These drums used to be made out of whale lungs until synthetic materials came along. Outdoors, in the biting wind, was an old lady called Mary making bannock, or sweet bread, in a frying pan. In Scotland, bannock is oatmeal bread but in Gjoa Haven it is something a little different. Mary's family were away camping and she had stayed behind. She burned some heather (which can take hours to gather because there is so little of it growing in the tundra) and heated some seal oil in the frying pan. Bannock and heather, how Scottish can you get? I felt bagpipes coming on.

When the bannock was done, I had some and it was delicious – all crispy on the outside with that lovely warm bready thing going on inside. I was a happy soldier. Bannock. That's a good Scottish word and I love that they still call it that all those years after the Scotsmen who went there first taught them how to make it.

I was so grateful to Mary and to those musicians and dancers. Meeting them was one of the joys of my life. I've always wanted to see the Ghost Dance by the Hopi Indians, which I've not achieved yet, but seeing the Eskimo drum dancers was on a par with that. It wasn't a tourist thing, either – they don't get enough tourists, not yet – this was the real deal. And the ladies who were singing were all born in igloos. I felt very fortunate indeed to have witnessed that. I had the privilege of shaking Mary by the hand before she disappeared inside her tent to get warm again.

* * *

> *INUIT CHILDREN PLAY in the dirt and that makes me smile. Someone famous recently said that what's wrong with children today is that people don't understand that a guy needs to dig a hole with a stick sometimes. And he doesn't need to be questioned about it, thank you. He likes to sharpen the stick and dig a hole right in front of him, shove the dirt around, then put it back in and go home. He doesn't know why. There's a lot to be said for that.*

I'm really fed up with people saying, 'The kids today aren't the same. They play on their computers all day and they don't go outdoors.' People have ruined outdoors for them, that's why they're inside. We've left them nowhere to go. Everybody's terrified that the trees are full of paedophiles that are going to drop on them the minute they go around the corner. So every bit of spare ground is closed off and everybody who goes into a park has to take three forms of ID with them in case people think they're mental cases.

I say let them play. Let them go. My God, I used to go camping with my friends on my bicycle. If you'd asked my father where I was, he'd have had to say, 'I've no idea. He's away camping.'

'Where?'

'I don't know.'

'East? West?'

'He went on his bike. He went round that corner and way up near Loch Lomond somewhere.'

All we had were blankets and bottles of water. We were completely ill-equipped. We'd get washed out in the middle of the night. We were freezing. But I'm still here. So, let them go. Set them free.

You see those lovely Inuit kids playing on their motorbikes in among all the traffic or digging in the dirt and being kids. They're very well brought up too; well mannered. Not in the please-and-thank-you way but they look on you, at the very

least, as an equal. They don't give you that crap. They don't shout and bawl and make your life a misery.

Although a bit of shouting and bawling and making your life a misery is pretty much okay, as well. I met plenty of that as a boy. You know, shouting rude things to people – I think that's part of the gig – and maybe a bit of vandalism. I don't mean like smashing all the windows in a hospital – but throwing a bicycle tyre over a lamppost so that no one's ever going to get it off isn't all that bad. Chucking sneakers over the electric wire isn't a hanging offence, either, which is just as well. ”

In Gjoa Haven, I bumped into Jim, a nice guy who worked for the Hudson's Bay Company, and who claimed to know me from back in my folk music days on the Isle of Arran. I asked what he was doing so far north and he said, 'It's a wonderful place to live.' He added that whenever he goes away, even somewhere like the Caribbean or the South Pacific, he can't wait to come home.

I don't get it myself, but I so remember living in places as a child that others would consider less than great, where everyone wished they could move away from and have a house with a bath on the outskirts of town. We loved it, though. It was where we came from. I regretted it when we left. Partick was where our hearts belonged and all the people we liked and the shops and the tastes and smells and noises. I can remember when the butcher was making up your order and if the meat was an ounce short he would throw in a sausage or two. It was a quick barter; the way peasants behave. They have a very strict way of living; a fair and a good way of living which I miss terribly, I must say. When I recognize it, my heart sings a wee song. I think that's really what home is all about. It's not how the place looks or whether the houses are grey or bright yellow. It's whether or not you like the people who live next door. Are they nice to you? Is your day good? Do you go to bed feeling okay? Or when you're away somewhere, do you look forward to going home, like Jim?

Then Jim told me that after his wife, an Inuit, died of cancer leaving him with two children, his son committed suicide. The lad shot himself with an army rifle. It's a real privilege to be the conduit for that sort of information, but I find it heavy on my heart because I'm not really equipped to deal with it. He was a total stranger but he felt he knew me through my DVDs and albums

Gjoa Haven

and said he'd liked me for such a long time. Then he just unloaded on me and sometimes I find that a burden. It will stay with me for years.

I couldn't help thinking about what had happened to Jim's son, but when I looked at the grey houses on one side and the terrain on the other; when I thought how far it was from the 'civilization' that kids come to know from the Internet or television, I kind of understood. These kids see everybody else in the world having a great laugh with rock and roll and boogie-woogie, but they're stuck there. It's not as if they can get on a train and go to any of those mythical places. It costs a lot of money to get precisely nowhere in Nunavut. This is beyond the magnetic North Pole, in a place where you have a couple of months a year of no light, plus nine months of winter. There are plenty of reasons for topping yourself.

I don't know if I have the right to look into the future but it doesn't look good for those who sit in such remote places, on dole money, with only an occasional hunting trip to look forward to. I keep thinking back to Amundsen who said, 'If you want to do these wonderful people a real favour, leave them alone to live the way they have always lived.' I think he was absolutely right.

Charlie Cahill, a Newfoundlander, gave me the grand tour of the town. He and his wife and kids moved there in 1990 to work for the government, and never left. Charlie told me that around eighty per cent of the 1,100 residents of Gjoa Haven are on income support. The rest work in education or health care and some work in

Waiting for the hunt

construction, but only for the three months of the summer, otherwise it's too cold. Strangely, global warming had deserted Gjoa Haven. Their summers have been getting colder in recent years and last winter was their coldest in thirty years, with six feet of ice on the ocean and temperatures of minus fifty degrees Fahrenheit every day and minus sixty-eight one day, plus wind chill. 'The local school only shuts when the temperature reaches minus sixty,' he said. I must remember to tell my kids that.

More than a third of the population are children as the region has one of the highest birth rates in Canada, which must be to do with the long winters. A dentist visits three times a year, a doctor covers seven communities over a huge area, and the local nurses diagnose most ailments, write prescriptions and treat patients. 'They do everything,' Charlie said. 'It's one-stop shopping.'

When Amundsen first arrived at Gjoa Haven in 1903, there was only a handful of people living there.

'The Inuit saw a big stick coming out of the ice, which was the mast of the ship,' Charlie explained. They had never seen a tall ship before, or a white man. Amundsen was a congenial guy who brought lots of blankets and pots and pans and knives and other things to trade with them. In a matter of months, about six or seven families moved up here, built igloos and decided to stay.

'It was good for Amundsen too, because he learned how to handle husky dogs and drive sleds and build igloos, all of which helped him years later when he went to the South Pole. This was his training ground.'

'The finest little harbour in the world'

Charlie added proudly, 'The great thing about Amundsen was that the men he took out with him, he always took back home.'

The teardrop-shaped harbour Amundsen described so lovingly is much smaller than I'd imagined; just five hundred metres at its widest point with a narrow opening, but it is a hundred feet deep and forms the only shelter from the wind, snow and ice for miles around. Amundsen found it in a time before there were maps to show him where anything was and the discovery saved his life. During the three years he stayed in Gjoa Haven, he and his men built a wharf, and an observatory to study the magnetic North Pole. The Hudson's Bay Company came later and added to the buildings. Now Gjoa Haven has schools and power stations and more than a thousand inhabitants.

Our vessel was only the second cruise ship to dock there in six years, so they don't get many visitors. Their only other callers are the giant barges that bring container loads of groceries, skidoos, televisions and fuel. Charlie described the transition the community had gone through in recent years as 'breathtaking', with better transportation and high-speed Internet offering more and more contact with the outside world.

'When the elders grew up they lived in igloos and they hunted and that was their life,' he told me. 'They may have traded something to buy a rifle instead of hunting with a spear but their lives were pretty traditional until the fifties.

'Now there are only seven dog teams left in Gjoa Haven. They are a lot of work because you have to feed dogs all year round and they can eat a lot. They are only used for maybe two months around April/May to hunt for caribou, so skidoos are far more practical.'

There is a monument to Amundsen in Gjoa Haven, to commemorate where he landed and spent time before opening up the Northwest Passage. It seemed to me that the broken down skidoo nearby it was as much of a monument to what is going on in this land these days.

Some of the residents have blue eyes and blond hair and are said to be direct descendants from Amundsen's men, or from the sailors who arrived after him. I guess the guys got together with local women and changed the gene pool a little with the high tide. George Porter, who was born in 1921, claimed his grandfather was the Scottish captain of a whaling ship. We Scots are everywhere. You think you're far away and then someone tells you their granddad's a whaler from Dundee and suddenly you're thumped right back home again.

Victory Point, King William Island, Nunavut

THE JOY OF Victory Point for me was that there was nothing there. Nothing is particularly powerful. There is nothing like nothing. The island is made of shale, bits of stone like terracotta, mountains of it, one piece on top of the other in a giant ploughing formation caused by the movement of ice. There was nothing else, except lichen – a kind of weedy life hanging onto the side of stones in the most impressive way.

It's always amazed me that life strives to carry on in a place like that. Every chance it gets, whether it's after a forest fire or a volcanic eruption or whatever, life starts to appear again, it hangs in there. When that is absolutely all there is, it makes the discovery of anything else very telling. And it was there, in all that nothingness, in what could be the most miserable place in the world that the final note from the Franklin expedition was found – made all the

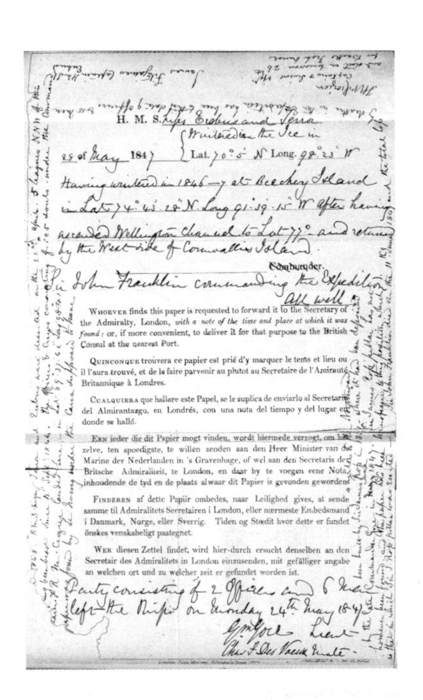

H. M. Ships Erebus and Terror

Wintered in the Ice in

28 of May 1847 Lat. 70° 5' N Long. 98° 23' W

Having wintered in 1846–7 at Beechey Island in Lat 74° 43' 28" N. Long 91° 39' 15" W After having ascended Wellington Channel to Lat 77° and returned by the West side of Cornwallis Island.

Sir John Franklin commanding the Expedition.

All well

WHOEVER finds this paper is requested to forward it to the Secretary of the Admiralty, London, *with a note of the time and place at which it was found*: or, if more convenient, to deliver it for that purpose to the British Consul at the nearest Port.

QUINCONQUE trouvera ce papier est prié d'y marquer le tems et lieu ou il l'aura trouvé, et de le faire parvenir au plutot au Secretaire de l'Amirauté Britannique à Londres.

CUALQUIERA que hallare este Papel, se le suplica de enviarlo al Secretario del Almirantazgo, en Londrés, con una nota del tiempo y del lugar en donde se halló.

EEN ieder die dit Papier mogt vinden, wordt hiermede verzogt, om het zelve, ten spoedigste, te willen zenden aan den Heer Minister van der Marine der Nederlanden in 's Gravenhage, of wel aan den Secretaris der Britsche Admiraliteit, te London, en daar by te voegen eene Nota, inhoudende de tyd en de plaats alwaar dit Papier is gevonden geworden.

FINDEREN af dette Papiir ombedes, naar Leilighed gives, at sende samme til Admiralitets Secretairen i London, eller nœrmeste Embedsmand i Danmark, Norge, eller Sverrig. Tiden og Stœdit hvor dette er fundet önskes venskabeligt paategnet.

WER diesen Zettel findet, wird hier-durch ersucht denselben an den Secretair des Admiralitets in London einzusenden, mit gefälliger angabe an welchen ort und zu welcher zeit er gefundet worden ist.

Party consisting of 2 Officers and 6 Men left the Ships on Monday 24th May 1847.

Gm. Gore Lieut.

Chas. F. Des Voeux Mate

The last Franklin note

Opposite: Victory Point

more powerful because it was backed up by such desolation. It must have been hellish for those guys who set out from the *Erebus* and *Terror*. They got eighty-five miles and decided they were going the wrong way so they went back and set out again on a second trip.

It was during those desperate attempts to find help that some of Franklin's officers wrote two notes in the margins of a page from a book. The first was penned by Lieutenant Graham Gore, who wrote: '*We put up in Beechey Island for the winter and now we've set out again and all is well.*'

Franklin was alive then and everything was okay. But round the margin of the note was another note by Captain Crozier a year later, dated 25 April 1848, who added that Franklin was dead along with twenty-four officers and crew. He said that a hundred and five of the survivors were setting out to try to get south and find help across the frozen tundra on a journey that would prove to be their last. What a fitting end to a miserable story.

There used to be a stone cairn where the note was found, but that had been decimated by everyone digging around it ever since and who never put it back together again. All of which says a massive amount to me about the whole affair and about the sailors, the great unsung, who put up that cairn in the first place. Those were the people with no names who were doing all the slogging and dragging boats across the snow, full of Franklin's button-polishers and ivory combs and French prayer books.

A place like Victory Point makes you realize how close you are to nothingness, which I'm always aware of in this area. You only need to step outside the door and you quickly learn. I had four layers of waterproof clothing on, as well as my underwear, a T-shirt, a shirt and a jersey – so eight layers in all. But my toes were freezing despite my Wellies and two pairs of socks; my fingers were freezing even with my lined sealskin gloves. I was molly-coddled by comparison to those poor bloody sailors out there who put up with it knowing that they weren't going to be warm any near time in the future.

And what about the guys who were sent to search for them? Like Lieutenant William Hobson, who went to the Arctic on a yacht bought by Lady Franklin, and found two skeletons, some abandoned clothes and the brief note rolled inside an empty food canister? Hobson and his crew were stuck in ice for four years. Four years! Imagine, if you were sixteen when you got there, you'd be twenty by the time the ice had melted enough to get you ahead.

Not to get you home, mind you, just to get you out of the ice. Only then can you think about going home. A commercial sailing from New York to London took thirty-six days. So by the time you're released in the Arctic, you still have to get through all the ice again and head south before you can even cross the Atlantic.

Those people were remarkable, as were the men who fought at Waterloo and walked home: Waterloo's in Belgium! Or the soldiers who fought in India or Turkey or Europe in the First World War who went home on foot – just as people had always done throughout the ages. It's extraordinary. Some of them would get the occasional lift but the vast majority walked. There are signs in Orkney and Shetland that say, 'The Second World War, 1939–1946' because that's when they got back – a year after the war had ended.

Prince Leopold Island, Barrow Strait, Nunavut

PRINCE LEOPOLD ISLAND, which used to be a Hudson's Bay Company trading post, is close to where John Ross overwintered at Port Leopold during his search for the Franklin expedition. Fourteen kilometres by eight, the island is also one of the most important migratory bird sanctuaries in the Canadian north. I never thought the words 'bird sanctuary' would escape my lips in my lifetime. In Glasgow a bird sanctuary is what they used to call a convent.

I've never had any interest in bird watching. I know other people do but it's not my cup of tea. But Leopold Island had some of the highest populations of murres, kittiwakes and fulmars (almost four hundred thousand), the young of which hurl themselves off sheer eight hundred-feet cliffs when they are old enough. That clinched it for me.

Our guide told us that the murres are known as the 'penguins of the north', even though there are no penguins in the Arctic. The eggs are laid on narrow ledges and can never be left alone, for fear of marauding gulls or in case they roll off. So each parent takes turns, like a tag team, to hold the egg between their feet. As soon as the young are old enough to leave the nest, they make a leap of faith off the monumental rock face and then try to glide a wee bit so that they hit the water and not the beach below, where they would quickly become a snack for a polar bear.

Birds wheeling above the cliffs

Once the babies have jumped successfully, the mothers leave the nests and fly south to Labrador, Newfoundland, but the fathers stay in the water with their chicks, feeding them as the current takes them south until the chicks are big enough to fly and fend for themselves.

My interest waning, I asked about the one bird I had been really interested in on my journey so far – the raven. There are a lot of ravens in the far north, which surprised me. A local guy told me the Inuit used to follow the ravens because the birds would show them where fresh food was. Once they had killed all the walruses and seals they wanted, they'd slit the carcasses open, divide up the meat and the ravens would come down to eat the spoils. Isn't that clever? It's one thing for a vulture or a buzzard to circle over dead animals, but a bird that will show you where live animals are so you can kill them and leave a bit for them is really intelligent, isn't it?

* * *

“*I HATE TOURISM and I hate being part of it. I hate being on a tourist boat. I don't want to be woken up by some laughing person with enforced gaiety. I'll be in charge of what mood I'm*

in at the start of the day, thank you very much. On cruise ships they have to do the 'Hi-De-Hi! Time to get up, happy campers!' thing, like at Butlins. It makes me want to puke. Sometimes you find yourself standing in line for something in among people with big long shorts and T-shirts with jokes on them and baseball caps and you think, 'How did this happen to me? What am I doing here?' It's like when you don't have a day job and you find yourself in a traffic jam and think, 'How did I end up in this? I don't belong here.'

I don't want to be one of those people spinning around the world in exactly the same temperature as when they left their house, even though they're travelling through the Arctic, Africa or Asia. On those sorts of holidays, the temperature doesn't change. They go from an aeroplane into the lobby of an airport, to a hotel, back into the plane and on to another place. Whenever I go on holiday, I try and avoid the tourist thing – those mass movements of people where everybody is doing the same thing together and there are rotten jokes and after every dinner, a lecture. You think, 'Oh God, not again.' It grinds me down. It makes me feel like an outpatient in a mental hospital and I don't like that feeling very much.

When I was on that Russian ship, just about the only good announcement that came over the tannoy was that a polar bear had been spotted shortly after we had arrived at Prince Leopold Island. I was amazed at the speed the dining room cleared. There were old people running for doors and dropping cutlery to see this Arctic superstar, which actually turned out to be just a dot on the horizon, albeit one of the most interesting wee white dots in the world. The bear didn't even know we existed as it stood throwing a bit of raw seal meat around.

It was great to see him, though – such a deadly thing, letting us know who was the boss. I thought it was wonderful that even though he was so far away, he still owned the enormous stretch of land he was on. Even from what we could see of him at that distance, we could tell he was in great shape and so impressive; eking a living, but doing it rather well.

We spend so much of our time being at the top of the food chain: wiping out the cod in Newfoundland, wiping out the herring, wiping out the haddock. Then a polar bear comes along and the game changes. Suddenly we're on the menu for a creature that is so amazingly good at surviving in those extreme conditions. That's what causes the exhilaration in us. Far from being afraid of it, people love it. They want to see the wild animal that's bigger and more powerful than them – the lion, the polar bear or the grizzly.

It was nice that everybody left him alone, apart from taking his photograph on great long lenses. We'd seen things being shot and slaughtered and skinned and eaten and had agreed with it because of the people who were doing it and why. But it was lovely to see the other side of the coin. It gave a nice balance and reminded me what we were there for. Good on him, I say. I'm on the polar bear's side. ”

Apart from spotting the bear, the saving grace of this part of the Northwest Passage for me was learning about Dr John Rae, the Scottish Arctic explorer sent to find Franklin. Rae is known as 'the hero time forgot'.

I got very excited by Rae, especially when I found how he was very obviously cheated. A fraud was committed, a crime, in my opinion, against a very good person by a very sly and ambitious person – Lady Jane Franklin (and her toff mates); not to mention the Admiralty and all those other people who are paid for the positions they hold. They pulled a flanker and it worked all the way to Westminster, so that John Rae was cheated of his glory. I mean, to give credit for the Northwest Passage to a guy who died along with a hundred and twenty-nine of his crew! Franklin should have hung his head in shame. And his family, who should have tried to hush the whole thing up, not claim the victory.

Dr John Rae

I felt like Inspector Clouseau as I unearthed the facts about John Rae, a remarkable man. It was a delight and very exciting to finally find a hero. Rae saved the Northwest Passage for me.

What happened to John Rae is a disgrace. It's going to have to be sorted. There was so much shameful behaviour at that time. If you go to Westminster Abbey you'll find the ornate marble memorial erected by Lady Franklin to her husband, whom she described as the 'beloved chief' of his lost men. The memorial claims Franklin '*perished in completing the discovery of the Northwest Passage*'. There's even a eulogy written by the then Poet Laureate Alfred Lord Tennyson, no less. If you go other places you'll find the Northwest Passage was supposedly discovered by a

JOHN RAE, who came from the Orkney Islands, trained as a doctor in Edinburgh. Employed by the Hudson's Bay Company, he was the surgeon at Moose Factory, James Bay, Ontario for ten years, where he took it upon himself to learn snow and survival skills from the Cree Indians.

In 1848, Sir John Richardson, a fellow Scot, naval surgeon and explorer, invited Rae to be his second-in-command on a year-long expedition to search for the lost Franklin crew. Their mission gleaned no new information but Rae did prove the existence of the Northwest Passage, succeeding where Franklin had failed. He was later sent to the northernmost fringes of Canada to map the area and 'fill in the gaps'.

Six years later, in 1854, on just such a mission, Rae met some Inuit on King William Island. Through Inuit eyewitness accounts, he finally learned the fate of the last of Franklin's men, including the disturbing evidence of cannibalism. He retrieved many of the dead men's belongings that the Inuit had kept and sent them back to London with a report, in which he wrote:

'*Some of the bodies had been buried (probably those of the first victims of famine); some were in a tent or tents; others under the boat, which had been turned over to form a shelter, and several lay scattered about in different directions.*'

He added: '*From the mutilated state of many of the bodies and the contents of the kettles, it is evident that our wretched countrymen had been driven to the last dread alternative – cannibalism – as a means of prolonging existence.*'

Lady Jane Franklin was so outraged when the news reached London that she started a vociferous campaign against Rae, which included the publication of articles denouncing him, some of which were written by her friend Charles Dickens, then editor of a magazine called *Household Words*. The famous novelist wrote that it was 'unthinkable' that the English Navy would resort to 'such horrible means'.

The fact that Rae often dressed like the natives, spoke their language and consorted with them was frowned upon in Victorian England. Lady Jane made much of the fact that he had not actually visited the site himself (which was several hundred miles from where he was and could not easily be reached), but had taken the 'second-hand' word of 'natives' against the stout moral fabric of Royal Navy men. It was even suggested that the 'savages' may have eaten the sailors themselves.

Dickens wrote: '*Had there been no bears thereabout, to mutilate those bodies? No wolves? No foxes? ... Lastly, no man can, with any show of reason, undertake to affirm that this sad remnant of Franklin's gallant band were not set upon and slain by the Esquimaux themselves. It is impossible to form an estimate of the character of any race of savages, from the deferential behaviour to the white man when he is strong. The mistake has been made again and again; and the moment the white man has appeared in the new aspect of being weaker than the savage, the savage has changed and sprung upon him ... We believe every savage to be in his heart covetous, treacherous, and cruel; and we have yet to learn what knowledge the white man – lost, houseless, shipless, apparently forgotten by his race, plainly famine-stricken, weak, frozen, helpless, and dying – has of the gentleness of Esquimaux nature.*'

Damaged by what was being said about him, Rae retired from the Hudson's Bay Company but continued to live and work in the Canadian High Arctic and the Northwest Territories. He became a student of several indigenous tribes. He visited Greenland and Iceland and was instrumental in exploring new territory, alone and in a dugout canoe, for a proposed telegraph line from the US to Russia. A strait, a river, an isthmus and two towns are named after him.

But his reputation in Britain was in tatters. While Franklin and his crew were all posthumously knighted, Dr John Rae became the only major explorer of his time not to receive a knighthood. He died in London in 1893 at the age of eighty and is buried in St Magnus Cathedral kirkyard in Kirkwall, Orkney. A stone memorial was later carved for him inside the cathedral, in which he lies recumbent in his Arctic clothes, a gun at his side.

man called Robert McClure. Others have their finger in the pie as well; people like Admiral Francis McClintock, for example, who also has a memorial in Westminster Abbey. He and McClure went to Rae for advice before exploring areas Rae had already explored, then they claimed to have made the discoveries themselves. They changed the names of places Rae had already named and they knew it.

I'm only too happy to be one of those shouting for Rae to be recognized. Roald Amundsen, the best and wisest of them all, was the first to say that the Northwest Passage was discovered by John Rae. I think we Scots should send a stonemason down to Westminster Abbey and make a few adjustments. I'll get back to you on that one.

* * *

" BEING RECOGNIZED IS *part of the deal of being who I am but what was funny about being in Canada was that so many people remembered me from so long ago. In a sitcom I did in 1990 called* Head of the Class, *I had much shorter hair and no beard or glasses, but people still recognized me from twenty years ago.*

A group of kids also remembered me from a cult movie I did ten years ago called Boondock Saints, *and a Canadian zombie movie called* Fido. *The barman on the Russian ship recognized me too, and asked, 'You play the banjo?' He told me that Solen, the man who organized the ship's kayak excursions, played but was a real beginner.*

I love meeting people who are less skilful than I am; they are so few and far between. I love to fawn over them and show them my great skill, which makes a change because normally I meet fifteen-year-olds who can lace me and I've been playing for seven thousand years. Solen was desperate to learn a few licks and he came on a storm. Two banjos make a great noise. There's a sort of chugga-lugga sound that's ten times better than one. I like to teach people by letting them play along with me rather than scorching over some little lick, trying to get it right. It's great being carried along with the momentum of someone else.

Solen played in a way that some people might think was wrong, but I come from the school of thought that nothing's wrong – you play like yourself and take it where it takes you and learn from other people and add what you've already got. I think that's where the art of it lies.

A guy called Ron Duff was the first banjo player I ever saw playing live. I was in the Territorial Army at the time and I'd seen Pete Seeger on television, which really impressed me. One of the guys told me about a folk club in Clydebank, so we went along. The band playing was the Tannahill Weavers, whose lead singer was Danny Kyle. Ron Duff played banjo.

Danny ended up being my best friend from that night on – a friendship which lasted forty years until he died. I asked him, 'Do you know anyone who can teach me to play the banjo?' and he said, 'Yeah, Ron will do it.' He called him over and away I went with my banjo and learned 'Cripple Creek', which is the tune I taught Solen. I ended up in Ron's band, learning from books and by asking people, 'How do you do that?' Some tell you to bugger off, some hide and others are really open and say, 'Oh, this is how you do that.' That's how I learned, through sharing. Sharing is the best. ”

Peel Sound, Nunavut

THERE HAD BEEN a disappointing lack of ice on my sea voyage aboard the *Akademik Ioffe* for my liking. Even when we had seen icebergs there had been something quite Disneyland and theme park about them, as if we were floating through a second-hand iceberg lot. There were times when I looked out the window of my cozy cabin and had to say to myself, 'That's the Arctic out there, and you're in the Northwest Passage.' It didn't feel like I've always thought it would, ever since I read about it as a boy. I felt like summoning a waiter: 'More ice, please!'

Then the captain suddenly announced that our way ahead was blocked by ice. The wind had changed, pushing pack ice into our path, and we would have to change our route. A request for an ice-breaker to help us get through had been denied. By turning back and travelling down Parry Channel and into Peel Sound instead of down Prince Regent Inlet, we would be going the way Franklin went. His captain on *Terror*, Crozier, who was a lot more intelligent and much more experienced in the Arctic, warned him against taking this route but Franklin didn't listen. So they sailed down

Ice in the Northwest Passage

Peel Sound – which was one big icy maze – with the ice closing behind them. It was here that they got stuck for two years, in mountainous ice that grew before their very eyes, making huge thundery noises. And it was from here that they tried all their escapes, towing their lifeboats full of things they didn't need.

When the Inuit saw those white men they thought they were mental. They knew they couldn't intervene because there were too many of them to save. At one point they did try to help but they had to leave them because they knew that helping them would end up killing them as well. The European sailors couldn't hunt for native food and didn't know how to survive in that harsh landscape. According to the Inuit, four of the crew lasted several years out in the frozen wastes. They could have been rescued in that time, but the reported sightings of them were completely ignored because they had come from the mouths of 'savages' and weren't to be trusted. That, to me, defines the expedition and everything that was wrong about the British and their Empire snobbery. Even though the Inuit knew where they were and kept them alive at times, their stories were dismissed. It's enough to make you vomit.

A melting iceberg

At Bellot Strait (named after the French Arctic explorer who went on one of the Franklin search missions), we all had to stay quiet onboard ship so that the officers could communicate easily with each other as we passed through the narrow channel, less than a mile wide. To our right was Barrow Point, the most northerly point of the American continent. In theory, I could have jumped ship there and walked all the way to South America.

Having navigated the Franklin Strait, our ship made a sharp turn around the bottom of Victoria Island in force nine winds and into the Beaufort Sea. Looking at the route we had taken on a map, ours looked like the most convoluted journey, but – just as when the explorers of the nineteenth century discovered it – there was no other way to go because of the northern pack ice clogging up the most direct routes.

After eight days, and with hardly any ice in sight, our historic journey through the Northwest Passage was over.

One of the stories which most delighted me about the hunt for the Franklin expedition was its extraordinary reliance on mediums and the paranormal in the search. In 1849, two years after the crew had been reported lost, Weesy Coppin, the four-year-old daughter of a sea captain died in Londonderry, Northern Ireland.

According to her sister Anne, Weesy started to appear to her after death. At first they communicated about girlie matters and things they were interested in as sisters and pals. Then one day, when Weesy had predicted the death of someone, Anne asked her about Sir John Franklin – who was big news in Britain at the time, like a rock star. According to Anne, the room she was in suddenly became a vision of snowy mountains and inlets and she could see a broken-down ship lying in a sort of a canal. Anne asked Weesy, 'Is he alive?' and the whole scene changed and the letters 'BS–PRI–NF' appeared on the wall. There was no explanation and at that point her father William stepped in and said that BS must stand for Barrow Strait, PRI for Prince Regent Inlet and NF wasn't explained. He thought it may have stood for Northern Frontier.

Captain Coppin got in touch with Lady Franklin and told her what his daughter had said. Franklin's widow had already been seeing a medium called Eileen Dawson who'd told her that Sir John was alive and well. Of course that was nonsense, he had died a year before. Nonetheless Lady Jane sent William Kennedy to follow the

THE DISAPPEARANCE OF the Franklin expedition coincided with a growing interest in spiritualism in Victorian Britain and several mediums contacted Lady Jane Franklin to tell her of visions they'd had as to the crew's whereabouts.

The Admiralty, which was honour-bound to follow up all leads, didn't hold with such paranormal claims and criticized the many 'malicious deceptions' as a hindrance to the real search. Among other things, they were inundated with messages purporting to have come from Sir John Franklin himself, maps and drawings positioning him and his crew in various locations many hundreds of miles apart plus the supposed 'discovery' of items from the *Erebus* and *Terror* said to have been found by assorted explorers.

Lady Franklin, however, so firmly believed in some of the clairvoyant messages that she tailored her plans for several search-and-rescue missions accordingly. It was due to one particular message 'from the grave' that she funded the second expedition to find her husband, captained by a former Hudson's Bay Company man and renowned Arctic expert, the Orcadian William Kennedy. His second-in-command was Frenchman Joseph Bellot, and his crew largely comprised Shetlanders.

leads given by Anne Coppin's information. Kennedy went to Londonderry to verify the story and reported back that he believed the girl's visions to be genuine.

Having travelled via Baffin Island and Prince Regent Inlet, Kennedy and his crew became stuck in ice. After an epic fourteen hundred-mile trek by dog sled, they discovered a new passage through the ice which Kennedy named Bellot Strait. The people of Britain went crazy with excitement that Kennedy would find the Franklin expedition, but he never did.

There's always one loony in a dog collar that shows up in an interesting story. This time some reverend or other claimed that Weesy Coppin's letters 'BS' didn't stand for Barrow Strait; that she meant Bellot Strait. He invented a whole new load of nonsense claiming that the discovery of the Northwest Passage was entirely due to voices from the grave. Personally, I think it's how you interpret BS. Is it Barrow Strait? Is it Bellot Strait? Or is it plain old ordinary Bull Shit. It's up to yourself.

NORTHWEST TERRITORIES

Tuktoyaktuk, Northwest Territories

TUKTOYAKTUK – a word not to be attempted if the adhesive isn't good on your dentures – is the first landfall after the Northwest Passage. Most people around there just call it 'Tuk', which is a lot easier on the teeth.

The big excitement in Tuk is not so much pingo, as bingo, which is the epitome of bohemian depravity there – but it's not like any bingo I've ever seen. Comparatively recently I was introduced to the concept of 'bingo lovers'. I didn't know there was such a thing but apparently it is the name for lotharios who show up at bingo and try to get off with widows and single, older women. They couldn't exist in Tuk because no one goes anywhere to have a good smoke and get their cards lined up and do a bit of showing off with the gay caller. (Why are so many bingo callers gay? It's one of those great unanswered questions in life.)

They can't do any of that in Tuk because they don't actually go to the bingo; they buy a card and a marker at the bingo hall (which isn't a bingo hall at all, it's an ex-radio station), and then they scuttle off home. A camera in the bingo hall broadcasts the numbers being drawn live on television at seven o'clock on Channel Five. Television Bingo is a big night out in Tuktoyaktuk. A woman called Dorothy Loreen runs the whole affair with a noisy bouncing ball machine. Her friend Agnes Panatalok is the caller. Agnes looked amazingly like little Madge, Barry Humphries's sidekick, who never says a word while he prances around being

TUKTOYAKTUK WAS CALLED Port Brabant until 1950 when it reverted to its Western Canadian Inuit or Inuvialuit name, which means 'it looks like caribou'. Legend has it that a woman saw some caribou wade into the sea to be turned to stone. Reefs on the shore, visible at low tide, are said to resemble the Arctic deer.

Long used as a site to hunt caribou and beluga whales, ducks, geese and fish, as well as being a good place for blueberries and blackberries, 'Tuk' – as it is more commonly known – had a sizeable population in the late 1800s until influenza brought by whalers almost wiped them out. Prior to the whalers' arrival, the local people had rarely suffered from even a common cold, but the incomers brought diseases such as measles, smallpox and diphtheria against which the Inuit had no immunity.

Situated on Kugmallit Bay, near the Mackenzie River delta, Tuk was established as a Hudson's Bay Company trading post in 1937. In the 1950s it became the venue for one of the radar stations on the Distant Early Warning Line, and still had the giant golf balls, scanning the northern skies. Twenty years later, the town became a major base for oil and gas exploration in the Beaufort Sea.

Known as the gateway to the Pingo National Landmark, Tuk lies just east of a protected site in which eight pingos, or Arctic ice domes, dominate the landscape. The highest is one hundred and sixty feet and there are more than thirteen hundred of them in the park.

Dame Edna Everage. I watched, fascinated, as Dorothy and Agnes went on air. Agnes began by reading notices to the community – prayers and good wishes for different families:

'To Ronald Norman Felix Junior, happy seventeenth birthday. Hope you enjoy your day, love Mum, your sisters and brother and Jenny,' Agnes read.

'There is a meeting tomorrow night at the school for all grade ten students and their parents starting at seven o'clock … To my little brother, happy seventeenth birthday to you. May you have many more years to come.'

Then the game began. Agnes announced:

'Your first game is one line or four corners for a hundred dollars. Any two lines for one twenty five.'

She read out the numbers and picked up the chosen balls, trying to get them into focus on the screen by holding them up to the camera. It was very funny. After a short time, Tuk TV Bingo had its first winner, a woman called Sandra, who phoned in with her numbers and won a hundred bucks.

The people of Tuk used to play bingo once a week in the city hall, but when someone came up with this idea they found that it

TV bingo

worked much better for those not keen to venture out in forty degrees below. It was all so amateur and lovely; such a communal event. I loved it.

After bingo, came pingo, something I'd never heard of before. A pingo is a little hillock thing made of ice, a kind of landbound iceberg. This part of Canada is one of the only places you'll see them in the world. It was explained to me a million times how pingos got there but I'm damned if I understand. For some reason, the ice comes bouncing out of the earth and makes a mini mountain covered in earth so it looks like a grassy mount or a pimple. Apparently, there's permafrost then ice, then moss and earth on top. I was lucky to have found a breeding pair.

I think pingo is an unfair name to give the poor wart on the landscape. It's kind of diminutive, isn't it? Pingo doesn't sound important enough. I was in a place in Canada once called Okanagan making a film and they had a lake there with a monster in it like the Loch Ness Monster but they called it Ogopogo. I immediately didn't believe it. Ogopogo? Give me a break. Now Nessie is a proper monster name, but pingo falls into that Ogopogo category.

There was a little notice in my hotel in Tuk, which urged people to stop going up and down the pingos in their all-terrain vehicles

A real-life pingo

because they're ruining them, but when that's the only hill for miles around and you've got a four-wheel drive vehicle I imagine it's kind of hard to resist a good whack up the pingo on a Sunday afternoon (although that sounds kind of dirty!).

When I first looked at a pingo from the boat I had to hop aboard to get to it, I wasn't that impressed by this lump on the earth covered in moss and pink primula-like plants. It didn't look like anything much. It wasn't big, it wasn't wide, it didn't smell particularly nice and you couldn't eat it. I decided to climb up one and take a look at the view from the top – not that climbing a pingo was on my 'bucket list' (things to do before I kick the proverbial bucket), but I thought it might be interesting. Pingos have a kind of breast feel to them; a mammary look but without nipples. The local people use them as landmarks in such a flat landscape. In earlier times, when they did a lot of whaling, they used to spot whales from up there. Of course, as I said before, the whales got wise and buggered off a long time ago because they knew when they'd been spotted they'd get a harpoon up their jacksie, which is another thing altogether.

Once I was on the pingo I began to appreciate the colours of it, which were sensational. After we'd spent so much time in the tundra and on stony ground with a complete lack of vegetation, to suddenly see a thing like this was absolutely beautiful. It reminded me of the autumn colours in Scotland or Vermont; all those reds and oranges and rusts, wild flowers and lichen. It was a thing of beauty.

TUKTOYAKTUK HAS A sizeable number of Catholics in its community, who worship at a little wooden church complete with a sealskin altar. Sitting by the side of the road not far away is the *Our Lady of Lourdes* mission supply ship. Built in Oakland, California in 1930, it acted as a supply vessel but was chiefly the ship on which thousands of Tuk's children were taken away from their homes and families and transported to residential Catholic schools.

The forced deportations went on for almost forty years. A plaque details the ship's history, giving the engineers' names as three holy Brothers, and states that it was donated to Tuk by Pope Pius XI. Many of the Inuit children who were sent away to have a Western, colonial-style education suffered physical and sexual abuse at the hands of their carers, the Christian Brothers. Some of the children never returned home and have become known as 'The Disappeared'. Mass graves of Inuit and Canadian Indian children have been found at a number of residential school sites. The Canadian Government has since apologized.

The one hundred and fifty-foot climb to the top also brought me to mind of Scottish hillwalkers, a breed of middle-class hill-walking types who really get up my nose. They call themselves 'Munro baggers'. Over a certain height (three thousand feet), a hill becomes a Munro, named after the Scottish mountaineer Sir Hugh Munro. There's a finite number of Munros and these people feel the need to climb them. I couldn't wait to confront them when I got back.

'Have you ever climbed a pingo? No? Oh, well, um, shame because I'm afraid that means your climbing career is incomplete.'

I'd like to be Scotland's first pingo bagger; the head of an elite society with secrets. No pingo – nothing.

My next excursion was a fishing trip on a freshwater lake with an Inuit named James Pokiak. The lake was created in the eighties by dredging designed to facilitate offshore exploration for oil and gas. The Mackenzie River feeds the lake, so the people of Tuk can draw fresh water from it, as well as from a nearby creek. In the winter, they fill buckets with ice and wait for it to melt; James told me it tastes a lot fresher than the chlorinated water that comes in by tanker.

The morning we set out was one of those magical mornings when the world seemed such a breathtaking place. James had put his nets out from a causeway between the lake and the Arctic Ocean the previous night, something he'd been doing since he was a boy. When we hauled the nets in he'd caught about twenty big fish, known as broad whitefish. He also snagged an unusual

Fishing with James

looking sculpin fish which had horns. In untangling the fish from the nets (some of which had been pecked at by gulls), I got sticky scales all over my fingers. James's response was, 'Well, go wash your hands.' But the place he pointed to was the Arctic Ocean and it was bloody freezing. Within seconds, I was in pain. There were no towels. Where was I going to get heat in the next hour?

James just carried on pulling in his net with an expression that said, 'You big Jessie. Dry your eyes and get on with it.' He said that some people go there just to be able to say that they've dipped their toes in the Arctic Ocean. My fingers were quite enough. My toes weren't going anywhere near it. I'm too soft for their life: I'm a big softie from the town. Every time I do things like that, it just shows up how little I know. It's one of the terrifying things about getting older. When you're in your forties, you think, 'Aye, I've picked up some things along the way. I know some stuff.' But then you get into your fifties and further on and you think, 'My God, I don't know anything! What have I done all my life?' This was one of those days. Left to my own devices, I would starve to death.

When we got home with our catch, James fed much of it to his seventeen sled dogs who literally wolfed it down. Each dog got a huge fish, crunching it down with a great noise that chilled the blood – eyes, tail, bum, the lot. Personally, I like my fish poached in a little milk. They were great looking dogs. One had different coloured eyes, like David Bowie. I was always a wee bit jealous of

A dog's dinner

David Bowie's eyes. I think it would be rather cool to have eyes different colours. The dogs had names such as Homer, but they weren't pets you'd open a can of food for at home. These were proper, working beasts, used for sledding and hunting polar bears which James tracks down for American and European clients.

I told him that I couldn't see what someone would get out of killing something as beautiful as a polar bear, but he countered that the hunting creates both food and employment.

'You get better payback for taking a client out to harvest a bear than you would just going out and hunting on your own,' he said. 'Our people have always been subsistence users and we manage our wildlife very carefully.'

Now that foreign hunters aren't allowed to take trophies home with them, the bear meat and hides are given to guides like him and divided between the townspeople. Fair point, I suppose.

There are also grizzly bears near Tuk. One was spotted three miles out of town a few days before I got there. The previous year, James's wife was attacked by one while she was out picking berries. As soon as she lay down and stopped picking, the bear left her alone and went on eating its fill. It was a territorial thing. Talking of territories, James helps conservationists attach satellite receivers to bowhead whales that swim in the waters near Tuk. The day before I went fishing with him, he'd received an e-mail from someone at the research base who told him that one of the whales

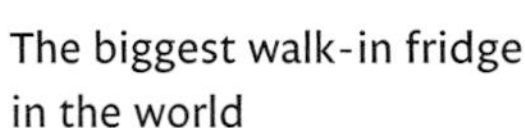

The biggest walk-in fridge in the world

they'd tagged a few weeks earlier was on his way to Russia, two hundred miles off Barrow Point in Alaska. I was impressed.

James told me he planned to dry some of his fish, freeze some and put the rest in his smoker. There are no trees in Tuk but he fishes logs out of the Mackenzie River, which have been washed downriver towards the Arctic Ocean. How good is that? 'We call it cod-wood,' he said. 'It is very soft and when you light a fire with it in the smokehouse, it makes a whole lot of smoke.' He can pull huge whitefish out of the sea every other day, then get his wood for free and go back and smoke it. I see something very right about all that.

James took me to the biggest walk-in fridge in the world. I had to wear a safety harness just to get inside. If you're pleased with yourself because you've a fridge with double doors, you'd better think again. This one was thirty feet down and cavernous. Reached by an ice-covered ladder down a narrow hole which led to a tunnel in the permafrost, the community ice house was carved with a pick and shovel by James's father and five friends in the 1960s – it took them about three months.

Funded by the local government and made of solid ice, the freezer had passageways and 25 rooms, 10 feet by 10 feet wide and 7 feet high, where James and others keep frozen seals and whale oil for winter dog food, as well as a mountain of fish. It was not a place for the claustrophobic. In the old days the government supplied lights and power to the freezer and charged people a fee to use it. When no one paid, they switched off the power and said anyone could use it for free with their own flashlights, which is what still happens.

The ice on the walls is in sedimentary layers, just like the rings in a tree. Each layer represented another winter, hundreds of years old, deep in the permafrost. It was brilliant. The strange thing is that in the winter, the freezer gets too warm, or at least warmer than out in the open air, so James and his friends bring all the food to the surface in crates to keep cold in the ambient temperature. Everything is back to front in the north. Oddly, too, this is a freezer they have to defrost, because at temperatures of between minus five and minus ten degrees just the act of breathing makes crystals on the ceiling which grow, same as in your fridge. Every few years, people come down and scrape the excess crystals off the ceiling and replace the floor with new snow. When I touched the twinkling, sparkling ice it made a great noise, a ting-a-ling-a-ling. It was like Santa's grotto in Harrods. Jingle bells, jingle bells, jingle all the way.

James invited me for lunch at his house: maktuk (beluga whale), smoked fish and turkey soup. He was living like a king. Everything was delicious, especially the smoked fish which we just ate straight off the skin. Where I come from, people would consider eating white whale an obscenity. Seeing me chow down on that lovely creature they'd treat me as if I'd eaten a giraffe or a black rhinoceros, but here I was in a different culture altogether. My experiences on this entire trip had me swinging back and forth about the killing of animals, about the way the Inuit kills something and survives by it and the way I look on it as a city boy. I've been wrong, but I've also been right.

Smoked fish

I don't think having feelings for animals is a bad thing, but I think there's a lot of tolerance needed by city people looking at those who live in the country. It's roughly the same as the argument about fox hunting in Britain. A lot of people are uninformed about the way the country actually operates and how animals behave. Because they've got a dog as a pet, they tend to have this attitude to dogs and foxes which the Inuit wouldn't understand. In the Arctic, they will eat the dog if they're hungry or if they're in trouble out on a drive. They'll feed one of their dogs to the other dogs. They would think nothing whatsoever of doing that.

There was something quite holy about my meal with James, beluga whale included. James was such a gas. He was a strong, iron man. His wife was a schoolteacher, he had three lovely girls, and there we all were eating fish and whale and drinking soup and laughing together in his house having just pulled his fishing nets in from the Arctic Ocean. What a brilliant day.

* * *

"*JAMES HAD A next-door neighbour, a guy called Johnny Walker from Perth, who had lived in Tuk working as a carpenter for about ten years. He knew who I was and he knew my comedy, which was nice. That's kind of like payback when that happens.*

It's a nice warm position to be in, to be respected by other people. It's that, and not the shining prizes, that matters. Of course, the shiny things are nice and I'm grateful for the bits that I've got but it is guys saying, 'You're my favourite' that counts, especially when they are comedians who think of me as a father figure and say that watching me made them want to do it. There's nothing better than that because it was lonely out there for a long time. I didn't resemble other comedians. I was so hairy and wild and weird, and my language and subject matter made me a kind of freak. I wasn't a media darling like the others. When I started, comedians wore blue mohair suits and talked about their mothers-in-law and Pakistanis. I came from another direction – from the folk music, left-wing politics side. I wasn't doing any of the racist, sexist jokes.

Comedy for me is a very organic affair. I have very little control. For a live performance I put on my stage clothes, comb my hair and then bounce around and try and get comfortable again. For some reason I can't think about what I'm going to say – I try to, but I just can't. I can't even remember what I did the previous night. It's a terrifying thing – like a test. As the witching hour gets closer and closer, I can feel it happening. As I walk up to the mic, I think, 'What am I going to say?' I try to think of the first words that will come out of my mouth, but invariably I just say something like, 'Hello, Manchester. Hey, what's happening? How are you doing?' Everything follows after that, like dominoes. Just that act of saying, 'Oh, it's lovely to see you—' then whoosh! out it comes, this thing that's inside me. It's like being in an accident. I don't have much recollection of leaving the dark and walking into the light. There's an adrenaline rush and the only applause I really hear is the one at the very end.

I've always described it as like surfing on a wave. At some point I step on the wave and psshht, I'm off again, talking, using it. I can even control it a wee bit – by moving backward and forward, off and on it. The next thing I seem to be saying is, 'Thank you very much. It's been a pleasure talking to you.' Coffee, anger and adrenaline drives it all forward. I'm an angry comedian. There's a lot of anger in my act. I go off on rants: 'I hate that fucking bastard. Do you hate him too?' I love being brave. People say, 'Oh, but so-and-so could sue you.' Yeah? Well, tell him to go for it. Aye, on you come, anytime you're ready. I see myself almost as a politician; making people aware of those whom I think are dangerous or dark. It's a joy, an absolute joy. I'm so pleased to be part of it and to be one of the movers and shakers to have driven it in a certain direction.

Sometimes people burst out laughing at something I didn't even think was funny. It might have been a combination of the way I said it, or the fact that my leg moved in a certain way. That's a great moment, like flying. There's something I particularly love when something untoward happens on the stage or I'm funny about it and then incorporate it into what I'm talking about. Then later I say it again and then maybe there's a bit of a space and I hit them with the third one and – boom – the audience just explodes. That's when I think, 'Yes! Now they can see me being a comedian. This is what a comedian should be doing. Three quarters of an hour later they're still laughing and it wasn't even funny in the first place.'

Lenny Bruce once said that comedians think funny things

and then say them. The people who have jokes written for them and then go onstage and tell them are actors. They may be extremely good actors (and they're not to be knocked) but they're not comedians. Comedians are naturals. My wife gave me some lovely advice once. She said, 'You've got to control yourself at dinner because you put the fear of death into people by being so funny. Some of them have got lovely things to say but they're scared. So pull your horns in and give others a chance.'

At first I thought, 'Oh fuck, but that's what I do! That's what I am!' But actually I was kind of showing off. Now I can't dominate at a dinner any more; nor do I want to because it is lovely to see how right she was. People flower in the room and I can see them enjoying being in my company and joining me laughing. There's a lovely thing happens to comedians: when someone tells a funny and I crack up you can see them thinking, 'Did you see that? Did you see him laughing? I made him laugh!'

I used to work with two guys in the shipyards where I was a welder. One was a plater and one was a carpenter: Lucas and Dalgliesh. They sounded like an end-of-the-pier Variety act. By God, I loved them. Jimmy Lucas is still alive but unfortunately Dalgliesh died a couple of years ago. I used to run back from my lunch because they were so funny. They'd put their arms on each other's shoulders in their duffel coats (which made it twice as good) and sing 'We'll Meet Again'. I can still see their lovely faces. I loved them. I loved what they stood for. I loved the fact that they were trying to make me laugh. These were married men with families, working in the rain and wind on the Clyde, trying to make an apprentice boy laugh. And they were both Rangers supporters and they'd teach me horrid songs and how to play the drums the way an Orange band does. I can do it to this day. I was a Catholic and dumb and I'd be there, marching and whistling with the band.

Those two taught me so much about being funny – that funny is something to share and that we should all enjoy. Humour is such a wondrous thing, and it's lovely to make a room laugh. Humour makes brothers and sisters and unites people. For me, making Lucas and Dalgliesh laugh was every bit as good as making the Albert Hall laugh. It was every bit as powerful. It's making your daddy laugh. It's getting approval and a million other things. I had a lovely e-mail from Jimmy Kerr of Simple Minds a few months ago. I'd done something on television that he'd found incredibly funny and he wrote, 'I was lying on the couch with my mother and we were killing ourselves laughing.' And I thought, 'Oh what a great thing! Lying on the couch with his old mother roaring with laughter. How good can it get?'

There's something about a shared joke and a moment of lightness in a dark time that is such a joyous thing. Like when someone tells me, 'My dad was dying and I would play your DVDs to him and I could hear him laughing all the way from the kitchen.' That has been immense in my life, to make dying men laugh. I carry that around like costume jewellery. I carry those dead guys with me. ”

Mary Ann Taylor knows a thing or two about sharing. She and her family of soapstone carvers have been making lovely little statues, tools and carvings for friends, family and tourists in Tuk for years. She sometimes uses Arctic soapstone from Cape Dorset, but usually has Brazilian soapstone specially shipped in from Edmonton because it has better browns and greens to it. Mary started carving when she was in her early twenties, having learned from her father who was a bone carver. She had taught her children and nephew how to do it as well. In her little house smothered in

Mary Ann Taylor's house

Mary and her 'blanket toss' sculpture

the antlers of caribou and musk ox, she crafts birds or little kayaks out of caribou antler and whale bone, of which there is a plentiful local supply. She makes beautiful ulus, the traditional Inuit knife (shaped like a fan), and carves little whales out of musk ox antlers, which – she told me – are solid all the way through and don't break as easily as soapstone. Mary has to use an angle grinder on the antlers, they are so hard.

One of her carvings featured an Inuit tradition called the 'blanket toss', which dates back thousands of years. She explained:

'When the hunters needed to see where the whales were, they would gather round and do a blanket toss. Whoever stood in the middle of the blanket would be tossed high into the air so they could check out where the whales were.'

Astonishing. How I would love to have seen that.

The Dempster Highway, Northwest Territories

I HITCHED A RIDE SOUTH with truck driver Bill 'the Fruitman' Rutherford who knows the Dempster Highway well. He should do – he makes the mammoth journey along the most northerly road in North America every three weeks in his eighteen-wheeler. He loads up his big Mack truck with fruit and vegetables then heads off to restaurants, shops and hospitals in great places with names such as Inuvik, Chilliwack, Fraser Canyon, Quesnel, Whitehorse, Smithers and Kamloops, many of which were first established as fur trading posts for the Hudson's Bay Company.

Stopping overnight only once at Eagle Plains, a town in the middle of the wilderness, it takes Bill a couple of weeks to get to where he's going, and then a week to sell all his produce. On the way home, he loads his empty truck with recyclable beer bottles, cans, bottle tops, juice cartons and plastics, which he cashes in to help pay for the fuel. How long his total journey takes each time can depend on anything from flash floods, avalanches and accidents to whether or not his truck breaks down. At some times of the year, the weather changes so quickly that he can hit three seasons in one trip if he times it right: on the way north, the trees will be green; farther north they turn yellow and on the way back home he can't see them for the snow.

'One time, on a section of road called the Horseshoe, I was

pounding through snow drifts three or four feet deep – in August! I was talking on the radio about how I might have to chain up and there was another driver at the side of the road about a hundred miles ahead. He heard me talking and called up and said, "Are you talking about snow chains?" I said, "Yeah, up on the Horseshoe there's four-foot drifts." There was a little silence then, a couple of seconds later, he said, "I'm going to bed." I passed him a hundred miles further on, asleep in his truck by the side of the road.'

Despite the hazards, Bill prefers to make his journey in winter because snow makes the road a lot smoother than the gravel top that

THE DEMPSTER HIGHWAY was begun in 1959 when the Canadian Government decided to carve a route through the Arctic wilderness to the Mackenzie Delta, an area believed to be rich in oil and gas. Political bickering, soaring costs and environmental concerns about the effects on caribou migration brought construction to a halt in 1961, with just seventy-two miles completed across terrain that was little known and often not even mapped.

Dubbed the 'road to remorses' by its critics and the 'road to divorces' by its construction workers, many questioned the need for a route which they claimed ran merely 'from igloo to igloo'. Seven years later, after the Americans found huge reserves of gas and oil at Prudhoe Bay in Alaska, construction began again in earnest and by 1979 the 450-mile long road was officially opened. With two bridges built by the Canadian Forces, and ferries at two river crossings – Fort McPherson (on the Peel River) and Tsiigehtchic (on the Mackenzie River) – the Dempster Highway now connects the major towns in this part of the Northwest Territories and the Yukon, and asserts Canadian sovereignty over the region.

Built on a gravel cushion up to two and a half metres thick in places to protect it from seasonal melting, the road was named after Welshman William Dempster (1876–1964) of the Royal Canadian Mounted Police (RCMP). Dempster was known as the 'Iron Man of the Trail' for his legendary dog sled patrols of the 475-mile trail from Dawson City to Fort McPherson in the early 1900s, in temperatures of up to eighty degrees below zero with wind chill.

Dempster was initially sent out onto the trail to look for four members of a lost RCMP patrol. He found the men dead: three had starved to death, despite having eaten their dogs, the fourth had shot himself. After the tragedy, Dempster was instructed to make the trail safe for future patrols. With the help of the local Gwitchin Indians, he found the best routes, built shelters, erected trail markers and hid food caches. He and his men used the route thereafter to administer the law and to deliver mail, news and supplies. Inspector Dempster died knowing that the new highway marking the journey he had made on so many occasions would be named in his honour.

Bill Rutherford's truck

he and I made our bumpy journey over – although the truck was surprisingly comfortable as I bounced around in my seat, which had its own suspension. He admitted that driving can get a 'bit hairy' in the mountains because the winds can flip a truck over.

'There are times when it can be blowing a hurricane on one side of the mountain, while on the other you could drop a feather and it would flutter to the ground.'

There are other dangers too. Like the time Bill hit a moose and in swerving to avoid it flipped his truck over on its side. 'I had that truck packed so tight,' he told me, 'that when it went over everything just shifted and lay up against the roof. I only lost one box of mushrooms and one box of tomatoes.

'Another time, a black bear came running out onto the road right in front of me in the rain. His mamma didn't teach him how to cross in a safe manner. It was one of those nights with poor visibility and about three inches of slop on the road. I took his head right off, and he was just a little bear too.

'He busted an airline off the front axle and the truck came to a stop right away. Soon as you lose your air the brakes come on. I had a tarp in the back that I could throw on the ground so I didn't have to lie in the mud to fix the airline but there was a really gross smell – I never smelt anything like that before – from the dead bear. I was looking over my shoulder all the time for his mamma.'

Bill sees a lot of porcupine caribou on his journeys and the hills are full of wolves and grizzly bears. He showed me a beaver house and we spotted some grouse and ptarmigan. The one thing he's seen on the road which most surprised him, though, wasn't animal:

'It was March, it was thirty below, and I was climbing up what they call the Ogilvies when I saw these tracks on the road that looked like a bicycle. I said, "No! It can't be!" A couple of miles up the road, there was this guy from Japan pedalling a bike in the middle of winter. He was sleeping in a ditch at night!'

In the winter Bill and his friends go jigging for fish on the frozen lakes.

'It's really funny because down south you hear about all these people with thousands of dollars worth of fishing tackle. Up here they use a stick and maybe four feet of white cord, a chunk of caribou or moose horn with a nail through it and a hook and they pull out fish after fish.'

They catch a bottom-feeder called losh, another called coney (like a salmon) and jack fish which they feed to the dogs: 'They call it dogfish unless there are tourists around, and then they call it the great northern pike.'

Before the Dempster Highway opened, people could only reach the northernmost communities by plane or boat. When the road was half done, truckers would drive to the Midway airstrip and load up planes to fly goods farther on. At nearby Midway Lake, there is an annual music festival in the summer where the region's best fiddle players entertain crowds who camp in tents and plywood cabins. Bill said it almost always rains but no one seems

The Dempster Highway

to mind: 'Last year they had one square dance that lasted forty-five minutes.' I can understand that. When you dance or play music for that length of time, you suddenly realize what it's all about. It becomes a kind of mantra and you get into almost a meditative state. The music starts to really mean something.

Bill began his business from scratch not long after the highway opened: 'I started off with a little single axle with an eighteen-foot box on it twenty-three years ago. That first winter, I built it up. I did Fort McPherson, Arctic Red River, Inuvik, Aklavik and "Tuck-di-tuck-tuck". I sold door to door.' Then he got himself a bigger truck and a set of stairs he hooks on to the side of the trailer, setting up like a store. Sometimes he trades, swapping oranges for his favourite char fish. He keeps each truck until it has done about six hundred thousand hard miles before upgrading to a newer model.

When Bill first started selling fresh fruit and vegetables to the people of the Northwest Territories and the Yukon, they thought his goods 'mighty strange'. Some had never seen the more exotic things like mangoes and yams – they were only used to onions, carrots and potatoes. Others complained that his cauliflowers were 'weird' because they didn't have black marks all over them.

'They used to say that I'd cause a rush at the hospital. Everybody had what they call the "green apple two-step" because their stomachs weren't used to the fresh produce.'

I was amazed by the idea that Bill could change the entire culture of what his customers eat by loading up his trucks in a particular way.

The scenery along the Dempster Highway was sensational, with the Richardson Mountains at the north end of the Rockies, all bathed in the most beautiful golden light. (I bet the First Nations people don't call them the Richardsons, though.) Some of the landscape looked like Scotland, then Scandinavia, then like New Zealand. It was absolutely beautiful and very silent. The rivers were like the ones you only ever see in pictures, with not a soul in sight. I kept waiting for a bear, but none appeared. They're very clever, are bears; they don't hang about posing for pictures.

* * *

" BEING IN THAT *big Mack reminded me of when I hitchhiked as a spotty youth, and happy jolly miles they were too. I used to go on holiday on my own – just my banjo and some clothes in a bag and away I would go. I hitchhiked all over Scotland and England, France and Belgium, and it was brilliant. I met splendid people along the way and learned a lot.*

In those days, people picked up hitchhikers. It was the sixties and there was a lovely mood and atmosphere about the world. It was before everyone was convinced that the trees were full of perverts and the woods were full of child molesters. I met a few weird people but the vast majority were lovely. I still stop for hitchhikers, especially going north in Scotland. They are usually students from Europe – Estonia, Latvia, Poland, Czechoslovakia, Hungary, and places like that. I think that, generally, their aim is true and I've never had a bad experience. Just once, many years ago, I picked a guy up and he had the temerity to tell me he didn't like my comedy, so I stopped the car and let him out. I told him I didn't like his company and so off he went into the rain.

When I was touring in Ireland this year, many more people hitchhiked than in Britain and I hope it's catching on again, because I think it's a lovely thing. People are not to be feared. People are to be joined in with. Let them join. If you don't like the guy, stop the car and let him out, but so many times I've met people I've really liked.

There's a vagabond feel to the road that you don't get on a plane or a cruise ship. You're on your own ground. You belong on the road. I never did the Transit van tour. We had a military ambulance instead, a lovely old thing with a goose on the front. And many a rollicking drunken laugh we had in it and many a strange hitchhiker we picked up and sent on their way rejoicing. I remember those days well, but I like these days better. ”

It felt good to be with Bill, doing what he was doing. It's probably the most ancient way to make your living – travelling around, taking goods from one place to another. It just happens to cover thousands of miles in his case, in a place that freezes solid every now and again.

To think that the extraordinary road we travelled along was once an old Indian trail, built on permafrost. To make it a road was the idea of John Diefenbaker, Prime Minister of Canada from 1957 to 1963, and the Dempster Highway is a kind of miracle. You can see it winding for miles and miles and miles through these incredible valleys. Those wilderness towns had been completely isolated until they got this highway; plus there's an ice road up there, which is the weirdest of them all – a road where they actually drive on a river in the winter. The whole thing's nuts; everything's in reverse. You can't get to the people at the end of the ice road in the summer because it's all marshy and boggy, but in the winter you can. You've probably seen it on television, with those truckers driving along it. I don't even begin to understand it.

I still find it hard to get over the huge vastness of the Northern Territories. And it was the vastness that made a huge difference to my attitude to the plans for drilling and mining up there. I had a very closed attitude to it until I went there and was slapped in the face by the sheer grand scale of the place. Canada can accommodate the industry; there's room. The wealth and the economy of nations has to be paid attention to, especially at this time. I've spoken to so many who are looking forward to the industry coming. In their history, so many crimes have been perpetrated against them, such as the taking of Inuit children from their families to try to educate the culture out of them. This is their payback.

At Fort McPherson, I stopped to see where the Lost Patrol men are buried. The poor men were trying to get to Dawson City in the winter of 1910. They set out on 21 December and the weather was atrocious – fifty below. Their bodies weren't recovered until the following March, which shows you what the winter was like. By reading their log book, the people who found them knew that by the time they had completed only a third of their journey they'd eaten half their thirty days' supply of food and were arguing among themselves because the head of their patrol had let the Indian guide go. Then things turned hellish. Instead of heading back, they kept trying to find the old Indian trail, without the guide. They did turn back eventually, but only when they were weak with hunger, exhaustion and frostbite, so they didn't make it. Funnily enough, they didn't resort to cannibalism like Franklin's men up in the Northwest Passage did (everyone seems to start eating each other up there), but they ate most of the fifteen dogs that were pulling their sled. People in Fort McPherson still talk about the Lost Patrol as if it happened yesterday; it had such a profound effect on everyone.

The lost men lie next to the tomb of a woman who went by the splendid name of Ellen Jane Snowshoe, and an Indian chief named

A different style of Arctic Circle marker

Johnny D. Charlie. The gravestones of the Lost Patrol men – Inspector Francis Fitzgerald, Constable Richard O'Hara Taylor, Constable George Kenney and their guide Special Constable Sam Carter – are unremarkable. I don't know which of them starved and which committed suicide. Poor guys. Dearie me.

From Fort McPherson we travelled south, and the further south we went, the better I felt. Crossing the line of the Arctic Circle made me very happy. I'd had enough of wearing layers and layers of clothes. That day was my first without long johns for more than a month. I had learned a lot of things about being so far north: don't go on a cruise; always remember your long johns; keep your woolly socks in good shape; keep your wits about you; have a fleecy near you at all times and, if you can, have a pillow or something soft to put your head on. Being in the north is nice. Being in the south's lovely. Being alive is nice as well. Being cold's okay but being warm beats it hollow.

Very few things grow north of the Arctic Circle because of the permafrost but after travelling just a few miles south we were surrounded by the loveliest colours – russet browns with yellows, a funky sage green – and fields of blueberries. It was absolutely beautiful; almost as nice as Scotland, although Scotland's got the edge. As a matter of fact, if that russetty-reddy colour had been a bit more purple I could have sworn I was in Scotland. And I loved seeing the rain on the mountains; the way the clouds hung down on them, raining down on the sinners. Did you ever hear that poem? '*The rain, it rains upon the just and also on the unjust fella. It rains upon the just because the unjust stole the just's umbrella.*'

I love that.

YUKON

Tombstone Territorial Park, Yukon

I'D ALWAYS WANTED to see the Yukon. I think it's a magic word – Yukon. This was the land of Dangerous Dan McGrew, the face on the bar room floor. Then there was Mexico Pete and Eskimo Nell— Oh no, that's something different, I think that was from a toilet wall in Glasgow.

If you look at a map the Yukon is such a huge area – twice the size of Britain – and yet there are only a few thousand inhabitants. A small place like Eagle Plains, which just has a motel and a gas station, has a thriving population of eight. Flying over Tombstone Territorial Park in a small plane, I thought I'd died and gone to heaven. My guide was called Lolita Welcherman and I felt like

Opposite: Autumn colours
Below: Tombstone Territorial Park

Right: Giving it the finger
Below: Lolita, my guide

Nabokov being whisked off into the mountains which were – Holy Jesus! – just phenomenal. They have jagged black granite peaks, alpine lakes and an explosion of colour in between. It took my breath away; it was amazing.

I desperately wanted to see the mountains from the ground and we landed so that I could but I was painfully aware that, as a city boy, I would be trampling on all these extremely delicate flowers. It happened at the pingo where we crashed through all these wild flowers clinging to life just to go up the hill and get a good view. It was the same in Tombstone Valley. There were staggeringly beautiful wee flowers and caribou antler-shaped lichen that I had to crunch through. I felt such an intruder in that world, looking like a bloody dandelion with my hair whipped up around my head by the wind. I had to question my motives, even if it was to see and show the world a staggeringly lovely thing. I made a commercial in Iceland once where I had to tramp through some flowers and the Icelanders made me walk backward in my own footprints. They told me it would take thirty years for the flowers to recover, which really slammed it home to me: I'm going to Botany Hell.

It is always the silence that gets me in places like Tombstone Valley. The whole earth must have been that quiet once. And the fact that it's been the same, century after century, ever since the mammoths roamed these primeval landscapes. Lolita told me that the bears that live in the valley now take priority. When a grizzly moved into an area, aptly named Grizzly Lake, to feed on the abundant berries, the parks' authority closed that area off to hikers and tourists. I was relieved that, in a place like that, the bear wins. A grizzly at Grizzly Lake? He was probably going to settle somewhere else until he heard the name of that place.

Lolita said that there were several lakes and mountains that didn't yet have names. I could see faces in some of them – one mountain looked like Marilyn Monroe, another looked like it was holding up a giant finger to the world. Another mountain looked like Snow White and the seven dwarves. To Lolita, one ridge resembled a howling wolf, although it looked more like a howling spaniel to me. I suggested calling it Yelping Dog Mountain or Irritating Squealy Dog Hill. Not much of a tourist attraction, I suppose.

I started renaming a few other places too; I thought it only my duty as an explorer. Flying over one ridge I named Inspiration Point I found inspiration for a song called 'Why Was I Born Delicious?' about being a pheasant. I decided a lake we flew over should be called Teddy Bear Lake, so that it would only attract teddies not grizzlies. I named another lake Thank God For That I Couldn't Walk Another Step. And thanks to me there is now an Ashtray Mountain, because ashtrays will be extinct in ten years and I think they should get some recognition. I renamed Mount

Monolith Mount Stogie because it looks like a cigar and it fitted perfectly with the Ashtray. They were born to be close.

We spotted some ground squirrels, and heard the distinctive whistle of a marmot. Lolita told me about the collared pika, a rabbity creature that collects grass all summer long and makes a little haystack under a pile of rocks:

'Sometimes the stacks might be two feet high and they guard them with their life. They're insane about their pile of grass because they don't hibernate so they need to feed on this grass-pile all winter long.'

She said that when she first heard the story of how the pikas are so protective of their haystacks, she instantly thought of the crazy gold miners in Dawson City, who – before the days of machines – used to dig holes in the ground by hand and then protect their little section. I guess that is the way of the Yukon – to dig up a fortune and make a pile.

I read a report of someone arriving in the winter at the height of the gold rush and being amazed at how silent the place was. Everyone was underground and there were no trees left. There was just smoke coming out of the various holes where the prospectors were living like moles, burning fires to keep warm. I wish I'd seen that; those human pikas protecting their stacks.

Dawson City, Yukon

DAWSON CITY, with its little streets and raised wooden boardwalks in front of the painted shops and houses was funky in a quaint way; although it's often a cruel thing to say about a place, that it's quaint. A lot of the 'q' words are cruel – such as 'quirky' and 'quaint'. Dawson seemed to be torn between being a real place and being a film set. With its shop windows full of things from the gold rush days that you couldn't buy, it was like wandering around in the wrong century.

Personally, I thought the place a bit sterile and dead. I could almost smell the mothballs: its function had gone, the gold rush had gone, even the majority of the tourists are gone. A lot of places were for sale and it was a bit windblown and tumbleweedy. Many of the buildings were propped up and on their last legs. It had its charm and the people there seemed to love it, but it had less life and was less raucous than I'd thought it would be. Sometimes,

DAWSON CITY WAS the epicentre of the Klondike gold rush, after a rich seam of gold was found in 1896 at a place called Rabbit Creek at the confluence of the Yukon and Klondike Rivers. The word Klondike derives from the Hän word *trondek*, referring to the hammerstones the Indians used to hammer home nets for fishing salmon.

The lure of gold (which had already caused the California gold rush in the 1840s and 50s) encouraged an estimated 100,000 'stampeders' to set out on the trail towards Dawson City, a town that didn't yet properly exist. Entrepreneurs hastily erected hotels, theatres, beer halls, brothels, casinos and dancehalls, many with elaborate frontages. The legend of Dawson City as the Paris of the North was set. By 1898, the town offered steam heat, running water and a telephone service.

This frontier city was named after George Mercer Dawson, director of the Geological Survey of Canada, who was one of the first to map the Yukon. Gold mining in the area reached its peak in the early 1900s, especially during the Depression, and the last dredge was closed in 1966. Dawson has around 1,500 residents, many of whom are still panning for gold, both literally in the surrounding creeks and rivers, and figuratively with tourism providing the richest seams.

Its reputation as the largest city north of San Francisco and west of Winnipeg has long been lost, but it is nonetheless the Yukon's second largest community after Whitehorse and is, in many ways, just as it was during the height of the gold rush. Costumed guides stroll the muddy streets and lead visitors to the town's heritage sites and museums, including the restored Palace Grand Theatre, the post office, the Yukon Hotel and Diamond Tooth Gertie's gambling hall.

One of Dawson City's most famous residents was the poet Robert Service (1874–1958), whose cabin on 8th Avenue is also on the tourist trail. Service, whose father (a bank clerk) was Scottish, was born in Preston, Lancashire, and educated in Glasgow. He gave up a job in a Glasgow bank in 1894 and emigrated to Canada with dreams of becoming a cowboy. Posted by a Canadian bank to the Yukon, Service fell in love with the wilderness and began to write poetry about it.

For three years he lived in the sod-roofed log cabin, which has been preserved to this day, on the city's 8th Avenue. Dubbed the 'Canadian Kipling', Service became famous for his poems about the Klondike gold miners, with titles such as 'The Cremation of Sam McGee' and 'The Shooting of Dan McGrew'. Returning to Europe a wealthy man, he became a war correspondent and war poet during the Balkan, Boer and First World wars, and died at his home in Brittany, France, having never given up his British citizenship. The American writer Jack London, author of *The Call of the Wild* and *White Fang*, also lived in Dawson City for a time, having travelled there with his brother to pan for gold.

Robert Service's poem

places suffer from being hooked in the past, and I think Dawson City is one of them. The people who would like to live there, the mining guys, can't afford it. The ones who can seem mad keen on preserving it in aspic. They are trying to get National Heritage status because, due to the permafrost, those wooden buildings built on stilts will blow away and fall down if they don't do something about them soon. They're locking the place in like an old photograph, but it would be much nicer if people actually lived in it or Dawson will end up being a replica of itself. It will be clad in fibreglass and plastic that looks like wood (which may not be a bad thing) but I prefer the slightly decrepit feel to it.

> Were you ever out in the Great Alone, when the moon was awful clear, And the icy mountains hemmed you in with a silence you most could hear; With only the howl of a timber wolf, and you camped there in the cold, A half-dead thing in a stark, dead world, clean mad for the muck called gold …
>
> FROM 'THE SHOOTING OF DAN MCGREW' BY ROBERT SERVICE

I stayed in Bombay Peggy's, which was once a brothel for the gold miners. I could just imagine the piano going, 'dink-dink-dink-dink-de-de-dee' in the corner. You know those pianos that stop the minute someone with a black hat walks in through the saloon bar doors? I've always wondered how that happens, because the guy playing the piano always has his back to the door and can't see the guy walking in, so it must be the piano that stops itself.

There was a picture on the wall of some of the hookers posing

in sailor suits and other costumes. These women were considered a necessary evil and divided themselves between Bombay Peggy's and Ruby's, named after a woman who looked just like someone's auntie or granny. I could imagine the miners going into Ruby's to shake off some of their gold dust in its many little dens and cots. Yippee! That place must have vibrated in the evenings.

My favourite spot in town was the Palace Grand Theatre which was a smashing place and just the way a theatre should look inside. They've been designing theatres for hundreds of years and they've come to the conclusion that deep red works. They're right. When I go to some modern theatres and they're all grey and white it gives me the pip. The seats in the Palace Grand were really close together so that you could feel the person next to you. It had a woodburning stove, which is a rarity in a theatre. It also had proper footlights to illuminate the actors from below, and a limelight from above. That's where the term 'green room' comes from, you know, because people would be so dazzled by being lit from the bottom and by the limelights from above that there would be a wee room off to the side, painted green, to get their eyes used to normal light again. Otherwise, they'd be staggering around half blind.

At the old undertaker's down the road there was a coffin and all the tools of the trade on display in the window. That's one of those things that you don't think about – that undertakers actually have tools; things they use to work on your body when you're dead. In Victorian times it would have been quite normal to display such tools; the whole death thing was such a ritual then. Now, people seem kind of scared of it. Back then, they even had mourning

Outside the undertaker's window

jewellery, such as rings with a lock of a dead person's hair in them, or watch chains made from the braided hair of a dead person. It sounds hellish, but it's actually very attractive and black and shiny. I've seen some. I would happily wear jewellery like that.

All the gear the undertaker used was in the window of that funeral parlour – the make-up, lip tint and face covering. Sometimes I wear mortician's wax when I'm filming, to cover up the very obvious hole in my ear where it's pierced. The wax goes on and they smooth it over and layer make-up on top of it. That's also what they use if your death was particularly scarifying. They'll tart you up a wee bit, so that you're better to look at.

The undertaker's window had a funny photograph of a funeral procession showing dogs pulling a sled with a coffin on it. A box of chemicals in front of it had a label which read, '*Alcoform: a concentrated liquid chemical for use in the preservation of the dead. Composed of the most approved germicidal preservative known to chemical science. Compounded by a method giving absolute preservation and lifelike appearance.*' So if you want to look lifelike when you're dead, that's the place to go. Next to it was some embalming fluid, 'semi-hardening'. Dear God.

It wasn't easy, burying people in Dawson. Sometimes they had to wait until a thaw came before they could even dig a hole. The following is an extract from a book called *I Married the Klondike* by a woman called Laura Beatrice Berton who worked as a school teacher in the Yukon in the early 1900s:

> One December the mercury hovered at fifty below for the entire month. There was a flu epidemic that year and therefore many deaths, especially among the half-breeds and Indians.
>
> But there could be no burials until the weather had moderated. The frozen bodies were stacked in the undertaking parlour.
>
> Indeed the winter's graves always had to be prepared in the fall, when it [the ground] could then be easily worked. As more people died during the winter than during the summer, there was always a good many standing open ready for the season. It was a grisly sight to pass the rows of yawning holes waiting for occupants and to wonder which of them were dressed in them before the long winter was over.

That's society for you and that's the way it ought to be. People should be in touching distance of death. God knows, I am myself. I'm not saying I'm close to dying, but I'm a lot closer to dying than I am to being born, if you know what I mean.

* * *

“THE LUST FOR *gold baffles me because I'm not big on it myself. I don't get the lure or the desire. The Indians have a lovely old saying: 'When you've chopped down the last tree, and you've caught the last fish, and you've poisoned the last river, maybe then you'll realize money can't be eaten.'*

I don't like diamonds either, even though I used to wear one in my ear. I got it from De Beers after I did an advertisement for them in Vogue *magazine. My wife was always kind of jealous of it. Then one Christmas my manager, John Reid, bought me another the same size and my wife nailed them both. I bought her a pair of diamond earrings so as I could get mine back, but they never reappeared.*

For a while I wore a black pearl dangling on a gold ring, which I liked to sport for a kind of piratical, buccaneer look. Then I had my traffic warden experience. I was outside Harrods and a traffic warden came along with an earring on and I thought, 'I think it's over.' I took my earring out right then. One occasionally makes its way back in, but wearing an earring is pretty much down the social scale when a traffic warden's doing it. That's when you know that it's no longer hip. ”

It's funny; you never think you'll find yourself in places like the Klondike in your lifetime. You kind of get to thinking that they only exist in literature and imagination. I've read about miners drinking coffee around the camp fire with wolves howling since I was a boy.

What I liked most about Dawson and the Yukon was that it had attracted the most extraordinary people over the years – my favourite kind too; those who just want to be alone. I could hardly imagine, though, that so many of them tramped all the way up there. Apparently, a hundred thousand headed north but only thirty or forty thousand made it. Dawson City was a very difficult place to get to in those days, especially if you were dragging heavy supplies which made it five times the journey over hill and dale, and those rocky mountain passes in the snow. A lot of people died, just for gold.

Out at the place where the gold rush started, there was a kind of *Star Wars* feel, with giant pieces of abandoned machinery in a barren landscape. The names of the different legendary locations were still painted on old dredger buckets – Dew Hill, Fox Gulch, Boulder Hill. Instead of having a little pan and scooping up water and silt to look for gold as it used to be done those dredgers,

An abandoned dredging machine

introduced after the First World War, scooped out the whole river so that they could examine the contents. They'd take huge bucketfuls and pour them into a pool in the middle of a machine then let the cogs and wheels shake it all around until the heavy gold fell through. The rest was thrown away, and you can still see the piles of dirty river that were dumped.

The people that operated those machines turned the land inside out on a grand scale, and they were taking out fifty pounds of gold every two days. That's serious money – and they did it right up until the sixties. The place is full of the ghosts of men with big moustaches and hats with badges and dreams of being rich. An immense number of them did get rich. The majority didn't, but that's the way of it.

They had names for the different levels of prospectors. A 'cheechako' was a guy who hadn't yet spent a winter there. Cash was regarded as 'cheechako money' because everyone else dealt chiefly in gold – or gold dust, specifically. Men paid in pinches of gold dust used to grow their nails long and rub hair oil into their fingers so that the dust would stick to their skin and they could grab a bigger pinch.

Once a panner had overwintered, he became a 'sourdough'. And to prove you were a real sourdough, you had to drink a sourtoe cocktail, which was Southern Comfort with a dead man's toe floating in it. Worse than that, you had to let the toe float up and touch your mouth. A tradition started in the Sourdough Saloon of Dawson's Downtown Hotel, those who complied became members of the Sourtoe Cocktail Club. I don't mind the petrified toe, I just don't drink. Those days are behind me. And it didn't seem right to ask for it with Coca-Cola.

When the first gold was discovered in the Yukon on 16 August 1896 it was like a lottery win. And this is how the gold rush started – it's an extraordinary story, even though the place where it all began looks like nothing more than a little stream bubbling over some rocks. A guy called George Carmack, who had married a Tagish Indian and lived like one, was camping near Rabbit Creek, which was well known to the Indians as a fishing spot. A fella called Bob Henderson, who was of Scottish heritage from Nova Scotia and an expert miner, told George that the river looked promising for gold. He said not to tell the 'siwash', a derogatory term for Indians derived from the French for savage. Henderson made the mistake of his life because George regarded himself as one of them.

Where the gold rush started

So George and his Indian brother-in-law went looking and they soon found some gold. The first pan they did brought up four dollars' worth, in the days when ten cents' worth was a good claim. In those days there was a sort of unwritten law that if you found gold you told everyone, so George decided to tell Henderson first and travelled a couple of miles down river to do so. When George and his friends arrived, one of them asked Henderson for some tobacco and Henderson called him a 'siwash' and refused. After that, George decided not to say a word.

George went back to the river and found a nugget the size of his thumb. Then he found several more in what he described as a 'gold sandwich' – slates with gold in between. George travelled to a place called Forty Mile Station and told everyone where the gold was so that they, too, could stake a claim – which they did. Even the barman became a millionaire.

The only person George never told was Henderson, who died a relatively poor man for his stupidity. Can you imagine the nights Henderson must have rolled around in his bed thinking, 'Why did I open my big mouth?' I'm not saying how much of the gold he deserved but it was his idea to pan there in the first place, so I think he deserved more than he got. It's a high price to pay for bigotry, isn't it? He felt desperately cheated.

George Carmack was the first to establish his claim at Rabbit Creek by writing his name on a tree. He made it very clear that was his claim and that everyone else could pan for gold all around him.

Each man was allowed fifty yards or something of a river that was soon renamed Bonanza Creek. They just staked out their claim and then went and registered it.

It was strange to sit in that little leafy glade with all its overgrown trees and trickling stream and imagine that was where the great Klondike gold rush began. On 16 August 1896, it was just a quiet little place where the Indians used to fish. By 17 August it was the hottest gold spot in the world. One word from George and a hundred thousand people started making their way there to seek their fortune. At a time of a world depression when people didn't think twice about dropping everything and heading for gold, Dawson City went from a tiny population to thirty or forty thousand virtually overnight. Even I found myself looking at the stones in the creek where it all began and thinking, 'Maybe there'll still be a bit of gold lying there?'

Now all the madmen have gone and the river just laps on as if nothing ever happened. The valley was raped but all these years later it doesn't look that bad. They've made a rather good job of covering up all that industrial wreckage. The place is so immensely vast that all their industry hardly left a mark.

* * *

" *THE PEOPLE FROM the time of the Industrial Revolution were remarkable. There was such a flowering of intelligence and ability, with the engineering of bridges and ships and aeroplanes and mining, that has never been equalled. We think of the Victorians as being a dull crowd, sort of grim and brown, but I think they've been judged a lot by the sepia photographs of the time.*

In actual fact they were the liveliest of people. Their music was fantastic. Their engineering was unbelievable. They loved bright colours. Photographs took such a long time to take, so if you smiled you looked an idiot by the end. It was much better to be stern, because you could hold it longer. But, really, they were a jolly bunch. "

Gold mining isn't dead in the Yukon; it's still very much alive. Especially now, when gold fetches something like nine hundred dollars an ounce, compared to the seventeen dollars an ounce in

George Carmack's day. David Millar, a second generation placer miner, showed me the ropes. Placer (pronounced 'plasser') comes from the Latin meaning 'loose' and refers to the fine gold loose in the gravel as opposed to a vein of it embedded in hard rock. The gold is blasted out of walls of mud and gravel by a huge, noisy, high-pressure hose, which first washes away what David called the 'overburden' or mud, then the permafrost, before it gets down to the green bedrock, or paydirt, where the gold lies.

Excess muddy water drains away into settling ponds, so that the silt separates before the fresh water is channelled into the local creek. There are no chemicals involved and it is all very clean. David goes so deep below the layers of earth and gravel that sometimes his hose exposes the bones of prehistoric mammoths and horses and other ancient animals. Each time he does so, he has to notify the government which sends archaeologists to excavate.

David is one of about eighty placer miners in Dawson City who work from April to September. Many of them are small family-run operations. David told me:

Hosing for gold

'The saying goes, you have a hundred days to make your money. I've almost used up my hundred days this year and I still haven't made any money, but there's always tomorrow.'

He described himself as an optimist. His father was a placer miner before him and used to make upwards of half a million dollars a year, with just fifty thousand spent on running costs.

'He'd sluice a hundred yards an hour, using five thousand gallons of water a minute and get around twenty ounces of gold an hour. Last year I sluiced a hundred yards an hour, using a thousand gallons of water a minute and I got a quarter of an ounce an hour. It wasn't a good year. My dad liked to live well and travel a lot, and it's a good thing because he died of cancer when he was sixty-two.'

David used to employ five people and work 'the wall' twenty-four hours a day, but these days he operates alone or with his two teenage kids during the school holidays because the gold is getting so scarce.

'I don't know how far into the hill I can go before I run out of gold, and if I move all of the equipment it costs me a hundred thousand dollars or more. If I do that and only get ten ounces of gold out, my wife might not be very happy.'

David told me he didn't watch the price of gold every day like some of the other placer miners do: 'It doesn't really matter what the price is, the fuel company don't want gold, they want money. It's not a really rich living, although sometimes you can do really good.'

Gold is nineteen times heavier than the water David uses to wash the gravel and mud out, so it settles at the bottom of the muddy pool he creates. He then scoops out a great mountain of muddy gravel and gold with a caterpillar track-type bulldozer and loads it into a hopper in his sluice plant – which is all giant hoses, wheels, conveyer belts and ball bearings with a big tray underneath to collect any gold that falls in the slurry. Then the spoil is pumped through another machine, with a series of fine meshes to catch the gold. The complicated sluicing process takes hours and has to be done over and over again. It basically does what panning used to do, but on an industrial scale.

This is hard, hard work for real men with hairy chests. Having watched David work, I think he is entitled to every ounce of gold he finds. There is something very appealing about the work and something very nice about these sorts of guys. Men like David are clever buggers; they have to know so much about so many things

David Millar

because, before they even look at any gold, they have to know about all the heavy plant and how to fix it. They can't run to the phone and call a mechanic every time something goes wrong so they have to know about water pumps and generators, about the earth and how it operates with its gravel, its bedrock and the overhang.

I told David he should have picked a gentler occupation, like being a watchmaker, or knitting or embroidery or writing children's books. But this career he called 'washing dirt for a living' was the one he'd inherited from his father. He liked working outdoors, especially with the chance of 'hitting the big time' always in the back of his mind. Even though he lived alone but for a pet poodle most of the year in the oldest roadhouse in the Yukon (his wife and kids lived in Whitehorse), he claimed he wouldn't do anything else.

When I spotted some gold glinting in one of his sluicing pails, I was strangely excited. I could feel the gold fever. A distinct change comes over you when you find gold. I wanted to touch it straight away. I wanted to get it up under my fingernails, but David was there in a shot, telling me sharply: 'No fingers'. His hackles went up and he changed. It wasn't an act. He had been working for months and months; blasting and digging and lifting and dumping and washing. All that money had been spent, with all that fuel it took to operate the pumps and the water. The timing had to be absolutely right because winter was coming and he had to be quick before it first slowed and then froze everything up. He wasn't going to miss an ounce. I thought he might have a rattlesnake in his pocket.

Holding that wee speck in my hand (with his permission) I realized that this was what all those thousands of people lived and worked and died for over the years: a small piece of gold that was once happy under the ground. After all that hard work, David eventually managed to get a bit more than an ounce of gold out of his muddy water and black sand, which would be worth around twelve hundred Canadian dollars. I had a new respect for gold and a new respect for gold miners.

David kindly gave me a wee vial with some gold in it when he was finished. I really appreciated that, to have a bit of Yukon gold that I got in a Yukon gold mine. I felt like a child winning a prize and I will treasure it forever because it represents such an optimistic day. The largest piece of gold his family ever found on

their claim was a three-ounce nugget his mother discovered in his father's sluicing box. He still had it and he let me hold it. 'I'll never sell it,' he told me proudly. 'That's a piece of our history.'

Dawson City

David had a lovely craziness about him that I really liked and fully expected from anyone who does something like gold mining. There's a great madness about the man who works alone. I can spot it in myself and my other friends who are painters and singers and actors. They get a certain wolfish strangeness in their eyes, a lupine look that is built on love and fear, coffee and passion.

Sometimes it's built on whisky but you're better to avoid that, in my experience.

A little goes a long way.

PART FOUR

There's a land where the mountains are nameless,
And the rivers all run God knows where;
There are lives that are erring and aimless,
And deaths that just hang by a hair;
There are hardships that nobody reckons;
There are valleys unpeopled and still;
There's a land – oh, it beckons and beckons,
And I want to go back – and I will.

From 'The Spell of the Yukon',
Robert Service (1874–1958)

HARLEY-DAVIDSON

YUKON

Whitehorse, Yukon

ONCE I HAD left the bumpy gravelled Dempster Highway and was on a tarmac road called the Klondike Highway, I swapped the bouncing seat of a Mack truck for the leather recliner of a Harley-Davidson and cruised towards Whitehorse through the most incredible scenery, exploding with late-summer colour. It was weird because it looked and felt like spring. The plants looked as if they were rejoicing but they were actually dying. This was their last fling.

Twenty-three thousand of the thirty thousand people who live in the Yukon live in and around the capital, Whitehorse. The rest of that Canadian state (which is twice the size of Britain) is virtually empty, but for mountains, trees and loneliness – described so beautifully by Jack London in his book *White Fang* which I read as a boy. Robert Service wrote well of this area too. His parents were from Glasgow which makes him Scottish – or at least he can play for Scotland which is the main thing. God knows, somebody should.

In one of his poems, Service used the line, 'a few of the lads chewing the fat' and I wonder if he was referring to the blubber the Inuit eat because I've eaten some myself and can honestly say that I have chewed the fat. I'll give you a bit of advice about blubber: if you're going to eat some have a really good mouthful and get into it; don't have little tiny bits because you'll think about it too much while you're doing it. Get a good mouthful and go for it. It's really

Left: On the road again

nice but I can't see it catching on. I can't see British people saying to their children, 'Come on now, stop complaining and eat your blubber. There are Eskimos starving in Greenland.'

Opposite top: Gold in them there hills

Service is one of those poets whose timing transfers wonderfully to dirty poetry. 'A bunch of the boys was chewing the fat…', there's your starter. Sit there and do it for yourself. I'll be what they call an 'occasioner of sin' – I'll lead you into it.

I felt pretty cool driving across part of the Yukon territory on my Harley until I met a bunch of bikers riding all the way from Fairfax, Alaska to Tierra del Fuego, an archipelago right at the tip of South America, near Cape Horn. They'll be a bit stiff in the arse when they get there. They'll be walking like the Hunchback of Notre Dame. I, meanwhile, was dressed in my Kevlar 'insurance trousers' in case I fell off and hurt myself.

If I was to say, 'Hand me my leathers chaps, I'm going out on my Harley,' that would be quite romantic, but the phrase 'insurance trousers' yearns for the word 'Nurse!' before it, as in: 'Nurse! My insurance trousers. Quickly! I feel an accident coming on!' You'll never see them appear in a romantic novel. Just imagine:

The hair on his chest showing just above his snowy-white T-shirt; the hint of a gold chain disappearing into it, he approached Dorothy in his insurance trousers. She went off him in a jiffy. 'Get away from me!' she yelled. 'I can't stand the sight of those.' 'But my mother said I should always wear them,' countered Steve.

No. It wouldn't work.

* * *

"PART OF MY *journey took me near the famous Chilkoot Trail, a thirty-three-mile hike across steep and difficult mountain terrain from Alaska to British Columbia. This was the terrifying route so many prospectors took to get to the Yukon during the gold rush.*

The Royal Canadian Mounted Police were so concerned back then that too many prospectors wouldn't survive crossing the Chilkoot Trail that they made each of them carry a ton of supplies, including food, tools, medicine, shelter and clothing. Mounties posted to the tent cities at the foot of the pass turned back those who didn't have the required items. Mule trains were set up to help ferry supplies. Can you imagine being a poor miner then, with holes in your socks, hauling a ton of

Right: Miners crossing the Chilkoot Trail

supplies over the mountains – and in that climate? That's what gold fever did to people. Some of them got rich, some of them got poor, but a lot of them died.

These weren't stupid men, either. People should never assume others are stupid just because they don't look as if they're very bright. Being bright may carry with it an image of someone wearing glasses with a waistcoat and a corduroy jacket, but bright comes in many disguises. I learned that in the shipyards. The men I worked with there were some of the most well-read people I ever met in my life. They were entirely self-educated; and they knew the really impressive stuff. They learned it down the library, because that was their escape route.

People often say that the great escape from poverty or a working-class background is sport or showbusiness, but they never mention the library. That's where the tunnel is, if you want to escape; that's the entrance to it anyway. Knowledge dispels fear – that's the motto of the Australian Parachute Training School, in case you're wondering. It's not mine. ”

Making my way deeper into the wilderness, I met up with Shawn Ryan, a modern-day claim-staker who is taking advantage of the fact that a huge percentage of the Yukon is still unclaimed for mineral prospecting. Camping overnight with him and his

fellow claim-stakers, I learned exactly how today's prospectors hunt for gold, copper, zinc, silver and whatever else they can find.

We sat around the campfire that night like gold prospectors from the old times. That was where the romance of it ended for me, though. My hands and feet were freezing, my shins were hot from the fire, I was stiff from being on the motorbike and all those men could talk about were bears and bear attacks. When I eventually crawled to my tent, I had the worst imaginable night. I was convinced there was a bear somewhere nearby so I never slept a bloody wink. I had my cayenne pepper aerosol spray beside me in case a three hundred-pound grizzly came crashing in, but I knew that would be like throwing meringues at a brick wall. When somebody started snoring in a nearby tent, I really thought it was a bloody bear. I actually considered going to sleep in one of the vehicles because, I thought, bears can't open car doors. Then I remembered something I'd seen on YouTube when a bear made a pretty damn good job of it. After that, I lay shaking in my sleeping bag, worried that I couldn't get out of it quickly enough if a bear came, or that if I didn't, the bear would think I was a giant caterpillar.

Top: Preparing to stake a claim with Shawn Ryan (**above**) and friends

It's like when you have a houseguest and in the morning he comes down and says, 'Oh, what a sleep I had!' And you say, 'Did you sleep soundly, then? I'm glad to hear that because it's unusual to sleep well in that room.' And he'll ask, 'What do you mean?' And you say, 'Oh, you know, some people have complained that there's a presence in that room, but it's probably nonsense.' Once you've implanted that thought, your guest won't sleep a wink the second night. It's the implanting that does it; it's not that the thing exists. That's always considered a good laugh in my house, and it is a good laugh until everybody splits and you're on your own and the laughing has to stop.

Shawn showed me his bear-banger the next morning, which he said kids love to set off like Chinese crackers. It was great fun, loading this thing that looked like a ballpoint pen with a cartridge, and flicking the end with my thumb. It made this great cracking noise and then shot into the air for thirty feet before exploding with a bang like a gunshot. The trouble is, it only really works if the bear is thirty or forty feet away and not bothering you. If the bear was intent on getting you it wouldn't be any good at all, unless it accidentally got up his nose or something. I wondered if there was a city version for thugs and muggers.

I'm not sure what I imagined it would be like watching these men with beards using modern prospecting techniques but the reality was even more unexpected. Sitting at a computer in their tent, I was given a sound lesson in chemistry, technological wizardry and geology. Shawn explained that prospectors these days spend more time scanning the Internet than they do walking the ground:

'It's like looking for a needle in a haystack but the government maps at least tell us where the haystack is.'

They call up databanks of satellite and aerial photography to check for structural patterns and strata anomalies, they scan endless maps, use sonar equipment to check rock formations and refer to more than six thousand soil samples from the government Yukon Geological Survey to check colour, chemicals and mineral content. Once everything comes together and they think there's a chance of a gold cluster being found, they will auction off a claim to one of the bigger companies who'll pay good money and decide whether or not to start digging.

'A prospector puts his whole pay cheque on the line, which a lot of people don't have the guts to do,' Shawn said. Working in teams of eight to ten, he and his colleagues can stake out eighty to a hundred claims a day. It can take up to two years before they know whether a claim is going to be worth their while. Shawn, whose business partner and budget controller is his wife Cathy, described it as 'a well-thought-out game of poker.' He added:

'If you don't do it the modern way, you're stuck with the

alchemy of the old way. I bet there are only six or seven serious old-style prospectors in the whole Yukon right now. They're a dying breed because they have a really hard time making a living.'

The way Shawn and his team work, if a claim makes what he calls 'a lot of zeros', then one of the zeros is his. Even when the snow keeps him out of the mountains he carries on looking for gold at home, sitting up late each night on the computer.

'All of a sudden, and it can be two-thirty in the morning, you're so pumped up – because you've found something in the middle of the winter time and you can't wait to get up there and go find it. I have to ask my wife if I can please have a budget to go out, and if she says yes, then I'm flying. It's like looking for the biggest Easter egg.'

Having had my mind boggled by computer science, I was taken up in a helicopter by Shawn, so that we could look at the contours of the land and scout out some more claims. It was such amazingly beautiful country that I wondered how the government felt about the prospect of this land being raped, again, as it was a hundred years ago.

'The government would love me to find a mine up here,' Shawn insisted. 'It would create employment, the price of houses would go up, and people who make money pay taxes.'

Despite all the soil sampling and the flood of research data analyzed by the latest software and GPS equipment, what really delighted me was that to stake a claim you still have to bang two four-foot long stakes into the ground and write on them, just as George Carmack did at the end of the nineteenth century. Taking me out to Skookum Mountain and a new claim site he was naming 'Billy Number One' in my honour, Shawn chopped some stakes out of a tree and chipped a slice off one of them for me to write my name on. Whenever he does this for himself, he told me, he adds a happy face. 'Happy to be in the bush,' he said with a smile. It felt like such a fantasy adventure – to hammer in my stake and write my name and the date on it, thus becoming part of that incredible Yukon history.

Once a post is in, no one is allowed to move it for a hundred years. Shawn flagged my posts with fluorescent tape so that they could be seen from the air by other prospectors, and we then paced the permitted claim, which is 1,500 square feet. As well as using GPS to make sure the claim was exactly the right size, Shawn still relied on the same technique used of old to estimate a mile – one thousand Roman paces. 'For me,' he said, 'a quarter of a mile is two hundred and forty-two paces, so I must be a little bit taller than a Roman.'

Finding quartz

Having paced it out in the style of James Dean, I declared myself the rightful owner of the Billy Number One claim. I yelled:

'To whom it may concern; to everybody anywhere in the world. This is the Billy claim. Keep clear. You hear?'

It's not every day you make a little bit of history or that a little bit of Canada belongs to you. Shawn then had precisely two weeks to make his way into the Mining Recorder's office in Whitehorse to register the staked land. Each claim costs ten dollars to make and then about a hundred dollars more in government fees. The two-week time limit was figured out as far back as 1898 when it was estimated that a prospector travelling back to Whitehorse could manage ten miles a day. I loved the way they'd hung on to that tradition.

Shawn showed me quartz glittering on rocks and in their veins. He often finds copper and zinc too – but, to him, that's like a second prize. Sometimes he quite literally stumbles across gold

WHAT IS KNOWN as 'free entry' mining dates back to the earliest days of the gold rush in the Yukon, when the government was keen to encourage settlers in to 'tame' the wilderness frontiers.

An estimated seventy-nine per cent of the Yukon is available for mineral exploration at minimal cost. Having staked a claim to a rectangular parcel of land and paid a ten-dollar fee, a mineral tenure is granted which allows the claimant unlimited access to prospect for minerals on that land, as deep as they can go. Under the terms of the Yukon Quartz Mining Act, a claim-staker doesn't even need a licence to prospect and anyone over the age of eighteen can apply. The only areas out-of-bounds are land set aside for national parks, near houses or registered to the First Nations tribes.

The right granted is indefinite, as long as the miner carries out a hundred dollars' worth of 'representation' work each year, which can include digging, drilling or conducting geological surveys. Alternatively, he can just pay the hundred dollars annually. Miners can build roads, airstrips, store fuel and erect underground structures on their claimed land. There are relatively few regulations and little that requires government approval.

If valuable deposits are found in a vein, or lode, the miner can apply to lease the subsurface for twenty-one years, renewable for another twenty-one after that, for a fee of as little as a few hundred dollars. The premise underlying the free entry system is that mining is the best use of public land: it encourages miners to stake claims over as much territory as possible. This had recently been challenged by environmentalists such as the Canadian Parks and Wilderness Society and by others who wish to see the land kept as a wildlife conservation area, the spiritual home of the First Nations people or for recreational tourism. The possible exploration for uranium rights in the future is a particular concern.

while he is pacing a claim. He digs around a little in the dirt until sparkling traces show up in his magnifying glass. We didn't find anything like that on my claim, although I still felt very proud. When I'm long dead, people will be able to look up the Billy claim in the files and read that I was there; I was that soldier. Shawn will have to explain in writing why the claim was named Billy, so there'll forever be a story about my visit in the record books too.

Shawn's enthusiasm was so infectious that I began to understand the gold fever that creeps into your soul. I found myself getting quite carried away. I could so easily see how people get into the whole gold thing, whether they're jokers and gamblers or those who think they've sussed the system by trying to put logic, mathematics and science into it. Either way, they're still coming up with it. Gold mining is one of the few trades where the norm is to fail. That's what they're up against and that attracts a particular kind of guy; someone who wants to buck that norm and live a dream. God bless them.

Most incredibly, the word that kept coming up between these savvy entrepreneurs in the midst of all their technology, wizardry and alchemy wasn't gold: it was another four-letter word – hope. That pleased me deeply. It's a very refreshing and enriching little word, based on their desire to find wealth. These men who laugh out loud and are playing many hands of cards in the hope that one will come up trumps are a rare breed. It made me wish I was twenty-five again, and full of such optimism.

Despite my fantasy about instant wealth – something Shawn described as a 'shamrock dream' – I'm still as poor as I always was. I'm not a zillionaire yet. But anything you want to know about gold mining, just ask me. I know loads. I've had at least two days' experience.

At a place called Ice Lakes, I went moose hunting with the unlikely sounding Romeo Le Duc, complete with Stetson, and Carolee Bateson-Koch, who was dressed in full camouflage gear.

Moose hunting with Romeo and Carolee

Carolee and Romeo? They sounded less to me like hunters than lovers or the subject of a Bob Dylan song. I could write it myself.

They were such nice, decent folk. Carolee was a masseuse, a naturopath and a chiropractor. Romeo was all cheekbones with a Clint Eastwood stare. He looked like he was made of solid steel. A trophy hunter and guide, he had a completely wonderful job, right down to chopping firewood in the winter. He carried a rifle that shoots with a calibre he invented himself to make sure it has enough power to take down the biggest and the best he can find.

'Yoo-hoo! Show us your hooves!'

Whenever he and Carolee kill a moose or caribou it is sliced up and taken back to Whitehorse and divided among their friends, just like the Inuit. That is so much better than the way some others kill things and just leave them or can't even remember what happened to them. There's nothing wrong with human beings killing animals and eating them; they've been doing it since time began. But if you ask any of those big-game fishermen what they did with the marlin they're so proud of killing, they say, 'Well, I'm not sure.' It could be lying at the side of the road as far as they know, and that's criminal.

We trailed up through the vibrant heather, ferns and brush into the hills above Ice Lakes carrying a decoy moose which is known as the 'blind'. Nothing more than a photograph of a moose stamped onto a flapping piece of canvas fixed to a lightweight wooden frame, the decoy, apparently, looked like a cow (a female) moose. It was mating season and we were hoping to attract a bull. I thought the decoy was kind of funny when I first clapped eyes on it, but once I saw it in action I realized that it was very effective indeed. In the breeze, it had a great way of moving just the way an animal would, and catching my eye as it looked over its shoulder. I quite fancied her myself. I felt like calling, 'Yoo-hoo! I'm in the heather over here in the long grass. Show us your hooves!'

Romeo told me that a moose will never be more than half a mile from water, so we stayed close to the lake. Carolee told me to spray some scent on the rear of the decoy – its rear, not mine, she stressed. I think it was Eau de Female on Heat. Ah, moose scent. I thought about spraying a little behind my ears when I next went out of an evening in Dawson. It could give me that special allure. Then I prayed I didn't actually get any on me or a moose might come crashing through the undergrowth and give me one. I wasn't prepared for that kind of action. My mother didn't raise no moose.

Romeo also had his rifle with him in case of wolves or grizzly

Hiding out in the hide

bears. He told me a bear will sneak up to a three thousand-pound moose and with just one swipe of its huge paw can break its neck. He personally knew five people who'd been mauled by grizzlies, including one who should have died because his skull was caved in. At that point, I wanted to go home.

Carolee had brought a crossbow with sights to shoot at a moose. Hunting with a bow has a lot going for it. There's a fairness involved there, and silence. I was also pleased to learn that there were almost gentlemanly codes of behaviour about hunting in the region and that people couldn't just fly in and blast everything they saw. They can only hunt bulls, and there are certain times when hunting is off limits so that everything goes back to square one.

Peering down the sights of her crossbow, Carolee told me that unless she aims for the heart or the lungs of a target, an injured animal can run for miles making it almost impossible to catch. 'If you hit him good, he'll run about twenty yards. He won't go very far and collapse – usually within thirty seconds.' With the decoy in place and Carolee and me in a purpose-built canvas hide, Romeo began his special moose call – not with a horn but using his voice.

It was a kind of low mooing. Indian food can bring out those same noises in me.

Twice, we thought we heard an answer but there was no action. I told him I didn't think his call was sexy enough. Whether it was that, or the fact of me being there, I don't know, but we never attracted a single moose – something I was secretly delighted about, although I would have loved to see one up close and personal.

As consolation, Romeo showed me a beaver house, beautifully made and insulated with sticks and moss. I'd never seen one of those before and it was brilliant, especially the fact that the beaver changes the world around him, damming the river to enable him to survive the winter. Romeo also showed me the bleached remains of a caribou that a wolf had eaten. We spotted some moose tracks, but that was the closest we got, so we had fried eggs instead and, eventually, went off into the sunset.

BRITISH COLUMBIA

Telegraph Creek, British Columbia

My next encounter, at the end of a seventy-two-mile dirt road near a quaint place called Telegraph Creek, was with a Mighty Mouse of a woman by the name of Nancy Ball.

Seventy-five years old, white-haired and incredibly beautiful, Nancy was born on a cattle ranch in Alberta but had lived on a homestead outside Telegraph Creek for the past fifty-two years. She was someone I had been very much looking forward to meeting and when I did finally get to, she was the most impressive woman I had ever encountered. Old and beautiful – there's an expression you don't hear much any more. Well, Nancy had it in sackloads, with her piercing, intelligent eyes.

Five-feet-nothing and made of wire, this powerhouse ran the Glenora Guest Ranch in the middle of a four hundred and eighty-acre spread, which was once the biggest hunting lodge in British Columbia. Since she separated from her husband, she had run it pretty much on her own – chopping wood, digging posts and setting up gravity-feed watering systems, in between dealing with wolves and bears. She did all the repairs herself and said most of her life was spent 'repairing the repairs'. She handled a motorboat like no one I have ever seen. Having met me at the river's edge, she jumped in, went at the outboard motor and took us off down the raging Stikine River with its wild current, totally unfazed.

We were met on the opposite riverbank by her rifle-carrying daughter Tammy, and loaded into a four-wheel drive all-terrain vehicle for the journey to Nancy's ranch. This midget woman drove us four and a half miles up a rutted track through woods, a rifle on her shoulder in case of bears. Her ranch was sensational; a series of little log cabins set in rolling acres with horses lolling about. I fell in love with the place the minute I saw it. It was a bit run down, with upsy-downsy fences, but that's what I loved most about it. Her house was covered in flowers and had a hand-painted sign which said, 'Wild Flowers Grown by a Wild Woman'. God love her! I felt like an old hillbilly in my lovely cabin with its woodburning stove, pile of logs and little oil lamp. Nancy had written a notice which read: 'Please note, you must have a good sleep. If you are cold, it is miserable. I advise warm nightwear and warm socks to be worn to bed.'

I sat on the veranda of my cabin and smoked a cigar until Nancy called me for what she called 'a trapper's dinner' of moose stew, which was sensational and absolutely delicious. I'm not a great red meat eater but moose is the man. There was also a bean stew, some carrots, potatoes and a raw cabbage salad. I loathe cabbage normally but I wolfed it down like a man possessed. Then she brought out a cake thing at the end. It was by far the best meal I had enjoyed on my travels so far. That night I slept like a stone at the bottom of the sea.

Nancy's ranch house was like something from your dreams, with antlers and a mountain sheep's bum mounted on the wall, as well as photographs of her many visitors over the years. She had a big cast iron woodburning stove which she got from the army

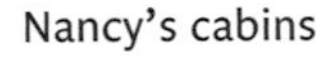

Nancy's cabins

Nancy cutting wood

when they were making the Alaskan Highway. How they got it back to where she lives is another story. The woman was just full of stories. She was a giant – a wee giant, but a giant nonetheless.

She split some firewood with amazing dexterity, despite complaining about weak wrists. Watching, I asked if she ever felt her life so far from civilization was too hard but she shook her head. 'Nope,' she replied. 'I like peace and quiet and I kind of like being on my own too.' In the sixties a few hippies built some small cabins near her ranch but they soon became what she called 'winter kill' and left as soon as the weather turned. Now, her nearest neighbour is fifteen miles away. She buys her groceries in bulk once a year and grows, hunts or fishes for the rest of her food, canning and pickling and preserving most of what she harvests. She has use of a freezer in Telegraph Creek and when she brings some moose meat home from it, she buries the meat in sawdust as insulation which keeps it frozen for up to ten days.

As well as breeding horses and growing, cutting, stacking and baling her own hay, Nancy raised four kids on the ranch, educating them via a correspondence course until they had to go to school. When her first three children were small, she had no communication whatsoever, no telephone or radio:

'Then I went through a really bad thing with my baby and said "I've got to get a radio", so I did. Of course it doesn't always work but at least it was something.'

Her children had little or no contact with other children until they went to school, which was a struggle for them:

'They knew a lot about the bush and they knew how to take care of themselves, but there were things in the outside world that they didn't know and I couldn't help them because I didn't know either.'

In the winter, Nancy can be cut off for months at a time, but said she kept busy and had her animals. 'I was one of the very lucky few who found where I belonged when I came here. I still feel that way. I've never got tired of it and I have never stopped appreciating the privilege of living here.' Looking around her wistfully, she added, 'The thing that bothers me most is I know some day I will have to leave.'

One night, wolves set about some of her seventy horses.

'I heard a racket in the middle of the night so I got the big flashlight and ran out the door. I saw a colt and two mares fighting off wolves. I'd forgotten my rifle. It was in the bedroom. One of the kids ran and grabbed it and another grabbed my shells, but of

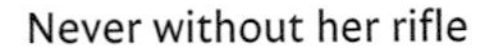

Never without her rifle

course it was dark and I didn't dare shoot except into the air, so that's what I did. The wolves took off.

'But then I had to get the kids up and go and gather up all the horses and put them in the barn.' She laughed. 'All in a day's work.'

Nancy took me for a walk to the top of a hill above her property, never once pausing for breath. She was never without her rifle but told me she preferred to frighten bears away, rather than kill them. She's shot several in her lifetime, including one she spotted running towards her four-year-old daughter innocently playing in the back yard. Nancy grabbed her gun and said, 'Goodnight Vienna.' I mean, that would be a war situation for me, but not for Nancy Ball. My God! I can't imagine my mother running and shooting a bear to save me. Nancy's life was so beyond my circle of experience.

She told me she gave bears three chances in a tight spot before she went for the kill. Once, she had to shoot at a female grizzly when it came upon her while she was in the woods gutting and skinning a moose. I mean – some moose are seven feet at the shoulder! So, there she was gutting one, as you do, when a hungry grizzly fancied a bit.

'The bear was about five yards from me and my rifle was over to one side. My hands were all bloody and I don't like to pick a rifle up with bloody hands. I hollered at her and she wouldn't go, so I went back a little way and hollered some more. Then I looked up and realized her two cubs were up a tree, leaning right over the moose carcass. I chased her away by hollering some more but I knew she'd come back for her cubs, which is exactly what she did.

'After she'd gone, I went back to my moose and I'd be darned if she wasn't there again, having hidden her cubs, so I shot over her head and she took off. I had never seen a bear act like that before and although I didn't want to shoot her when she had cubs, if she'd come back a third time I'd have had to. Lucky for her – and for me – she stayed away.'

Looking down on the spread of her property with her, I could see Nancy's immense pride in it all. She showed me where her daughter was building a house; a woman who is also immensely admirable and whose husband is paraplegic. The house has been fifteen years in the building so far, but I wouldn't care if it took fifty. To build your own house from logs is just a dream. On the way back down the hill, Nancy showed me a beaver dam, joking, 'If I ever find a man that can work like a beaver I'm going to take him home.'

Wild Flowers grown
by a Wild Woman

Nancy taught me so much in one day. Her genuine humility touched me. Her optimism shone over me like a prayer. I watched as she chopped down a jack pine tree 'to cook with' and started to clear away brush from a three-mile trail down to the river. So strong in the things she believed in, she lived in a staggering place, completely organically in the old-fashioned sense – she'd never used a chemical spray on anything. Back at her ranch this human dynamo made us a delicious lunch of salad, cold meat, potatoes and apple crumble. I never wanted to leave.

If anyone is qualified to speak about ageing, Nancy Ball is the person. Like me she believes that if anyone should tell you to act your age, you should treat them with the disdain they deserve. If you take their advice then you need professional help. There is no sense in it, because if people had any control over Nancy they'd have made her retire ten years ago, only to be miserable. I learned so much from her about living and how to age properly. Spending those few days with that remarkable woman was a life-changing experience. I don't know how it is going to change my life, but I'm determined to take on some of her optimism and strength.

I don't think Nancy Ball will ever leave me.

Opposite top: 'Some day I'll have to leave'
Opposite bottom: Wild flowers grown by a wild woman

* * *

"NANCY MADE ME *feel good about my age and I don't even have a problem about that, it's just something that crosses my mind every now and again. I sometimes wonder if something is okay for me to do 'at my age' – which is a very stupid thought. Age has nothing to do with anything. Not that I think people should be out dancing all night, or maybe if they should they should sleep more during the day. But there is this constant hammering on in magazines and newspapers about age; how employers insist that they won't hire people over a certain age. It is a crime. It might even be a sin. People should be allowed to do whatever they bloody want. Go on, get it on. Shake your tail feathers. Look good for your partner. Go for it.*

Take my word for it, it works. If it doesn't work for you, come and see me and I'll tell you how to do it right. You don't need to look pretty, just look like you. I don't look pretty. I'm only attractive – well, maybe a bit, remotely.

No one ever claims to have grown up. Growing up is always

Joie de vivre

someone else's idea. They say, 'It's time you grew up!' and all that bullshit. Don't grow up. By all means grow old, but don't grow up because that means being beige or grey. When they talk about older people's spending power they call it the 'grey' pound. What utter nonsense. Grey? What about primary colours? Don't listen to people like that, they don't know what they're talking about, and I do.

Yes, I do. ”

Telegraph Creek was genuinely old and lovely, perched on the edge of the Stikine River gorge. The place would make a lovely pattern for painting-by-numbers. I half expected to see John Wayne strolling down the street.

But it was also a Heartbreak Hotel town because for many of the original would-be gold miners this was their last chance saloon. Having arrived by boat, the vast majority didn't make it much beyond there; they died or turned back halfway through hauling their ton of supplies on the thousand-mile journey north along Indian trails into the heart of the Yukon.

The town is named Telegraph Creek because it served as a

The Stikine River gorge

construction access point during one stage of an ambitious plan for the world's first complete telegraph system to link Europe and America; it was to stretch across America and the Bering Straits at Alaska, across Russia, and then across Europe to London. After they had spent three million dollars and installed almost two thousand miles of it, somebody beat them to it by completing the transatlantic telegraph system, and that was that. Then there was a scheme for a huge railroad to the Yukon which also started and failed, so Telegraph Creek was the venue for a series of failed ventures or grand schemes that ran out of steam.

Maybe because of its history, Telegraph Creek was a place where loads of religious nutters flocked to try to convert the indigenous people, who (they didn't realize) were already delirious with joy. The Seventh Day Adventists were among those cuckoo people who had the terrible presumption that the locals didn't know what was right. I don't think these missionaries acted maliciously, but they did immense damage around the world just cancelling existing beliefs as if they didn't matter. They would come charging into a place and spoil it by destroying the original culture. There was a great deal of corruption involved as well. Some of those so-called missionaries took a lot of the Indian artefacts, ostensibly to be burned, but then actually sold them – many turned up in museums and auction rooms all over the world.

There was too much of that creepy religion in Telegraph Creek for my liking, with three or four churches vying for attention in what was effectively a ghost town. Generally speaking, I think ghost towns are best left to the ghosts. The walls of some of the ramshackle buildings were covered in biblical quotes, too – great chunks of it. There is something rotten about that; something intrinsically wrong.

* * *

“*I UNDERSTAND WHERE religious belief comes from and that it can be very pleasant and comforting for some. It's having a daddy looking after you. You remember your dad's big hairy hand when you were walking along the street as a kid. You never forget the strength of that hand, with its fingers twice the size of yours to guide you around. That's the God thing. People get the pulse from him, and for everything that is good, from above. I understand that completely.*

Telegraph Creek

What I don't understand is the anger-driven, born-again thing. I think that comes from disillusionment. People say, 'I didn't get what I wanted from life, but not because I was an underachiever but because I was on the wrong track. It's all in the big book. Invisible friends in the sky are in control and everything that I do is written down in there, so it's out of my hands.'

It is peculiar enough to have invisible friends – that's not normal – but if the religious surround themselves with other people and convince them they've got them as well, it makes them feel better about their beliefs. Neither is it normal to think your life is written in a book somewhere and that you don't have control of it. Then to run around trying to convince others that it's you who's right is frightening, to say the least.

Having been brought up as a Catholic, there are times in severe turbulence when I fail the atheism test. I don't believe I will suffer a major change of heart on my deathbed, but who knows? The fear of death is a powerful thing with the invention of Hell and the idea of burning for eternity. They've done a great PR job on it. I can completely understand deathbed Christians leaving that window of opportunity open. I don't know if my views would change. Right now I don't think so, anyway, but right now isn't the end. ”

In the landscape around Telegraph Creek, I was once again struck by the amazing colours in the trees and bushes. I'd seen beautiful autumnal scenes before but usually only for a brief time. I had never been in the midst of them for such an extended period. It was like art, or like a movement of music, the swelling and gradual descending. It was a lovely thing.

On the Stikine River, I was shown ancient fishing sites belonging to the First Nations people who fish for salmon using booms out on the river. They then dry and smoke their catch in the same way as their ancestors did. Each section of the river has rights that belong to individual families, based on which family had been fishing there for so many generations.

The gorge was unnavigable in places for larger boats, so during the gold rush someone clever invented a winch system fixed to the rocks to pull smaller boats up to Telegraph Creek. There were three gold rushes in that area during the nineteenth century, which involved some ten thousand people passing through that strange village to follow their dreams. They used the river like a road and it was so busy with paddle steamers that they had traffic lights. I'd never seen traffic lights on a river before but there was such chaos and, as the gorge narrowed, it was the only way to stop the boats crashing into each other. The pioneers back then were so incredibly resourceful.

On the road out of Telegraph Creek, which followed the route of an old Indian trail, I don't think I'd ever seen so many trees in my entire life. Of course, I knew that Canada had lots of trees and lumberjacks, timber and lumber, but it wasn't until I was confronted with it that I realized the scale of the thing. I spotted two huge eagles, including a bald eagle which flew in and landed halfway up a pine tree and just sat there looking at me, all bald-eagley. That was a phenomenal thing to see.

I was relieved to be in a sturdy four-wheel drive vehicle on such a difficult road because it wasn't the kind of place you wanted to be stuck, with all those wolves and bears and wolverines. I was convinced that there were all sorts of weird hairy things lurking behind bushes. People shuddered when I said I was going to drive along that road – which didn't fill me with confidence. They're different people from us, though. After all those years of being in the cold they have a completely different mindset about winter. I got the idea that summer is a kind of intrusion in their lives that they don't particularly look forward to. Summer brings

Beaver country

mosquitoes and all sorts of other nasties. Like the Inuit, I think they prefer winter, when they function better.

New Aiyansh, British Columbia

IT WAS AT A PLACE called New Aiyansh that I met a remarkable Indian called Alver Tait, a member of the Nisga'a, Canada's only self-governing First Nations tribe. Alver is a woodcarver and totem pole maker who is trying to bring a bit of the culture back, and the language. I think that's where these people's strength lies; in knowing who they are again.

It was the missionaries who first discouraged the woodcarvings of the indigenous people because when they saw them making totem poles and writing on them they thought they were worshipping pre-Christian idols. They completely failed to understand that it wasn't idolatry; that carving images in wood was a way of recording both their mythological and their factual history because they had an oral tradition made pictorial by carving.

I found myself thinking a lot about the way the Indians had been treated over the years and it really was shabby. Their land was taken from them and they had been used and abused. They must feel so unhappy about that, deep down. They must sometimes look around and think, 'What happened? We had all of this and now we have none.' It is only relatively recently that reparations have been made.

With Alver Tait

The lava beds

The landscape around New Aiyansh is dominated by miles and miles of extraordinary moon-like lava beds. They form the base of the Nass River valley, beneath snow-capped mountains. A volcano erupted two hundred and fifty years ago and wiped out the village, killing two thousand natives. By law, no rock can be removed from this sacred site. The record books catalogued the eruption as a major geological event, but the Nisga'a has its own story. Nisga'a legend claims that a naughty Indian boy slit open the back of a salmon and put flaming sticks in it to make it swim around, which was a great insult to the fish. He was warned against doing it by the tribe but he kept on. The punishment from the gods was to make the volcano erupt and destroy most of the village. A god appeared (whose name I can't pronounce because it's one of those words with hardly any vowels), and he came down and stopped the lava flow and saved a lot of them. I love all these ancient myths and legends.

Alver was an interesting man who told me about his older brother, Norman, who seemed like a very impressive guy. Norman travelled the world to find as many as he could of the Nisga'a artefacts that had been lost or sold by missionaries. Then he brought them back to New Aiyansh and used them to teach young people the old ways and how to start carving again. Alver was the only one who persisted in Norman's original class and is now a master carver and teacher himself.

There was such an air of goodness and optimism about New Aiyansh. It didn't have that faded, defeated feel that so many of the frontier towns had. People took pride in their homes and gardens once they knew they wouldn't be taken from them again. Alver didn't seem at all bitter about the way his people had been treated. On the contrary, he seemed grateful for the way things were. 'We're very fortunate that we got part of it back,' he told me with a smile.

'A certain percentage of something is better than a hundred per cent of nothing. We're taking control of our own lives now. We're taking it in strides; we're not crying about it and we're happy we're governing ourselves. No longer are people pointing at us saying, "The government is looking after them and putting food on their table." Now we're doing it ourselves, just like we always did.'

They have their own government building and their own council, to whom they can go to speak about fishing, forestry or other problems. Alver had been to the council earlier in the day to ask for permission to cut down four red cedar trees to make some new canoes. Some things they can't change, though, like the disappearance of the region's wildlife and fish:

'We have to accept that and try to work around it. I remember when I was a child fishing with my dad, we could fish seven days a week, twenty-four hours a day if we wanted. Then, later, it was reduced to about five days a week and after a while to four.

'Now we've got about six hours to go out there and catch some salmon and that's it. They give us a certain amount for our own use; not to sell but for ceremonial purposes, as well as for our survival through the winter.'

Alver's totem poles were things of great beauty. Just as in the old days, each pole tells a story. Once, such poles might have given the history of a chief's life after his death, or some other major tribal event. 'Now we mainly make ones which identify which tribes live where,' said Alver. The six thousand or so Nisga'a are divided into four tribes represented by an eagle, a killer whale, a raven and a wolf. These four animals are carved into every pole.

Long after the volcanic eruption on Nisga'a land, a terrible flood devastated New Aiyansh in the 1940s, leaving 'Old' Aiyansh frozen

Below and opposite:
Alver's totem poles

Aiyansh Old Town

in time across the river, rusting and rotting. Alver showed me a story pole which depicted one of their gods holding a rainbow: 'The story goes that after the great flood, there were a thousand rainbows around the whole valley and these rainbows signified hope.'

In the late 1990s Alver was asked by the chiefs to make another totem pole, to bring unity to the village. Beautifully sculpted and unpainted, as they all were, it stands proudly in the heart of the community. A dance group was formed and villagers regularly dance around the pole to remind themselves to work and live in harmony. Alver formed a new carving group to teach the young people the old skills, along with the old language which forms part of the process.

'Once you get into carving, everything else starts to fall into place,' he said. 'There is so much pride in it, you see. A totem pole belongs to the people; to your ancestors. When we raise a totem pole we are bringing back your ancestors.'

I loved the idea of his totem pole bringing the village together like that, and the fact that Alver is invited all around the world to speak and carve and show others his great skill.

Alver and his brother Norman were both victims of the disgraceful residential school system. For six years, they were sent away to Edmonton and never saw their parents.

'It was like sending us to Russia,' said Alver. 'We didn't know anyone and we were just kids. All we heard was other children crying every day in the dorms. Many were abused by the staff. A lot of people who went through what we did just drank themselves to death and are under the ground now. That or on Skid Row.

'I think what gave my brother and me strength was my father's teachings when we were young about how to be strong and not to buckle under anything. That, and my mother's love. She was a Christian so that helped us quite a bit. They were both strong people and they told us not to lay down and die.'

When Alver was eventually returned to his village he didn't know anything of his culture or language but he was determined to learn. He soon spoke the language fluently. He spent a lot of his time trying to counteract the effects of drugs and alcohol on the young of the village by encouraging them to learn the language and to carve, especially canoes.

'It gives you such pride to be able to paddle a canoe that you have carved yourself. That gives people a lot of strength,' he said.

Keith Tait, who was another residential school victim, guided me through the next part of my adventure, which involved spending some time in a sweat lodge – a kind of meditative steam bath taken in company with a handful of other people. Steam from hot rocks is used for physical and spiritual cleansing in a group therapy setting. I'd heard about sweat lodges and always thought

Inside the sacred lodge with Keith Tait

I'd like to try one some day, even though I'd been warned it could be a rough ride emotionally and physically. When my day arrived, I was very unsure. Shawn, the gold miner, had told me he'd tried it and it took him right to the edge of his endurance, being in the pitch dark in this screaming heat. He thought he couldn't take another second of it until the release began.

All I really knew was that I was going to be boiled and steamed and I didn't know if my body could stand it. I felt as if I was about to be covered in herbs, cooked and eaten in a tent. I was going to have to trust the people involved. I hoped I'd be up to it. I didn't want to look like a wuss. I am a basket case emotionally but I really hoped to learn something from the experience.

Before we started, Keith took me out to the lava beds to gather the right stones to heat on the fire inside the lodge.

'The lava rock is very significant to us,' he told me. 'It comes from the centre of the earth and Mother Earth is where everything begins for us. Whenever we take something from its own element we give thanks to the Almighty for that part which sustains us.

'The principle is that when you take you also give, reinvesting. We Nisga'a have always done that, whether it is a fish or a moose or the chopping down of a tree. The policy is to never take too much of what you want. It is those principles that keep us in harmony and balanced.'

Keith told me that in the sweat lodge they heat thirty-two rocks because they like to do everything in fours:

'Everything in life is in fours. There are four directions and four seasons, so we use eight rocks at a time in four different rounds.

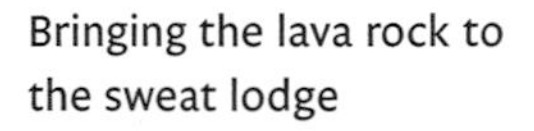
Bringing the lava rock to the sweat lodge

The sweat lodge is where we feel comfortable; it's where we bring in our issues or whatever's weighing us down and we start to build ourselves back up to a positive frame of mind.'

As evening fell, he led me to the isolated lodge, considered a sacred, secret place, and introduced me to those who'd be sweating with me – a girl called Kate and five others, including a man named Herbie. The rocks we'd picked were blessed and then heated on a fire pit in the middle of a tent. Before we went inside, Keith gave me some final advice:

'This is a place where we can extend ourselves spiritually. If you go in with a negative frame of mind, you're going to want to give everything away that might be in your mind or hurting your body. So go in wanting to absorb the steam and the cleansing and that's what you will do.

'If you start to panic and hyperventilate then you're breathing through your mouth and you're not in control, so breathe through your nose and mouth; slow breaths that keep your heart beating normally. For first timers it often feels like a shock to the body. I always tell people that if they start to feel they're having difficulty the coolest place that you can be is close to the ground because the steam always rises. Okay?'

Now I was really scared. I had meditated many times in my life before and was hoping that I could draw on that experience to keep calm. Keith explained that, having been assigned a place in the seating order, we would sit and meditate as if in a church, building ourselves up to what he ominously called 'the final act'.

'It gets you down to a level where you are just part of your surroundings,' he added. 'You are no better, no more and no less. You're as good as a mosquito. This helps you prepare so that when you do extend yourself spiritually, your focus is not just on yourself. You're just part of the universe. You came from somewhere and you want to end up somewhere. Any time you disrespect any other living organism you are disrespecting yourself.'

Sounded okay to me.

Then he told me that sometimes the sweat lodges continue until the early hours of the morning. My God! As they say in Glasgow, my arse was making buttons. I didn't want to be the big silly white boy that couldn't cut it. I was really afraid I would panic and run out screaming after a while. I certainly didn't know if I'd be able to share any of my worries – I get shy at such events – but I did want to take part. Just like life itself – you don't want to be an observer,

Heating the blessed rocks

you want to be in that number when the saints come marching in. Fortunately, Keith was an understanding kind of guy with that incredible fairness of heart that the native people of North America all seem to have.

Once stripped of all our clothes and seated in a circle inside the dark tent, we burned sweet grass and sage for all those who had died, and those still with us, and we smoked some tobacco mixed with roots. I did the Bill Clinton thing and didn't inhale, because I wasn't sure what was in the pipe and I didn't want to get stoned. When they closed the doors there was total and absolute darkness except for the glow of the coals. There wasn't even enough glow to reflect faces. I couldn't see a thing. I could only hear.

Keith said prayers in his own language, and then in English for my benefit. The burning sage, he said, would bring down a spirit to listen to our prayers and take them back to the creator. Ash was smudged onto my skin and blown onto me and I had to get it in my hair as it was wafted round me with a feather. Water was splashed onto the sacred hot rocks and the heat became intense. My skin felt like tissue paper and my hair like candy floss. As Keith gave thanks for our beautiful surroundings I could hardly breathe. The more water they splashed, the more pain I felt as it scorched my mouth and throat. I remembered one of the guy's advice about taking it slowly and it worked.

You've no idea how much your body is desperate to inhale even when you know that if you do, it's going to roast your insides. Everything in your being is telling you to inhale a big bulk of air but it doesn't work and you feel so cheated; you feel alone and abandoned. I thought my head was going to burst but it was amazing to sit through and not give in and lie down. It was a case of breathing right and dealing with it like a man. As I was being baked, I could feel myself turning a funny lobster colour so I said to the guy next to me, 'Does this make me a redskin?' He roared with laughter.

They started pouring cool water on me and, oh my God, it was like being struck by lightning. I knew from the Buddhist mindfulness of breathing that I had to get my breathing sorted. Once I did, and got used to the darkness and the heat, it was one of the most moving things I ever did in my life. It was nothing remotely like I thought it was going to be. I began to develop such a deep respect for the Nisga'a beliefs of sharing and fairness, balance and love. I caught part of a prayer which stated that no one

Left: Go in like a man, come out like a baby
Below: A changed man

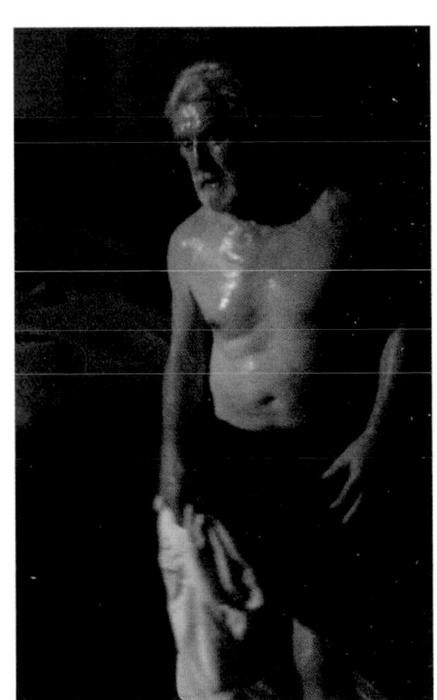

is completely evil; there is always good in someone. The rest was in their own language, with some singing and chanting – that wonderful wailing they do – and the beating of small drums. I had never met such extraordinary people. Their philosophy is so full of love and understanding.

These Indians have a tempo that is different from mine or yours. If you asked what time something started, they'd say, 'When it starts.' Or if you asked when it ended, the reply was, 'When it ends.' There was no schedule. They didn't wear watches. Their tempo made the sweat lodge experience intense and relaxing at the same time. Keith had told me that time would pass faster than I imagined. To begin with I thought, 'I can't sit like this for long', but I was astonished at how much I could stand.

I had always seen myself as a wimp but I'm not really. It was all about control. We are born with it but it's a question of accessing it. In our world, we're not really asked to and so we forget how. Before I knew it, and to my disappointment, the session was over. It had lasted almost four hours.

The whole point of a sweat lodge is that you go in like a man and come out like a baby. When they opened the door, I literally had to crawl out. Sweat was belching off me and when I tried to stand, I staggered about like a toddler, but I felt such a sense of achievement. I wanted to go back and do it all again.

* * *

I SAW LANCE ARMSTRONG, the cyclist, interviewed once and he was asked, 'What you do must be so painful?' He replied, 'You have to own your own pain.' I always liked the poetry of that – owning your own pain – and now I think I get it. You have to take the pain. It is yours. It doesn't belong to anyone else. You have to take it and use it and put it back out as something else that's good. That's what I learned in the sweat lodge and it was a phenomenal lesson.

Keith had told me, 'Embrace the heat. It's your friend. If you don't, it will hurt you.' I was quite taken aback by the level of goodness and humanity in those people after all the atrocities that had been performed against them. Each of those men individually told me of the physical and emotional hurt they'd endured. The guy sitting on my right still suffers terribly from his experience, psychologically and spiritually.

I think the abuse thing comes back in cycles to him. I have some experience of that myself and it does come back to you in a kind of cycle, if you allow it to. The trick is to put it somewhere in your mind where you can access it when you want information about it for yourself. Otherwise it's a bit like grief. You never get over the death of someone, ever, but you do get to a place where you can put it somewhere, access it and then live without it dominating your life. That's what those guys were doing.

I have a little thing I've invented – an invisible windscreen wiper in my head. When I am trying to get to nowhere and a thought comes into my mind, I just re-enact my little windscreen wiper. It never takes more than three swipes to get rid of the thought and I am back to nothing again. It's a bit like wiping the blackboard with a duster, so my little wipers come in really handy.

Being with those people brought a great happiness to me. I learned from them that the only way to get rid of the pain of it is to think it away. And it was lovely to see that I could still do that.

I had a wonderful night in the sweat lodge, chanting and sweating in extreme heat with those incredible people. I will never forget it as long as I live. Everyone gets a few once-in-a-lifetime chances and that was one of mine. It had a profound effect on me.

It felt such a privilege to be among the Nisga'a and to share their lovely wisdom. It had been such a long time since I'd been in the company of so many people just saying good things and enthusing so much.

When I bade them farewell, I was genuinely sad to be parting from their company. They told me they have no word for goodbye in their language. Instead, they always say, 'We will see you again.' Isn't that lovely?

* * *

I LOVED THE naturalness of the way the Nisga'a lived. There was nothing fake or phoney about them. They didn't worry about the insignificant things in life, the way people in the West do, like how much water we should all be drinking, for example.

When the world was new and everything was fun and fab, you didn't get people wandering around with bottles of water. When Britain was at its most creative point in history, no one was drinking litres of water. They were drinking plenty of other things, maybe getting a good pint down them, a nice Scotch or a bit of wine, but no one was pushing this water nonsense. Peeing like a racehorse doesn't make you attractive. Just look at people who jog and drink water. Don't they look such miserable sods running about in nylon clothes? Can you imagine how they smell every day?

So my advice to you is don't buy into that water thing. It's a con. Have a drink in the house before you leave; have a drink before you go to bed, but only a wee one. You don't want to go and pee the bed. A drink now and again to keep you hydrated is all you need. The rest is nonsense, and you know who's spreading it? Nutritionists – the biggest liars on the planet. They are fakers and frauds. They say eggs are good, eggs are bad; cheese is good, cheese is bad; marge, butter, potatoes, bread – all good, then bad. Bullshit! Whatever next? You're scared to eat, for Christ's sake!

So, scrub the water and stop eating. Drink Guinness instead – it's a three course meal in every pint. Or finish off your day with a working man's Black Velvet – a bottle of Mackeson's with a spoonful of Andrews Liver Salts. Get that down you. None of this champagne and Guinness bullshit; Mackeson's and Andrews fizzes like a mad thing. That'll do you the world of good. ”

The Nisga'a paid me the ultimate honour. In a traditional naming ceremony as part of an annual music and dance festival, they inducted me into their tribe, making me an honorary member of the killer whale chapter. How cool is that? I might get myself a stamp of approval; maybe a killer whale tattoo. I still can't easily pronounce the Indian name for my new Nisga'a moniker, which is Sikibou (or something like that). I'll have to rehearse it. Translated, it means 'Prince of Laughter', which is such a compliment.

As part of their philosophy of balance and exchange, I had to offer the tribe a blanket before my name was given to me in return. The killer whale matriarch Sherry Bejar and her mother, Nisga'a chief Lorene Plante, presided. The Nisga'a have long had women as their chiefs. Tribal status passes down from mother to daughter, while the uncles and fathers do the teaching. Sherry effectively adopted me and became my tribal mother. By accepting my new name, I took on an obligation to her and to the tribe, which she can

call upon any time. I could just imagine it: 'Billy! There's a whale on the phone for you. She says to tell you it's your mother.'

My first obligation to the tribe would be to help supervise a canoe race by some of its younger members across Lava Lake. First, the elders named the two canoes, which were a gift to them from the government as part of the healing process. Thinking about the suffering that the healing process referred to, I found the naming ceremony deeply moving. I got all wobbly and thought I was going to burst into tears. I had to get a grip of myself. I couldn't understand what was doing this to me, but of course it was my recent experience in the sweat lodge, which people had told me would last for a few days.

Standing by the banks of the river, I then had to don the regalia of the tribe – a black waistcoat and long fringed skirt, each decorated with the red tribal crest. Black, I was told, signifies the darkness in which the Nisga'a once lived, and the red signifies the dawn of a new day. One of the speakers spoke of Scotland and said that he loved whisky. My whisky days are over. I drank my whole share at once. I didn't know it was meant to last a lifetime.

When they sang my name to accompanying drums I was once again overwhelmed by emotion and gratitude. I felt so very proud, but could hardly speak to say thank you because I so wanted to cry. I had to put my hand up to my mouth and hold my face because I was going to blubber when they sang my name. That sort of affection and generosity always gets right to my heart. I've got no apologies to make for it. It was a beautiful moment.

Above left and opposite: Naming ceremony
Above: A killer whale in tribal dress

Eventually, I pulled myself together enough to say a few words and told them how great my experience had been. I promised that as I went through life I'd carry the good news about the Nisga'a and always speak very highly of them. When it was finished, I felt so good walking around in my regalia. It was like walking in my kilt for the first time; you know when you get a new kilt and you look down and there is this movement on your legs? It's a funny feeling; as a man you're not used to this broadside movement you get from a skirt. It felt great and so did I. There was a level of happiness still in me from the night before that I hadn't felt in a long time. Those people treated me so incredibly well.

Their culture of sharing and of giving something back is so genuine and so deep. Herbie, my friend from the sweat lodge, had told me that when he was fishing one day as a little boy, his uncle came by and asked if he'd caught anything, which he hadn't. His uncle told him, 'Give it your whole self, not just the hook and line.' He taught him a little fishing song which Herbie sang for me in the sweat lodge and which kept going around and around in my head for days. Before long, the fish were tugging Herbie's bait. Through song and tradition, he learned how to fish properly and communicate with the river and the whole thing became one.

It was such a nice moment to hear the man talking like that and singing me the song. The land gives you something, and you give the land something back. You hear a lot of that from hippies who've read it in the magazine or something, but when you actually spend time practising that philosophy it really starts to mean something.

After the naming ceremony we ate salmon and fresh blueberries and the combination was delicious. Smoked fish and blueberries and jolly good company. You don't get many days like that.

Williams Lake, British Columbia

I KNEW I WAS HEADING back to civilization when my mobile telephone buzzed into life just as we landed at Williams Lake airport. I heard the phone make a noise for the first time since I'd crossed the Arctic Circle at Auyuittuq National Park and thought, 'Oh, I am back in my own world again.'

I called Pamela straight away and she told me she was in Samoa judging a cross-gender beauty pageant. I could only begin to

HOTEL
CITY OF WILLIAMS LAKE
WILLIAMS LAKE

WILLIAMS LAKE IS known colloquially as Billy's Puddle. It is British Columbia's stampede capital and host to the annual Williams Lake Stampede, in which North America's top rodeo riders and cowboys compete in events such as steer wrestling, bull riding and chuckwagon races.

With a population of more than 10,000, Williams Lake is the largest town between Kamloops and Prince George. Named after a First Nations chief called William, who prevented an uprising against the settlers in the Chilcotin War of the mid-1800s, the town was a natural resting point on two pack trails to the gold fields during the Cariboo gold rush. Having become the bustling municipal centre for miners, merchants and travellers, the town lost its status when a bypass was built around it in 1863.

The town's fortunes were rejuvenated by the construction of the Pacific Great Eastern Railway in the middle of the twentieth century. Its primary industries are now forestry, ranching and mining.

Williams Lake is also home to the British Columbia Cowboy Hall of Fame.

imagine that in my head. She was furious because the people there knew all my DVDs and she was introduced as 'Billy Connolly's wife'. Oops.

A long-horned Hereford

Williams Lake is a cowboy kind of town. It looked prosperous enough from the outside. They mine for copper and zinc and a bit of gold at a place they call the White Cliffs of Dover because they have taken the whole face off the rock in open cast mining and it is dazzlingly white. There is a pulp mill where all the logs are brought in and shredded to a pulp for paper and other products. There is also a huge livestock market.

I think being a cattle farmer is no longer what it was when it all started during the gold rush years. In those days, they could buy cattle cheap in America and sell the meat really dear but now they have come upon hard times. First of all, the cost of foodstuff for cattle has risen sharply and farmers can't make the profit they used to. Then they've had some cases of BSE (bovine spongiform encephalopathy) or mad cow disease, so the American market has closed down and they'd relied heavily on it. People are just about breaking even, which is really hard luck if you've spent the whole winter seeing your cattle through and then feeding them all spring and summer and you only break even. It's not really the point of the exercise.

I visited a livestock auction to assess the profound influence that cowboys and ranchers have on the area. I was surprised to find two

At the cattle auction

Scotsmen in charge – Wilf Brimley and Robert McGregor. Wilf was every inch the cowboy with his big buckle, the hat and the boots. His mother came from the Royal Mile in Edinburgh and she was sitting there too, this wee woman who looked up and said, 'Oh, it's Billy Connolly!' Wilf showed me all around the place. Robert, who was in the ring conducting the auction, was also from Edinburgh and used to be a cop. I couldn't understand a word he said. His auction banter sounded to me like a song, but he guided me skilfully through the whole game, which he knows from hoof to horn tip. He pretended I'd bought something after I asked him, 'If I blow my nose, will I end up with a herd of cattle? Or if I scratch my eye, have I bought a cow? Is there any danger of that happening?' We had quite a laugh about that and it turned out to be the happiest of mornings.

The cattle buyers who travel to Williams Lake buy meat for butchers and wholesalers all over America and Canada. Many buy online, via a live computer link. More than fifty thousand head of cattle are auctioned off there every year, most of which have been raised organically on wild grasslands and in the most stunning surroundings. There were fifteen hundred head for sale the day I was there, including the best bull I have ever seen in my life: a long-horned Hereford. Holy bloody Moly, it was a monster. The sheer power of it was impressive. This was vegetarian Hell. There were scores of calves and cows (or 'coos' as we call them in Scotland) as well. One big heifer with a strange hairdo reminded me of a former girlfriend who used to chase me around the schoolyard.

Cowboys wearing Mexican heels and hats moved around the auction rooms in that slow way they have, looking every inch the Marlboro Man. When these men shook my hand, they squeezed real hard. Despite what they were going through, there was a great deal of optimism in Williams Lake. I think the people there were born or bred with it because not every year is great in that industry, but there could always be a better year ahead.

Quesnel Lake, British Columbia

MY NEXT STOP was a town called Likely on the western fringes of Quesnel Lake. I was meeting a man called Gary Zorn, who worked as a wilderness guide and knew more about bears than most.

Quesnel Lake is the largest lake in the Cariboo region and, at more than five hundred metres, is one of the deepest fjords or glacial lakes in the world. Gary took me out in a boat early one morning to see if we could try and spot some grizzly bears feeding on migrating salmon. It was the most beautiful September dawn,

Bear-spotting with Gary Zorn

a day which Gary called 'just dandy' as we watched the sun rise over the snow-covered Cariboo Mountains.

He told me that the fish run the river upstream to the lake in four-year cycles in what is one of the largest salmon migrations on earth. In the first, or major run, there are as many as four million fish; by the fourth cycle, or minor run, there would be around fifty thousand. The bears arrive each year to catch the fish as they jump the rocks and rapids to make it upstream to spawn. Gary said the bear population had doubled in the past fifteen years, something Nancy Ball had already told me.

'The winter mortality rate has gone,' Gary said. 'We used to lose a lot of the juvenile bears in minus forty-five degrees but now that we barely hit minus twenty, the bears survive.'

He and his fellow guides had kept track of the bear population around Quesnel Lake for twenty years, watching them grow from cubs until they were old enough to have families of their own.

It was sunny but cold as we left the lake and headed in a jet boat up the Mitchell River towards the salmon spawning beds. The

Above: Quesnel Lake
Below: Wilderness guide Gary Zorn

Amazon-style inlets

landscape became much more jungly and rainforesty; like something in the Amazon, only much colder. I wished I'd brought my nice Arctic hat but I forgot it, so I had a Jungle Jim camouflage hat with flaps that made me look such a Charlie. A bear would probably have died laughing before it ate me.

Once we approached the spawning beds, Gary came over all serious:

'Everybody remain in the boat and stay calm and quiet,' he said, speaking in a whisper.

'No hollering, no loud voices and no sudden movements. If we're approached by a bear, do exactly as I say.'

Twice, he'd had bears trying to get into his boat and three times he had been mauled.

'I broke the leg on one bear. I dislocated the hip on another and bit a toe off another,' he told me, as if it was nothing at all. His wife hit a bear on the face with an oar once until it bled from its mouth and scarpered. Gary didn't carry a gun, he just had one of those bear sprays but I felt a hundred per cent safe.

The air was full of circling bald and golden eagles. I had never

seen so many in my life. By spotting where the fish-eating birds are Gary could lead visitors straight to where the bears were feeding. Gary said the birds wait for the bears to take their fill of their favourite parts of the fish – the brains and roe – then swoop down to feast on the remnants. As well as eagles, there were also hooded mergansers, a type of duck with a lovely crest that looked like a cloth hat tweaked down over their eyes. It reminded me of the Scottish soldiers who wear their berets tilted down over their faces.

He cut the engine and got out of the boat in his waders and pulled us through the shallows by a rope. I was impressed. I'd met so many people on this journey who were immensely strong; it made me feel such a weakling. Guys like Gary who are probably my age but who have worked with their muscles and their bodies all their lives.

The sockeye salmon were all around us in the clear water, hundreds of them flying upriver. They are like designer fish, in neon red with a green head and a green tail. Gary told me that there are so many of them the bears just take what they want and

Top: My first full frontal grizzly
Above: Waiting for leftovers

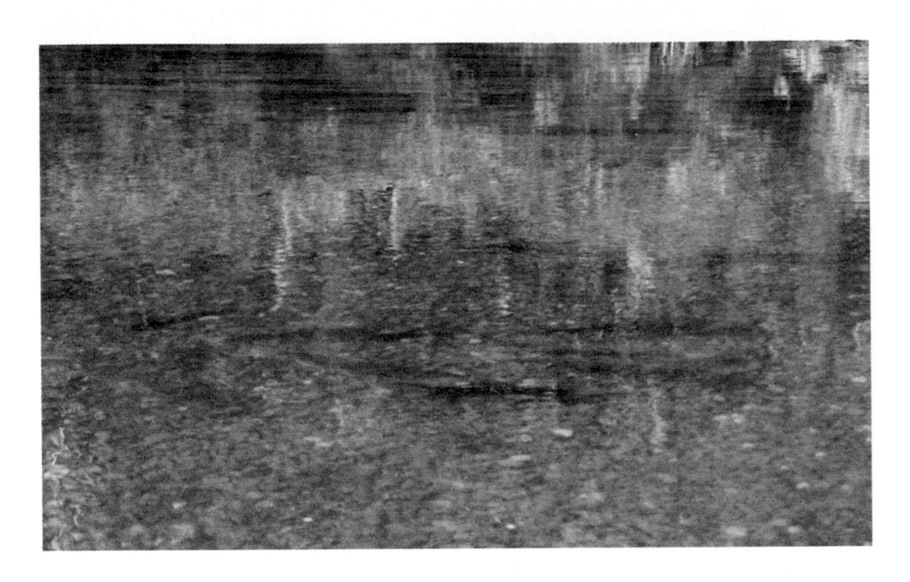

Sockeye salmon

throw away the rest for the birds. What a country Canada is, booming with these things.

We rounded a bend in the river and came to a little promontory of gravel along which was scattered driftwood and logs. Sure enough, we spotted a big bear, and what a beauty he was. We startled him and he looked up and then stood up on his hind legs. He was sensational, maybe seven feet tall with a big teddy bear face. He was hard to take seriously. I wanted to smile at that great face, peering at us just ten feet away. Then he turned and made off into the woods. We saw his big backside disappear into the bushes in that lovely, wobbly way. It was a rare privilege; I had never been that close to a bear in my life.

We turned round and jetted along the river and came around another corner to find a bear running in a semicircle. It looked as if it was coming towards us at first, but then it cut across and into the bushes so that we got a lovely view of it. Drifting farther down we came across a third grizzly, on a log, looking for fish. It saw us but it wasn't sure what we were. It showed curious interest, as if it was thinking, 'What the hell's this?', with that short-sighted way bears look at you. Then it got up and walked along three or four logs before shuffling off into the bushes. It was a beautiful thing.

There is something wonderful about seeing a big hairy-arsed creature on its own territory and in its own world, just being a wild beast. It is so deeply impressive that it can hunt that well and make itself that huge muscley beast just on a diet of fish. What an extraordinary animal it is that can live in such a climate and survive in it by sleeping through the winters after building up enough fat to endure months and months of cold. Gary had names for some of the bears we spotted, including Sad Bear, who he said looked as if she was about to cry all the time, poor thing. What a great day I had in the wilderness. I often dreamed of doing that. I plan to go back one day and catch myself a few of those amazing designer fish.

* * *

"IT IS SUCH A LUXURY to be so close to a beautiful wild thing. It happened to me in Nairobi once, when I was in Kenya for Comic Relief. I got into a taxi at the airport and we drove straight out into a national park, and there was a giraffe. I said to the driver, 'Look! There's a giraffe!' and he looked at me like I'd just farted. 'Yeah?' he said, as if I'd spotted fuck all. But I was so impressed. It wasn't a giraffe in a cage at a zoo; it was a giraffe just being a giraffe, you know, walking around doing giraffey things. I changed the subject, but I couldn't stop looking. I couldn't believe I had just come out of a plane and was seeing this big thing being itself.

I feel the same whenever I see a rabbit or a mouse. I can get as much a buzz from spotting a weasel or a lemming as I do from seeing a wolf. I have been like that since I was a boy, since I first started peering into rivers to see fish. There is something

about a creature's ability to survive without me, or any of us, probably not even knowing we exist, that amazes me. It is a privilege to get a glimpse of this alien world, which is why I fish in the first place.

I am sure it will feel the same way to the first guy who gets a message from outer space. 'Hello?' It will blow his socks off. And it's the same with the bear. It comes from a place that I know nothing about and it feels so special when it lets me have a look every now and again. ”

Gang Ranch, British Columbia

I'VE BEEN A cowboy most of my life. I've worn all the clothes and played my banjo and sung the songs, I just never actually did the real thing. At the million-acre Gang Ranch, on the Fraser-Chilcotin Plateau west of Williams Lake, I was finally given my chance.

Run by Larry and Bev Ramstead, the ranch was established in 1865 to feed the hungry gold miners flooding into the province. At its heart, Bev runs the only post office and store for more than fifty miles. Shortly after arriving, I was introduced to Dustin Sippola, the ranch's chief cowboy and rodeo champion. Dustin is such a great name for a cowboy. He had the best walk you ever saw and a big plug of tobacco on his bottom lip. I asked Dustin how long he'd been chewing tobacco and he said since he was thirteen and his dad showed him how. His father had a small

Gang Ranch

ranch in Alberta and Dustin had wanted to be a cowboy ever since he was a kid.

Chewing the fat with Dustin Sippola

* * *

> PEOPLE THINK A *vocational job is to be something like a priest or a schoolteacher, a doctor or a lawyer, but there are a lot of great jobs you can do that are vocational. To be a cowboy is one of them and so is comedy.*
>
> *I knew exactly what Dustin meant when he said he'd wanted to be what he is since he was small. I could hear and see the shipyards from my school in Glasgow and I always thought it would be nice to work there one day. There are so few people in the world doing what they should be doing, that it's such a joy to meet them. It's almost a holy thing. It's vocational. It's a bit like comedy, or anything that will bug you for the rest of your life if you don't do it.*
>
> *I remember a guy called Willy at the shipyard who was one of the first I ever spoke to about being a comedian. He told me, 'Well, you'd better do it this year, because if you don't, you'll be an unhappy old man here wishing you did and haunting me.'*
>
> *The key is to stay open to all possibilities and I tell my kids that. I tell them, 'Beware of people who know the answer. Seek the company of people who are trying to understand the question. Stay open and you will find that you're drawn to things naturally.' A lot of people miss mountains of things that could make their lives lovely. If they don't go out and try something, they'll miss out. That's also the cowboy way.*

A million acres is an unbelievable amount of land. The owners have a helicopter they sometimes use to help them round up cattle far away but Dustin told me he'll regularly go out on five- or six-night camping trips, making his own food.

I asked him, 'But aren't you fed up with that?' And he just laughed as if to say, 'How could you get fed up with home cooking?' He didn't say, 'I get cold and wet rolling up the tent in the snow.' He never said anything remotely like that.

He told me that a few days previously his friend and fellow cowboy spotted a grizzly bear. He took measures to go around it

and was riding downhill on his horse when he heard a noise and turned around and the bear was charging him. He bolted off on his horse and rode into a wood and hurt his leg against a tree. Then he peed himself with fright, as I would myself.

The previous week Dustin and his colleagues had killed three wolves which had been slaughtering lambs up on the hill. What an extraordinary life they lead. Killing wolves and running from grizzly bears. I'd like to have been a cowboy in my thirties – to have been riding and roping and branding. To see them rope a calf around its ankles is a joy. It's not about being a macho manly man with a droopy moustache; it's about being awfully good at what you do. I love people who are good at what they do – I don't care what it is, even if it's putting string up one nostril and pulling it down the other.

Dustin took me down to the corral where I warned him I was very rusty on a horse: I've only ridden one in movies; I don't do it socially and I was more than a bit nervous. He said he would go easy on me and pointed out a wonderful palomino called Trigger, which was the same golden colour as Roy Rogers's Trigger. I only hoped this one had the same temperament.

* * *

“I SAW TRIGGER ONCE, *in a Roy Rogers show at the Glasgow Empire when I was about twelve or thirteen. I watched that horse dance with a kilt on. Lots of people haven't believed me when I've told them that story over the years. They've said I'm nuts and that I never saw such a thing. I even began to question it myself.*

Years later, during the publicity tour for the Mrs Brown *movie, I was asked to collect an award in Los Angeles, not far from where I was living at the time. To my dismay I found the place full of Christians. They'd published a magazine in which they'd reviewed films that were safe to go and see with your children – you know, so that there were no blow jobs lurking in the middle – and* Mrs Brown *was among the films they picked.*

One of the guests at the event was Dale Evans, Roy Rogers's widow, who was in a wheelchair. I told her I'd seen Roy's show at the Glasgow Empire and she said she remembered that tour. I said, 'Could you put something right for me? Did or did not

Trigger dance, wearing a kilt?' She laughed and said that he had.

'Thank you!' I cried. 'I've been telling people that for years and they think I've got acid flashback or something. They accused me of inventing the whole damn thing.' It was such a pleasure to meet her and to finally put my mind straight. ''

Larry, the manager of the Gang Ranch, tried to find me a decent Stetson to wear but they couldn't find one that fitted, so I ended up with a bashed old black thing of Dustin's which suited me just fine. I also wore a red neckerchief. Larry lent me his chaps and they were beauties; burgundy leather with fringes. I thought, 'My God, I've got all the gear. I'd better not fall off.'

Dustin entered the corral full of horses and went up to Trigger and made eye contact. It wasn't a horse whispering thing – I hate that. Everyone who's good at anything suddenly gets called a 'whisperer' now – a bear whisperer or a horse or a dog whisperer. I wish people would get off that shite. Dustin, that real deal of a cowboy, quietly separated Trigger from the other horses by just a quick left and right movement, which was a great example of how

Dustin tells Trigger to go easy

Riding out with the herd

to work an animal. He roped the horse and brought it over and set it all up for me. Then he went and got himself one. I was a bit jumpy, so he got on Trigger first and rode him round the paddock and it looked fine. When he brought Trigger back it was my turn, and we went for a walk. Within minutes, I felt really great. It was very comfortable in the big western-style saddle. We loaded the horses into a trailer and drove out to where we were going to round up some cattle.

I wasn't sure what to do at first but Dustin said simply to hang back and keep the cattle in formation as we herded them along at a gentle walking pace. My horse kind of bucked up at one point and the cattle were getting scared but I kept on nudging the outer ones into line. All of a sudden, a young, black calf dived into the woods. I thought, 'Let's go!' So I gave it some left and then some right, yelling, 'Whoa! No, you don't!' and I got it back in. It was the best feeling because everything I tried, worked. We came to a big field where we had to steer the cattle through a narrow gate; Dustin and I worked it with the other guys, and through they went. There

One of the boys

was a lot of riding down and cutting out and bringing back but it all worked.

I decided to try a bit of roping and I discovered I was actually quite good at it. I could handle myself and I felt very confident. It was such a joy and a deep relief not to make an arse of myself, and not only that, but also to be in a position where I was actually good enough to really enjoy what I was doing. And the cowboys relaxed in my company, once they realized that they didn't have to look after me. I felt I was a cowboy, too, moseying along with the other guys, and it was a deeply satisfying feeling.

I would like to get better at riding horses but I don't want to spend my life running around on them. I don't like galloping because I always think that if there's a gopher hole, I'll be dead. You never see a horse falling when there's no one on it so it must be the rider's fault. Not that any of those cowboys I met would make a mistake like that. Those men know who and what they are and they don't care what anyone thinks – they would much rather you like them but if you don't, it's nothing to them. I can live with that attitude because I've come across people before who've said, 'I don't like what you do and I don't like what you stand for.' I reply, 'Well, avoid me then. In fact, let's avoid each other because I don't think I like you either.' It seems so incredibly simple, although I can never understand why anyone should feel duty bound to tell anyone else that they don't like them.

The cowboy does so many things that are considered antisocial by other people. He likes his wife to stay at home while he goes out on freezing nights to tie up calves and all sorts of other things. He likes to drink whisky and enjoys getting drunk from time to time. He likes to chew tobacco and spit. What I loved most, though, was their attitude to one another. There were always roars of laughter coming from where the cowboys were. It seemed to me that they deeply respected one another and enjoyed each other's company. The vast majority I met had, like Dustin, wanted to be cowboys since they were boys and they loved their job. Apparently, it doesn't pay that well, they only make maybe two hundred pounds a week, but they get their keep and they get well fed into the bargain, plus they can save a lot of money as they are usually living well away from spending places.

Not everybody can live with that kind of lifestyle. It takes a particular kind of wife or friend. Dustin, who is married with two small children, told me that in general, it's often easier to be unmarried and a loner. His wife had been a cowgirl at a neighbouring ranch, so at least she understood the life.

I loved the cowboys' style. I loved all the special clothes they wear to do the job. They get into their clothes and the mindset follows. They buy the right jeans and custom-built boots with great spinning spurs. They have their saddles specially made for them, some of which can cost a third of a year's wages. They've got

Cowboy spurs

Two real cowboys

people they trust to make those things and they send away their sizes. They'll wear a scarf a particular way or a certain type of snap-button shirt and jacket, it's all so well thoughtout – whether they are walking out, riding on the ranch or attending a barbecue.

I think that sort of country attracts a definite kind of man. It attracts someone who likes to work with other people but to spend a lot of the time on their own, doing their job, without a foreman looking over their shoulder. There is an appeal in such openness and trust, and the fact that people have entrusted you to do a job and then allowed you to do it without checking up and judging you twenty-four-seven. I don't care if you are a clerk in an office or a cowhand; there is something deeply uncomfortable about being watched all the time. It carries a presumption that someone thinks you're not very good and are going to correct you as you go along.

I am a loner. I do what I do. I need space to do it and I identify heavily with welders and truck drivers and cowboys who feel the same. It's all to do with the thrill of doing just what you should always be doing. Most people have a purpose in life and when they're not doing it they feel incomplete. That's what those cowboys were like. I love what they stand for, emotionally and spiritually. I'm glad they're still there.

Horsefly, British Columbia

NEXT TO COWBOYS, lumberjacks probably have the most rugged image. Cecil Morhart, the mayor of Horsefly, who calls himself a 'tree faller', and Leonard Elzinga, a retired logger turned logging teacher, took me into forests in the northern Cariboo region to show me the ropes.

Now, I'm a tree hugger from way back, and when I was first told I might be chopping down a tree I kind of panicked because that's the last thing on earth I would like to do. Some of the trees in that forest are eight hundred years old, the most magnificent cedars and Douglas firs. Leonard told me he'd felled trees twenty-four feet across in his time. But this is one of the areas worst affected by the bark beetles that are destroying the forests of British Columbia and much of North America. Diseased trees need to be cut down and burned before the bugs infect neighbouring trees. The whole idea is to keep the forest growing for future generations.

It's just a fact of life.

Having been introduced to the other tree fellers, who sat around a camp fire in baseball caps just as I expected them to, I had to don another pair of Teflon safety trousers, to prevent me accidentally

HORSEFLY, WHICH USED TO BE called Harper's Camp, got its name from the swarms of horseflies which plagued the gold miners when they arrived in this region during the Cariboo gold rush of the 1850s and 60s. Horsefly Lake and Horsefly River were similarly named.

Horsefly was the nearest small town close to the site of the first major gold discovery in the Cariboo region. The first deposits were found by an American led to the spot by some local Indians. The discovery, in 1859, sparked a gold rush in this region which drew thousands of Canadians, Americans and many British.

The boom led to the Construction of the Cariboo Wagon Road, along which gold bullion could be transported safely out of the area (and not to the United States), to help maintain British Governmental authority over the region.

chopping my own leg off with a chainsaw, which was not a price I was willing to pay. Once I was kitted up in all the gear, I started to look and feel like a real lumberjack. I had on a big pair of boots with spiky soles (like on golf shoes) for walking around safely on logs, and I was shown the special way loggers tie their laces so nothing catches as you're making your way through the forest. I had a hard hat and leather gloves and ear muffs. A first aid kit sat ominously near.

Then Cecil talked me through how the chainsaw, a fearsome machine, worked – what the various bits were and what they did. All this while it was still lying on the ground! He also showed me a big scar on his neck where a chainsaw once kicked back and bit him. Leonard, who said he'd been a logger 'since Jesus was a cowboy', spoke to me about having respect for the machine and for the trees. And he showed me his hand where he had lost a thumb, aged fourteen. I asked him if anyone chopped trees down with an old-fashioned axe any more. He said, 'When you've got chainsaws, why work with an axe? Unless you really, really hate yourself and just want to go out and work up some sweat.'

Under Leonard's expert supervision, I started by cutting through dead wood on an old stump just an inch or two (a couple of centimetres) in diameter. He suggested I buff up a slice and take it home to mount on my wall as a memento. Oh, how the wife would love that!

'Hi, honey. I've got a big chunk of wood for the living room – just what you've always wanted.'

Cutting my teeth

The men demonstrated how a tree was cut down; by making a horizontal and then an angled undercut in the trunk, depending on which direction I wanted it to fall, then taking the wedge out so that the tree acted on itself like a hinge. They used the saw at right angles to where a tree was going to fall, working one side and then the other so that it fell in a straight line, which is known as the 'sight line'. It was hard work, especially after they told me to imagine a carpenter's level balancing on the blade to keep it horizontal at all times.

It turned out I was quite good at this as well – so good, in fact, that they let me cut down a couple of trees by myself; the second one was a beauty and fell flat as a pancake. I didn't know you could be so specific as to where a tree falls just by the positioning of the chainsaw. The accuracy is staggering. I was very disappointed, however, to discover that they didn't cry 'Timber!', like in the movies. Leonard said that if they did, they'd be yelling all day and would soon run out of breath.

I'd been saddened earlier on my journey to learn that the Inuit don't yell 'Mush!' at their sled dogs, either. No wonder the world is in the state it's in.

After two trees, I was getting tired and my arm was sore. I couldn't imagine how they did this for six hours straight. For the last tree I would fell, Cecil showed me how to use the weight of the tree against itself to my benefit. I did a really good first cut, the second was my dream cut and then the tree started to go. Cecil cried, 'Let's go!' – we'd chosen our escape route before we'd started – then, from a safe distance, I watched that big tree start to come down and, oh my goodness me! There was a great loud creaky-squeaky breaking noise and then the earth shook as the tree came crashing to the forest floor.

Since the days of *White Fang* and all those books I loved as a child, I'd always wanted to chop a tree down but I'd always thought it to be vandalism. As I got older, with the increasing lack of trees in the world, I believed that even more so. The last thing the planet needs is eejits like me cutting trees down. So it was the greatest feeling to fulfil a childhood fantasy with a completely clear conscience, because the tree I was felling was sick and had to go. When an opportunity comes along like that – oh Lord, what a feeling! You have to grab it. Something you may do only once before you die.

THE DECIMATION OF great swathes of pine forests from British Columbia to Mexico has been caused by an epidemic of the mountain pine beetle, *Dendroctonus ponderosae*, which bores into the trees' bark and lays its eggs, the hatched larvae then feed on the sap.

Within two weeks of an infestation, trees are overwhelmed and begin to show signs of dying as their needles turn orangey brown. They literally starve to death as their water and nutrients are eaten by the beetle young. Colonies of the beetles thrive in long, hot summers and – as climate change raises winter temperatures – they are also surviving the winters to double the population.

Experts estimate that the current outbreak of pine beetles is ten times larger than ever before and claim that more than thirty-six thousand square miles of forest have been lost in the past decade. If not stopped, there are fears that the Western United States and parts of Canada could lose ninety per cent of its forests. Controlled burning, a method once used to eradicate the beetles, is no longer possible in many areas because of the proximity of houses and towns.

I was becoming such a roughtie-tuftie. I was driving pickup trucks through the woods, eating steak like a total carnivore, smoking cigars and riding horses. I was a rambling, jambling, outdoorsy, hairy-arsed man. Like in the song, I was a lumberjack, chopping down trees and going to the lavatory. What the hell was becoming of me? That's what the great hairy-arsed outdoors will do for you. I was such a nice tree-hugging hippy when I left home. My wife wouldn't have recognized me, not least because I looked like Grizzly Adams. In my defence, there was a great shortage of tofu to eat in those parts.

Cecil and his gang were funny and good men who laughed easily and loudly. I have been blessed with the ability to communicate with strangers but they made it very easy for me. It's a particularly nice thing to share a laugh with someone you don't know. The joy of communication could save the world: if people would only communicate better and have a laugh; if politicians weren't bound by diplomacy and that silly language they use, but had deep meaningful conversations instead. I want to hear the American president saying, 'I just met the Russian president and we roared with laughter.' I would be so hopeful if I heard that. The language of diplomacy is the language of lies and subterfuge. 'Cursiflage and obfuscation', as we say in the biz that we call show.

In that picture postcard part of Canada with its trees and beef and cowboys, I felt very much at home. That part of the world breeds a fantastic type of man – hard-working and strong but also very nice and kind. The tree fallers and I all roared and howled, and my day spent in Horsefly was one of those lovely ones when everything worked and I was among good people who did a good thing very well. The harder a job gets, the more passionate people seem to be about it. The cowboy life is hard and the forestry life is hard, especially as it gets colder. These men work long hours in the most inhospitable conditions but they love what they do and that's what comes screaming across.

* * *

" *I LOVE THE camaraderie of men, and I miss the people that I've had it with in the past. I miss my welder friends; I miss my cigar store friends; I miss my army friends. There is pleasure in men's company, a real manly thing that a lot of men miss out on. For some reason, men keeping the company of men is frowned upon by bullies (male and female) who don't know what it is because they don't have any friends because they're wankers.*

People assume when we are in men's company that we talk about sex all the time, which is the most ludicrous thing I've ever heard. We talk about all sorts of wonderful things – politics and football and sport and life generally. There is a special contact between men – as I am sure there is between women too, many of whom I have seen rolling around and having a whale of a time. Unlike women, men tend not to speak about their feelings, but they do have other problems to be getting on with, like being the providers or dealing with matters of the soul. Or like how not to be humiliated or belittled. Men don't want to be fired, or left out or have promotion bypass them. They have status problems and worry about their position in society, in the family, at work. Talking about that gives rise to all sorts of great conversation.

Some of the highlights of my life have happened in male company: roaring with laughter, being deeply moved or listening to somebody talking about the death of a parent in a way he wouldn't open up to with a woman. Men are a deeply misunderstood species, and the situation doesn't seem to be

Cecil Morhart and the tree fallers

getting any better because we have enemies within, especially in the media, who perpetuate pish about men and a stereotype of them which is untrue.

Some people think you have to take sides – men, or women. I disapprove of that kind of thing. It's like when you tell anyone that you like Arabs, they immediately think you don't like Jews. I mean how did that little equation pop up? People are frightened to be seen to be less than hairy-chested. We're afraid to confront these things but the truth is that some people are homophobic in the worst imaginable sense.

Like the banning of men's clubs, for example. What's that about? Then they open women's clubs – where men are banned! I think there is a word for that and I think it's fascism. Get out of my face and leave me alone. It's like smoking. I smoke cigars. I am happy to smoke cigars. I don't give one shit what anyone else thinks about me smoking cigars, it's none of anyone's business. But suddenly there's nowhere indoors in the world I can do it now, because of them. *Even if I belong to a private club, all of whose members love to smoke, we're not allowed to by those who won't even be there when we're doing it!*

The last time I was in Vancouver my favourite smoke shop, the Havana Room, had to close down. We were no longer allowed to smoke in this most beautifully ventilated place in the middle of a cigar store. How anyone could wander by and accidentally inhale this smoke defies gravity never mind logic. In the same week they opened a place where you can go and fix heroin.

In smoking my cigars, I am doing something completely legal. It is a luxury. It may harm me but that's my business. Driving a car may harm me. Crossing a road may harm me (and that harms a darn sight more people than cigars do). But they, *in their infinite wisdom, have decided I'm not to do it, even though I am prepared to pay to do it, because they don't like it. I can't wait 'til the health warnings that read: 'Fat bastards!' start appearing on a cheesecake box. I can see it coming.* ”

Nootka Sound, Vancouver Island, British Columbia

WHEN I WAS A BOY in Glasgow, there was a guy who used to sing a song about Canada. I think his name was Hawkins. The song was called 'When it's Springtime in the Rockies'. I made up my mind then and there to see the Rockies one day, the way everyone does I guess, but not everyone makes it. As I headed west towards the end of my journey and drove past the blue Canadian Rockies, I realized how fortunate I was. Following the course of the Fraser River, I couldn't take my eyes off the legendary snow-capped peaks while that song echoed around and around in my head.

There is something quite romantic about following a river to the ocean. At the point where the Fraser and the Thompson rivers

White Pass and Coast Mountains between Alaska and British Columbia

The Fraser River

meet and thunder towards the Pacific, I was struck by the fact that the rivers in Canada have been the destiny of the place: the mighty Hudson, Mackenzie and Saint Lawrence rivers were the making of Canada. On a journey marked by three lesser but, still, very grand rivers, I had traversed this extraordinary country: from the Gander to Disappointment River to the Fraser.

When you say 'ten thousand miles' it just rolls off the tongue and doesn't sound that far. But when you've travelled that distance from Nova Scotia and Newfoundland, up through the Arctic, down to the Yukon and still farther west, you realize it is one hell of a distance and one hell of a country. Just looking at my boots I could tell where I'd been. I had the Dempster Highway and Dawson City and Whitehorse and the frozen desert and the forests and the mountains caked all over them. There is a size and beauty to everything in Canada that takes your breath away – mile upon mile of fjords and mountains and forests and rivers.

The overpowering scale of the country really came home to me when I realized that it had taken ten weeks to cross and I hadn't been hanging about, either. I'd been tearing along in helicopters and aeroplanes, on Harley-Davidsons, in trucks and in four-wheel-drive all-terrain vehicles and on all sorts of boats. If I'd taken my time I'd have seen even more than I did, and yet I'd seen so much.

Canada has so much to offer, and it's ever changing. Everywhere I'd been I'd heard people speaking of better times before and of changing times ahead. They admitted that the cod-fishing days were behind them, that the salmon aren't running the way they used to and the seals are not coming so much; coal mining isn't what it was and the gold is drying up; there is not so much demand for their cattle, people don't buy Canada's wood any more. Plus the climate is warming, or there is a beetle eating all their trees. With Alberta riding an oil wave and the Arctic opening up with potentially lucrative mineral rights, this place is going to change quite radically, and soon. Not least will be the struggle between

NOOTKA SOUND, on the rugged western shore of Vancouver Island, is home to the Nuu-chah-nulth First Nations people, whose name means 'all along the mountains'.

In 1778, British Royal Navy Captain James Cook sailed HMS *Resolution* into Nootka Sound, where he traded furs with the Mowachaht Nuu-chah-nulth people under the auspices of Chief Maquinna. For the next twenty years, as more fur traders and explorers followed in Cook's footsteps, Nootka Sound became one of the most famous trading posts on the west coast of North America.

Cook, who was killed by natives in Hawaii a year after discovering Nootka Sound, had the distinction of being the first to chart much of Newfoundland and the north-west coast of America on world maps. On several occasions he had attempted to find a way through the Northwest Passage via the Bering Strait, without success. Instead, he laid claim to parts of Alaska and neighbouring regions to fend off Spanish and Russian bids.

Fierce competition between Britain and Spain over the control of Nootka Sound led to the Nootka Crisis in 1790. Ships were seized and compensation refused, as both sides prepared for war. Ultimately, the Spanish conceded and abandoned exclusivity claims to the area, an event which marked the beginning of the end of their empire. In contrast, the British won important rights which paved the way for colonial expansion in the region.

Traditionally hunters of whales, bears and wild deer, the Nuu-chah-nulth captured and traded slaves, including two English crewmen from an American vessel who were held captive for three years. An estimated ninety per cent of the Nuu-chah-nulth people were systematically wiped out in the early 1800s by a combination of smallpox, sexually transmitted diseases and malaria. Caught up in the conflicts between colonial interests, a large number were also killed in battles.

Friendly Cove

Canada, America and Russia about who wins sovereignty over it all.

Change is the norm. Sometimes change can be good. It doesn't have to always be for the worse. Best of all, the things we can't change will always be here to enjoy: the way the sun comes up in the morning; the way clouds cling to mountains; the way the world starts another new day, every day – these are what make life jolly.

Captain Cook, too, was looking for the Northwest Passage. Well, wasn't everybody? Of course, he never found it but being a bit of a businessman he did a deal with the local chief, Maquinna, and bought some land to establish a fur trading post. It nearly caused a war between the British and the Spanish, but there you go – so did almost everything.

At a place called Friendly Cove (whose native name is Yuquot, which means 'wind comes from all directions') on Nootka Island, Cook set up a busy port for exporting fur and importing other goods. And it was this that started everyone jockeying for position in that part of the world. Now there is just a lighthouse and one house. I wondered if the Friendly family live there? Actually I was told that the guy who lives in the house is a direct descendant of Chief Maquinna who kept Friendly Cove as his tribe's coastal

Looking out to the ocean as the sun sets

village. Maquinna not only traded directly with Cook, but also with all those who followed him. I read somewhere that Maquinna died of having a good time – I think from alcohol – as so many of the First Nations people did.

Sitting on an old log and staring out to the Pacific Ocean at the end of my epic voyage gave me a strange and pleasant feeling. My journey to the edge of the world had started ten thousand miles ago, way over in Nova Scotia on the Atlantic Ocean. Now here I was right across on the other side of that vast continent. It seemed such a long time ago that I'd been at Pier 21 talking about Canadian immigrants or that I had wondered at that head-shaped hole in the church window; so long since I'd visited the *Titanic* graves – so moving – and an age ago that I'd been listening to the pipe bands and the Cape Breton fiddlers.

All those people I'd met – cowboys, Indians, lumberjacks, prospectors, fakers, Quakers, mother-haters, fathers, lovers, religious nutters and joyous nutters – what of them now? I'd encountered a lot of hairy, smelly people and I was a bit hairy and smelly myself having worn the same clothes throughout much of the journey, but I didn't care. And my wife wasn't there to complain.

I'd been to St John's, Newfoundland – that jolly town down at the docks – and had a day fishing in Gander with Dave. As a matter of fact, I spent a lot of time doing things with guys called Dave. I'd jigged for cod with Ralph and Bobby, met fiddle-playing Chester and his scarecrows, then flown into the Arctic and to Iqaluit to travel in a hearse with Bryan and to see lovely Rebecca cooking maktauq. I'd listened to the incredible noise of throat music and sat with wee Tookie watching old movies that showed how happy the Inuit had once been. What a journey!

Then I'd trekked up to Pang to listen to that lovely man Simeonie playing his accordion. At Pond Inlet I'd gone hunting for seals with another Dave and his family. What a time was had by all. In Igloolik I'd become a friend to wise old Abraham, who had taken me to his old magical site and the grave of Alexander Elder, that Greenland mate, or expert ice sailor. Then I'd boarded a ship and sailed the Northwest Passage – one of the few people ever to do so – stopping off at those extraordinary places along the way. Beechey Island with the graves of those sailors, long-dead, will always remain with me – those three, lying there, exactly the same as they were when they were buried a hundred years ago. What a wonderful thing to have seen.

The Northwest Passage was kind of ordinary by comparison. I had hoped it would live up to legend and be full of ice and thunder and lightning, but there was mostly just grey sea and a big sky. But it had been a joy to learn about John Rae, who discovered so much about that region, and a revelation to discern that John Franklin was rather an incompetent fraud with a pushy wife. Then I'd travelled down through the Yukon to the one-time gold rush boom town Dawson City, then on to Whitehorse to swish for gold – with another Dave – and then I'd staked that 'Billy' claim up in the mountains with Shawn. I'd bumped along the incredible Dempster Highway in a big truck with Bill and flown in a helicopter over the breathtaking Tombstone Mountains with lovely Lolita. What a time to have! Then to British Columbia, the flower of them all, with its cowboys and Indians, its bears and its eagles.

My time in the sweat lodge will remain with me for the rest of my life. Keith and Herbie, Kate and all the rest. That experience, above all, really changed me emotionally. I seemed to have been touched far deeper than normal. My feelings seemed much closer to the surface than they had ever been before. Beautiful things moved me to tears. I hope the feeling hangs around because it really was a nice thing.

I got my new name, too – an Indian name I am very proud of. A member of the Nisga'a people and their killer whale tribe, my emblem was carved on a pole by Alver. Then to ride Trigger and round up the herd with Dustin and the cowboys, and then to chop down trees with Cecil and the boys. What a gas! Not many people get such chances in a life and I am really glad I did. Nancy Ball was one of the great highlights of the trip for me, running that remote ranch all on her own. That woman, that wee bolt of lightning, she, too, will remain with me forever.

Sitting on that old log, I felt kind of sad that my travels were over. I felt that I had seen Canada at its very best. If it is down to its people, then Canada is in good shape. They've got some lovely folk there and I never met helpfulness or had a welcome like it anywhere in my life. I think there is going to be abundant wealth up in their northern territories and they're entitled to it: it is theirs. My main hope above all is that the native people get their share. But the Canadians are very good people with a good history and I believe that, ultimately, they will do right by them.

Just one thing, though – I do have one little complaint.

People should shout 'Timber!' when a tree falls down. That's one of those things that has to be put right.

'*Timber!*'

It's Canada for goodness sake! This is what the world expects.

I'll give them lessons if they're stuck…

CREDITS

Extracts from 'The Shooting of Dan McGrew' and 'The Spell of the Yukon' by Robert Service reproduced with permission of the estate of Robert Service c/o M. Wm. Krasilovsky.

Map and line drawings by Andrew Farmer

Archive Illustrations

p. 155 Engraving from *The Voyage of the 'Fox' in the Arctic Seas* by Captain Francis McClintock, 1859

p. 160 Photograph of Sir John Franklin (© National Maritime Museum, Greenwich, London)

p. 184 The note found on King William Island by Captain Francis McClintock, discoverer of the fate of Franklin's expedition, from *The Voyage of the 'Fox' in the Arctic Seas* by Captain Francis McClintock, 1859

p. 195 Engraving after the painting *'They Forged the Last Link With Their Lives', The North-West Passage: HMS Erebus and Terror* by Thomas Smith, 1895 (Mary Evans Picture Library)

p. 242 Packers ascending the summit of Chilkoot Pass, 1898, photo by E.A. Hegg (Library and Archives of Canada, c-005142)

p. 299 Dying pine trees in Banff Springs, Alberta (© George Rose/Getty Images News)

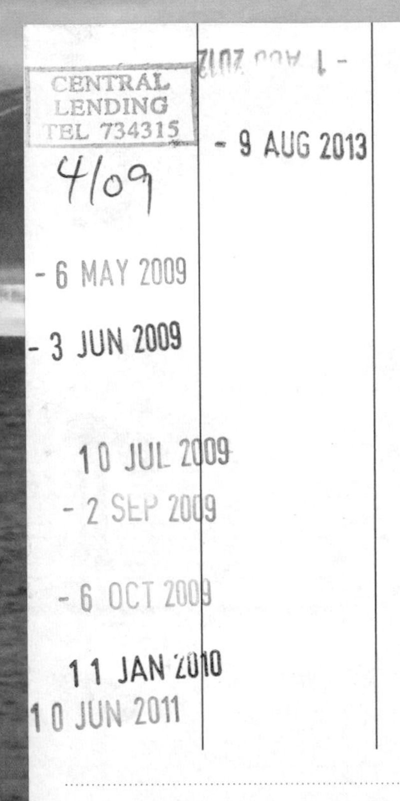